George Sand

Twayne's World Authors Series
French Literature

David O'Connell

Georgia State University

TWAS 761

George Sand

By David A. Powell

Hofstra University

Twayne Publishers
A Division of G.K. Hall & Co. • Boston

George Sand
David A. Powell

Copyright 1990 by G.K. Hall & Co.
All rights reserved.
Published by Twayne Publishers
A Division of G.K. Hall & Co.
70 Lincoln Street
Boston, Massachusetts 02111

Copyediting supervised by Barbara Sutton
Book production by Gabrielle B. McDonald
Book design by Barbara Anderson

Typeset in 11 pt. Garamond
by Compositors Corporation, Cedar Rapids, Iowa

Printed on permanent/durable acid-free paper
and bound in the United States of America

First published 1990.
10 9 8 7 6 5 4 3 2 1

Library of Congress Cataloging-in-Publication Data

Powell, David A.
    George Sand / by David A. Powell.
        p.   cm. — (Twayne's world author series ; TWAS 761. French
literature.
    Includes bibliographical references.
    ISBN 0-8057-8260-5 (alk. paper)
    1. Sand, George, 1804–1876—Criticism and interpretation.
I. Title.   II. Series: Twayne's world authors series ; TWAS 761.
III. Series: Twayne's world authors series. French literature.
PQ2417.P6   1990
843'.7—dc20   90–30538
CIP

For . . .
Q. B.

Contents

About the Author

David A. Powell received his Ph.D. in nineteenth-century French literature from the University of Pennsylvania, where he completed a dissertation on the function of music in the works of George Sand. He has presented several conference papers on Sand at MLA and International George Sand colloquia. He has published articles on Sand in *George Sand Studies, Le Bulletin des amis de George Sand,* and conference proceedings of a George Sand colloquium. He has also published many book reviews on George Sand, music and literature, and various other topics, in *Nineteenth-Century French Studies, The French Review,* and *George Sand Studies.* He is currently working on a book on music and Sand.

Preface

George Sand, author of over eighty novels, twenty plays, numerous political tracts, and a staggering amount of correspondence, is still relatively unknown, and misunderstood, by most of the general and a large portion of the professional reading public. Yet Sand reaped the esteem of Balzac, Dumas père and fils, Flaubert, Musset, Sainte-Beuve, Chopin, Delacroix, Liszt, and many others of the romantic age. Her relationship with these major artists was at once professional and personal: she discussed politics, art, music, and literature with them; she went to the theater and to concerts with them; she was a member of their elite group. Being a woman did not necessarily enhance her position in the group; rather she became a prominent member of the literary community despite her sex.

No one aspect of George Sand's character can fully explain the individual place she held in her profession. Certainly her provincial background, crossed with her aristocratic blood, predisposed her to the romantic predilection for social antithesis. Her relentless and moralizing idealism has caused many to misconstrue her liberalism as condescension. While often didactic, she always strove to represent life in a social context, which she thought put it in its best light. She wrote to Balzac, "You paint man as he is; I prefer to paint him as he ought to be." Social injustices, along with human relationships, formed the mainstay of her thematics. She freely wrote of the plight of workers, women, and artists, seeing them as misunderstood and mistreated by society in general. Idealism, for George Sand, provided an effective means for communicating the need for social reform.

Sand's first novel, seen by some as Balzacian in concept and style, soon gained public and critical acclaim and became an important addition to the novel tradition. Sand was one of the most widely read authors of her time, and several of her stage plays enjoyed great success. Yet, after her death only the "rustic" novels could be found in bookshops. Although they were recommended to girls, no one seemed to notice their value as important examples of social, romantic prose fiction. This state of ignorance continued for three-quarters of a century before the critical world slowly began to uncover the dusty volumes. The recent movement to disinter Sand's literary contribution and to disentangle her renown as a writer from her amorous reputation alone arises from three principal organizations: L'Association des Amis de George

Sand, directed by M. Georges Lubin; L'Association pour la diffusion de l'oeuvre de George Sand, founded outside of Grenoble in 1975 and directed by M. Jean Courrier; and The Friends of George Sand, founded in 1976 at Hofstra University and directed by Natalie Datlof. Each of the three organizations produces a publication, respectively *Bulletin des amis de George Sand*, *Présence de George Sand*, and *George Sand Studies*. I should like to express here my debt to my fellow *sandistes* for their unflagging encouragement in this and all endeavors to bring Sand to the attention of the reading public.

The work is far from accomplished, however. Only once has a George Sand novel appeared on the list for the *"agrégation,"* and that nearly thirty years ago. School manuals still portray Sand as the writer of "rustic" novels, traditionally read by girls and promptly forgotten. The number of doctoral theses consecrated to the study of the works of George Sand is finally increasing in France and elsewhere. That a volume on George Sand in this series is only just now appearing indicates the difficulty in admitting the Berrichon author to the canon.

In the last decade and a half scholarly research on George Sand has taken a positive turn. Moving away from voyeuristic accounts of her liaisons, contemporary criticism is beginning to show Sand the respect that it accords to all great writers. This general study does not pretend to be an exhaustive commentary on the life and works of George Sand. As an introductory overview, its goal is to impress upon the reader the volume of writing Sand produced on topics of great importance to her contemporaries as well as her unique stamp on the tradition of French literature.

David A. Powell

Hofstra University

Acknowledgments

This volume could not have been accomplished without the dedicated work of M. George Lubin, to whom I am forever indebted. I should also like to thank Professors Priscilla Parkhurst Ferguson and David O'Connell for their initiative and support. I owe thanks to Hofstra University for a travel grant and release time. I should also like to express my unending gratitude to Mr. Thomas R. Pileggi for his counsel and editing skills.

Chronology

1804   Sophie Delaborde marries Maurice Dupin 5 June. Amantine-Aurore-Lucile Dupin (George Sand) born in Paris 1 July.

1808   Maurice Dupin is killed in a riding accident.

1809   Contract between Sophie and Marie-Aurore Dupin gives the grandmother the charge of Aurore.

1818   In January enters the Convent of English Augustinians in Paris, where she will stay until April 1820.

1821   Grandmother dies at Nohant 26 December.

1822   Marries Casimir Dudevant 17 September.

1823   Son, Maurice, born 30 June.

1828   Daughter, Solange, born 13 March.

1829   Writes *Voyage en Espagne* and *Voyage en Auvergne*.

1830   Meets Jules Sandeau 30 July.

1831   In January leaves Nohant for Paris for three months. "La Prima donna," written with J. Sandeau, appears in April issue of *La Revue de Paris,* signed J. Sand. *Rose et Blanche,* another collaboration, also signed J. Sand.

1832   Publishes *Indiana* and *Valentine* under the name G. Sand. In December contracts with Buloz for a regular collaboration.

1833   Meets Alfred de Musset in June; leaves with him for Italy in December. *Lélia.*

1834   Musset falls ill in Venice. Sand has affair with Dr. Pagello, returns to Paris, and begins *Lettres d'un voyageur. Jacques* and *Leone Leoni.*

1835   Signs a separation agreement with Dudevant 15 February. Meets Michel de Bourges 9 April. Files for legal separation in October. *André.*

1836   Wins custody of both children in separation trial in February. Final agreement signed 29 July. Musset's *La Confession d'un enfant du siècle.*

1837   Mother dies in August. *Mauprat.*

1838   Balzac visits Nohant in late winter. Sand meets Frédéric Chopin; travels to Majorca with him, October–December. *Spiridion* and *Les Sept Cordes de la lyre*.

1839   In February departs Valldemosa for Barcelona, Marseilles, and eventually Nohant. Second version of *Lélia*.

1840   *Le Compagnon du tour de France. Cosima,* Sand's first play, performed and published.

1841   Legal proceedings against Buloz. First issue of the *Revue indépendante* appears in November. *Un Hiver à Majorque.*

1842   *Consuelo,* followed the next year by *La Comtesse de Rudolstadt.*

1844   Chopin's father dies 3 May. First issue of *L'Eclaireur de l'Indre* appears 14 September. *Jeanne.*

1845   *Le Meunier d'Angibault* and *Le Péché de Monsieur Antoine.*

1846   Chopin returns to Paris alone in November. *La Mare au diable* and *Lucrezia Floriani.*

1847   Begins *Histoire de ma vie.* Solange breaks off previous engagement and marries the sculptor Jean-Baptiste-Auguste Clésinger 19 May. *François le champi.*

1848   Jeanne-Gabrielle Clésinger born 28 February, dies 6 March. Sand's last meeting with Chopin 4 March. Hippolyte Chatiron, Sand's half-brother, dies 23 December. *La Petite Fadette.*

1849   At Guillery Solange's second child, Jeanne-Gabrielle, born 10 May. Chopin dies in Paris 17 October.

1851   Leaves Paris after the coup d'état 4 December.

1852   Sees President Louis-Napoléon 24 January.

1853   *Les Maîtres sonneurs.*

1854   Clésinger and Solange are legally separated in December. *Adriani,* the play *Maître Favilla,* and *Histoire de ma vie.*

1855   Jeanne-Gabrielle Clésinger dies in January. Sand travels with Alexandre Manceau and Maurice to Italy in February.

1857   Discovery of Gargilesse. *La Daniella.*

1859   *Elle et Lui.*

1860   Suffers serious attack of typhus in late October, which leaves her very weak. *Le Marquis de Villemer.*

1861   *Valvèdre.*

1862 Maurice marries Lina Calamatta at Nohant in May.

1863 Maurice's son, François-Marc-Antoine, born 14 July. *Mademoiselle la Quintinie.*

1864 Leaves Nohant with Manceau under Maurice's supervision and they take a small house in Palaiseau. François-Marc-Antoine dies at Guillery 21 July. *La Confession d'une jeune fille.*

1865 Manceau dies at Palaiseau 21 August.

1866 Maurice's daughter Jeanne-Claudine-Aurore born in January. Sand visits Flaubert at Croisset.

1868 Maurice's daughter Jeanne-Lucile-Gabrielle born in March.

1870 Sand and her family leave Nohant in autumn because of an epidemic of smallpox.

1871 *Le Journal d'un voyageur pendant la guerre.*

1872 *Nanon.*

1873 First volume of *Contes d'une grand-mère.*

1876 After a short and painful illness, dies on 8 June. Buried two days later in the family cemetery. Second volume of *Contes d'une grand-mère.*

Chapter One

George Sand's Life and Works

Knowledge of George Sand's life is for her reader both an advantage and a disadvantage. She fascinated her contemporaries after her move to Paris in the early 1830s; people often read her works because of what they knew about her life. Yet biographical information has prejudiced many readers, resulting in unfair judgments of her fiction. The investigation of Sand's life and times must reinsert itself into a wider social context and a narrower textual framework. A limited biography is, however, in order.

A Mixed Lineage

Amantine-Aurore-Lucile Dupin was born in Paris to Maurice Dupin and Antoinette-Sophie-Victoire Delaborde, on 1 July 1804. The next day she was baptized at Saint-Nicolas-des-Champs as Amandine-Aurore-Lucie. Aurore started life with a family tradition that combined two separate worlds: Maurice Dupin could trace his ancestry back to the king of Poland, and Sophie Delaborde was the daughter of a Parisian bird-seller. As George Sand would later devote more than five hundred pages in the Pléiade edition of her autobiography to her ancestry, a few words concerning her mixed heritage are appropriate.

Louis-Claude Dupin de Francueil, the recognized natural son of Frederic-Auguste de Saxe, King of Poland, and Aurore of Koenigsmark, a Swedish countess, was given the title Maréchal de France by Louis XV to demonstrate the French government's gratitude for Maurice's instrumental role in the wars for the Polish succession. His affair with a beautiful actress, Marie Rainteau, produced a daughter in 1748, Marie-Aurore.

Marie-Aurore enjoyed a cultured upbringing in Paris with her mother and aunt, who now called themselves the de Verrières damsels. She was put into the convent at Saint-Cyr until the age of eighteen. She petitioned Parliament to be registered in civil court as the natural daughter of the Maréchal de Saxe, which made her marriageable. After an unfortunate marriage, failed petitions, and the like, Marie-Aurore married her aunt's recent lover, Louis-Claude Dupin de Francueil, aged sixty-one; she was then twenty-nine. One year later, in 1778, she gave birth to a son, Maurice, the father of George Sand.

In 1793, five years after her husband's death, Mme Dupin de Francueil purchased Nohant. But "citoyenne" Dupin (Marie-Aurore) was imprisoned later that year for hiding jewels and silver. When the nobility was exiled from Paris, Maurice could only communicate with his mother by letter. George Sand includes a large number of these letters, many rewritten in her own literary vein, in her *Histoire de ma vie*.

After the Reign of Terror Aurore Dupin was released from prison. She returned with her son to Nohant, where they started life anew, making the best of their reduced status. Maurice had a son, Pierre Laverdure, known as Hippolyte Chatiron, with a local woman, Catherine Chatiron, in 1799. But he was inspired by the noble prospect of military achievement; he responded immediately to the Directory's general conscription. Maurice enjoyed steady promotion in the military and was first lieutenant in Milan when he met Sophie Delaborde, the mistress of his superior officer. Sophie was five years older than Maurice, had had a child at the age of sixteen, and another child, Caroline, with a different man.

Maurice married Sophie in Paris on 5 June 1804 without his mother's knowledge. A month later Aurore Dupin was born. Maurice's mother tried to have the marriage annulled, claiming that Maurice was not of age to marry without the consent of his parents. But once she saw her own granddaughter, she was so charmed by her that she dropped the suit and accepted her son's marriage.

Youth and Marriage

Aurore's childhood centered on the absence of her father, whose military career was flourishing in Napoleon's army. With him gone, Aurore's world was peopled with her mother, her Aunt Lucie, and Caroline, her illegitimate half-sister. But in 1808 Sophie, seven or eight months pregnant, took Aurore and went to Madrid where Maurice had just been stationed. They lived there for two months. Aurore was only four years old, but the sojourn left her with many memories, including the recollection of dressing in a military uniform that duplicated her father's.

Sophie bore a blind son. He was very weak and suffered gravely from the trip to Nohant, where the family moved after the Spanish uprising. The son died and was buried at Nohant. Sophie, fearing he had been buried alive, had the boy exhumed and reburied; the next day, Maurice went to La Châtre and had a riding accident on the way home and died.

The issue of guardianship now posed serious problems and the rift between the two Mme Dupins widened. Finally an agreement was settled upon: Aurore would stay with her grandmother at Nohant and her mother would receive an annual allowance of a thousand francs and would live on her own in Paris. Thus in February 1809 Aurore found herself without father or mother, living in a strange place with a very strict grandmother.

It was during these difficult years that Aurore invented the deity Corambé. Corambé was an androgynous, Christ-like figure for whom Aurore built a natural temple out of brightly colored pebbles and shells, moss, ferns, and birds' nests. She worshiped Corambé and told him/her her deepest secrets; she called this oral ritual her "roman" (novel). But one day a little friend discovered her secret, and Aurore destroyed the altar and internalized Corambé.

In the Convent of English Augustinians, where she continued her education, Aurore developed in opposing directions. On the one hand, she became a favorite member of the "diables," the mischief-makers of the convent. On the other hand, she befriended Sister Marie-Alicia Spring, whom she adored for her beauty and fine manners. This quasi cult for Sister Alicia transformed Aurore into a devout girl, who, at the age of fifteen, had a vision while contemplating the words "Tolle, lege" in a painting of St. Augustine. Her sudden conversion as a result of this vision moved her to contemplate taking vows, but both Sister Alicia and Aurore's confessor, Abbot Prémord, discouraged this action. Mme Dupin, very concerned with her granddaughter's recent penchant, removed her from the convent.

Aurore's grandmother fell ill in March 1821. Her condition deteriorated quickly, and she died the day after Christmas, leaving Aurore with these words: "You are losing your best friend." The prediction proved to be true, for at the reading of her will both sides of the family revealed their true colors. The Villeneuve side of the family from Châteauroux (Maurice's relatives) attempted to force an agreement that Aurore would never see her mother again. Sophie determined to take Aurore to Paris with the firm intention of taking control of Nohant. The law of maternal right prevailed and Aurore went to live with Sophie in Paris.

Aurore felt trapped. During her grandmother's illness she had functioned as the mistress of the château at Nohant; now, at seventeen, she found herself once again a child, answerable to her mother. Aurore went to the suburbs to stay with Sophie's friends, the du Plessis family. They treated her as their adoptive daughter, and on a trip to Paris they ran into an old friend, Casimir Dudevant, the illegitimate but recognized son of Baron Jean-François Dudevant.

Aurore and Casimir seemed to have much in common: they shared almost the same birthday, both were of mixed heritage, both were from families with illegitimate children, and both stood to inherit an impressive sum of money and some land. Despite Sophie's misgivings, a marriage contract was drawn up that reserved Aurore's inheritance for her although it would not be under her own control. The contract was signed 24 August 1822 and the wedding took place three weeks later. Aurore was eighteen, Casimir twenty-seven.

After a brief wedding trip, the couple established themselves at Nohant. Aurore soon became pregnant, but a delicate condition caused her to keep to her bed. She took to needlework while her husband went hunting with Hippolyte. On 30 June 1823, in Paris, Aurore gave birth to a son, Maurice Dudevant. She decided to breastfeed him, which was rather unusual for a woman of her class.

After Maurice's birth, Aurore grew despondent, and Casimir remained unresponsive and insensitive. So, when two former convent friends contacted Aurore and invited her and Casimir to accompany them on a trip to the Pyrenees, Aurore welcomed the change, and her spirits soon rose. She relaxed with the new friends she had made, Zoé Leroy, a young woman from Bordeaux, and Aurélien de Sèze, a young lawyer who immediately fell in love with Aurore.

Although Aurore might not have returned the passionate love that Aurélien felt for her, she did encourage his emotions. Together they shared a heightened sensibility. Aurore admitted her feelings to Casimir, but she assured her husband of the chastity of the relationship in a long letter, now known as "the confession letter."[1]

With the return to Nohant in 1826 also came the return of a childhood friend, Stéphane Ajasson. Aurore began seeing Stéphane again after her trip to the Mont-Dore spa in Auvergne (August 1827). There seems to be every reason to suspect that the daughter that Aurore bore on 13 September 1828, named Solange, was the result of her union with Stéphane.

It was at this time that Aurore began to write fiction. With a pet cricket at her side, she produced "La Marraine" (The godmother), an unpublished novel about the courage of a loving woman. This novel, which Aurore never sought to have published, demonstrates an important thematic initiative in George Sand's works.

Writing in Paris

Just after the July Revolution Aurore met Jules Sandeau, a young Berrichon man studying in Paris who was home in La Châtre on holiday. He was good-looking and clever—exactly what Aurore felt she needed to rescue her from her dull life with Casimir. Aurore and Jules were soon involved in an affair they scarcely hid from anyone, including Casimir.

In November of that year, Aurore happened to run across an envelope in her husband's desk addressed to her, but not to be opened until his death. Aurore did not waste any time opening it and, much to her dismay, she discovered exactly what her husband thought of her.[2] Confronted with this letter, Casimir could only plead guilty, and together they devised a financial agreement whereby Aurore would receive an annual allowance that would permit her to live half the year in Paris. In January 1831 she left Nohant to spend the next three months in Paris.

Aurore arrived in the capital full of verve and hope. There was already a well-established Berrichon community in Paris, she would be with her lover, Jules, and she already had a novel practically finished (*Aimée*) with which to make her debut in the Parisian literary circuit. She wanted to fit in with other writers, so she dressed just like them: a long, square morning coat in gray wool with matching trousers and vest, a big grey cravat, and metal-tipped boots. She could easily put her hair up into the gray top hat that students were wearing. Dressed thus, Aurore found she could come and go in public as she liked without the constraints placed on women's dress and deportment: "I was no longer a *lady,* nor was I a *gentleman;* I could walk around in *man's desert.*"[3]

Aurore's first disillusionment in the world of literary marketing came shortly after her arrival in Paris. She went to see Henri Delatouche, a Berrichon who had tried his hand at all forms of literature. Now bitter, he ran *Le Figaro,* at this time a four-page polemical and satirical paper of the opposition. Delatouche read *Aimée* and counseled Aurore not to write novels, but he did hire her to compose a few columns for his paper.

Aurore sought other routes into the world of literature. She garnered an introduction to Count Auguste de Kératry, a deputy from Brittany and the author of a violent novel.[4] He was less than encouraging. According to Sand's romanticized version of the story, he seems to have advised her that women should not write, and that she ought not to make books, but babies.[5]

Nonetheless, Aurore was not discouraged. Inspired by her admiration for la Malibran, the famous soprano Maria Garcia Malibran, Aurore collaborated with Jules Sandeau on a story for *La Revue de Paris,* "La Prima donna."

The story was signed simply "J. Sand." This piece won Balzac's approval, and Aurore began to believe there was a future in writing. She collaborated with Sandeau on a second short story, "La Fille d'Albano," which they sold to the small paper *La Mode* one month later. Later that year a novel came out under the name of *Rose et Blanche,* signed "J. Sand." This pseudonym served the purpose of hiding their collaboration, and Aurore's sex, behind one name.

It was only with the writing of her first solo work, *Indiana* (1832), that Aurore was forced to find another name. Jules was no longer willing to share his truncated name when he was not contributing to the work. With the advice of Delatouche, Aurore kept the surname under which she had already published, and she took a different Christian name: "I quickly and resolutely took the name George, which seemed to me synonymous with Berrichon" (*OA,* 2:138–39). It also placated Casimir's mother, who had asked if Aurore insisted on publishing what she wrote, that she not use the Dudevant name.

Musset and Italy

The immense success of *Indiana* marked the arrival of George Sand the writer. She no longer collaborated with Jules Sandeau, who had become somewhat jealous of her good fortune. He realized that she had more discipline and perhaps even more talent than he had. He was further discouraged when she published her second novel, *Valentine,* in November 1832, and she was frustrated by his lack of work. It is thus not surprising that the relationship began to suffer. Sand moved into another garret apartment in late 1832, about the same time that she signed a contract for regular collaboration with François Buloz, the director of *La Revue des Deux Mondes.* Jules tried to continue in Aurore's good graces as long as possible, but she finally rid herself of him by financing his trip to Italy.

George Sand soon met the famous actress Marie Dorval, then the mistress of Alfred de Vigny. Sand was captivated by the actress's sensitivity and art and asked to meet her; Dorval came to her apartment the next day. They discovered they had many things in common, especially in the domain of art. The two spent much time together. Sand often went to see Dorval in her dressing room after the evening's performance to be alone with her. They became known as "les inséparables." Sand and Dorval's correspondence bears witness to an intimate relationship about which we can only conjecture, but it is clear that the two women were very close.[6] It is of ironic interest that when Sandeau published his novel *Marianna* in 1839, the success of the novel turned the heads of many women, but it was Marie Dorval who won his heart.

In the beginning stages of her relationship with Dorval, Sand was writing her new and innovative novel, *Lélia,* a disturbing work about a woman desperately seeking a meaning for her life. With the dual heroine Lélia-Pulchérie, Sand reaffirmed a marked attachment to double characters and doppelgänger, and to the dialectic of sexual frustration and the asexual yearning for love. Buloz reacted badly to the preliminary form of this work, a short story entitled "Trenmor." Sand decided to give the manuscript of *Lélia* to Dupuy, with whom she had already published *Indiana* and *Valentine.*

It was at this time, April 1833, that George Sand and Prosper Mérimée met and exchanged some letters. He promised to cure her of the headache that her husband had caused her by showing up in Paris with Maurice. Mérimée took Sand and Solange to the Opéra to see Meyerbeer's *Robert le diable.* They then spent either one night, forty-eight hours, or seven days together, according to different versions of the story. Mérimée apparently did not impress George Sand as a lover, and the "affair" was very short-lived. Mérimée never accepted the rejection and is said to have cast many aspersions on the reputation of George Sand.[7]

Lélia appeared in July 1833. The reaction was mixed: Sainte-Beuve admired the novel; Capo de Feuillade called it a worthless piece of filth.[8] Generally the reviews showed either admiration or confusion; there was little middle ground. Sand, who had given a lot of herself to the creation of a truly original work, was dissatisfied with the critical reception.

One positive critic was Alfred de Musset. Sand had met Musset at a dinner at Sainte-Beuve's. They exchanged several letters, and shortly after the publication of *Lélia* they became lovers. In early August 1833 they enjoyed a brief sojourn at Fontainebleau. While George Sand was grateful to get away from her critics, Musset was probably reliving an experience with another woman. During a walk through the woods one day, Musset was struck with a fit of trembling while he stared into space with a glassy expression in his eyes. He had an hallucination: he saw himself as a pale man, unkempt and in torn clothes, his hideous face deformed by hatred and disdain. Although they ended their visit at Fontainebleau cheerfully, this incident would not soon be forgotten.

Musset and Sand felt they had found the incarnation of their respective romantic dreams. Their liaison advanced quickly and they planned a trip to Italy together. Maurice was in boarding school in Paris and Sand took Solange to Nohant. She arranged a financial deal with Buloz whereby he advanced her money on the next novel she was about to write, an "Italian" novel, *Jacques.* On 12 December 1833 Sand and Musset left Paris for Lyons, where they boarded a steamer down the Rhône. On board they met Stendhal, who was also en route to Italy; the meeting was cordial, but nothing more. Musset was seasick on the boat from Marseilles to Genoa, but once in Genoa it was Sand who fell ill while Musset sought his amusement on the streets. This habit stuck with him in Florence and later in Venice, where they arrived on New Year's Eve.[9]

Once in Venice, George Sand fell ill again, this time with sick headaches. Musset, exasperated, left her alone and finally admitted to her that he no longer loved her. Had she not been too weak to travel, Sand might have left Venice then and there. But she stayed on, requesting a doctor; the physician was Dr. Pietro Pagello.

Musset then fell ill. Not only had he contracted a "nasty disease,"[10] but he now was victim to uncontrollable fevers and seizures. Dr. Pagello was called in to treat him. The diagnosis was typhoid fever and pneumonia; his state was dire and he tottered on the edge of death for several days. It was during this period, while Pagello cared for Musset, that George Sand developed an admiration for the young doctor's sensitive and virile demeanor. In moments of lucidity, Musset imagined he saw the two of them embracing or planning the trips they would take after he was gone. However many of the details Musset might have imagined, Sand's feelings for Pagello were a reality.

Finally, after Musset was out of danger and following many bitter quarrels and jealous rages, he left Venice on relatively good terms with both Sand and Pagello. Even though she enjoyed the time spent touring the Veneto with Pagello, Sand still yearned for Paris and Musset. She and Musset had once again begun to exchange letters, first on practical concerns of health and accommodations, then on their despair over lost romantic dreams. Sand left Venice, accompanied by Pagello, in late July 1834. His intention was only to accompany her on the long and difficult voyage; he never entertained illusions of a new life in Paris with George Sand.

Sand agreed to see Musset a few times in Paris; the meetings were painful but passionate. Musset left for Baden Baden uplifted and full of plans for the autobiographical novel that he would dedicate to the woman who inspired this love, *La Confession d'un enfant du siècle*. George Sand left Paris on the same day; Pagello remained in Paris. Once in Nohant, she realized how little she felt for the Venetian doctor. This was the summer of Sand's thirtieth birthday, and her thoughts turned to Mme de Staël's *Réflexions sur le suicide*. Instead of convincing Sand of the value of life, this metaphysical text caused her to become more despondent.[11]

As Sand had expected, she had a dreadful quarrel with Casimir, and she returned to Paris with both children. Solange's presence in Sand's apartment created an obstacle, or the pretext of one, for entertaining Pagello there. Musset's imminent return to Paris promised renewed problems. In short, Pagello recognized his awkward position and, quite simply, packed his bags and left.

The following months constitute a tumultuous series of reconciliations and quarrels between Sand and Musset. They alternately sent each other locks of hair, refused to see each other, fell passionately into each other's arms, and so on. The last scene of this quintessentially romantic series of episodes took place at Musset's mother's, where he lay ill in bed, requesting that George care for him. Although she came, she deftly engineered her escape after Musset pulled a knife on her and she threatened suicide. Once again off to Nohant in March 1835, she could finally turn the page on this chapter of her life.[12]

Perhaps the most important newcomer to the group of friends who were privy to these vicissitudes was Franz Liszt, whom Musset had invited to dinner in the autumn of 1834. Musset had grown jealous of him when he observed how much Liszt and Sand had in common. Sand had even gone so far as to ask Liszt not to visit her for fear Musset would interpret their relationship as more intimate than it was. This friendship would develop into a strong emotional and intellectual bond.

Separation and Freedom

Near the final breakup with Musset, George Sand drew up an agreement with Casimir wherein he agreed to give her full rule and responsibility of Nohant by the end of the summer of 1835. Casimir deplored the contract and wasted no tact in displaying his feelings about it. George Sand was furious at the rumor that she had accepted charity from the likes of Casimir Dudevant when, in fact, this matter concerned her own inheritance. Consequently, she ripped up the document, a rash reaction that she soon regretted.

Sand sought legal advice in Gabriel Planet, a young Berrichon lawyer who had welcomed Sand and Sandeau many times in his Berrichon-club home in Paris. He advised her to put her children in boarding schools to spare them from future scenes and to protect them from being used as pawns. Along with his legal advice, Planet shared his republican ideas with Sand. He told her of the republican newspaper he had founded with a Louis Chrysostome Michel, a famous lawyer in Bourges.

George met Michel, known as Michel de Bourges, in April 1835. Their first conversation lasted until four o'clock in the morning. He was appalled that she had not as yet shown any effort to postulate republican-liberal prin-

ciples in her novels. She was dismayed that he should expect literature to
serve purely political and didactic ends. The flame of what was to become a
passionate yet consoling conflict had been kindled.

Dropping plans to rewrite her short story "Mauprat" as a novel, and leaving her manuscript "Engelwald" unfinished,[13] Sand dashed off another
Lettre d'un voyageur, the sixth, dedicated to "Everard," a code name for
Michel. In the letter she attacks blind political faith, yet, at the same time,
her passion is clear. Michel went to Paris in May for the most important trial
of his career, the famous trial of the Lyons silk workers that put Michel in
sickbed and later in prison. Sand stood by him throughout his difficulties.

By mid-October 1835 conditions at Nohant had grown intolerable.
Casimir's scenes were well known, but on one occasion he had to be physi-
cally restrained from striking his wife. George Sand immediately consulted
François Rollinat, a Berrichon friend and lawyer, and Michel, who was at that
time serving a prison term in Bourges. Both lawyers advised her to file for
separation without delay. To avoid weakening her case, she left Nohant while
Casimir was taking the children to Paris.

The court decided in George Sand's favor: the legal separation gave her
custody of both children and advised the separation of property. Casimir appealed this decision, establishing a long list of grievances against his wife, including her affairs with Sandeau and Michel de Bourges. Ironically, instead
of arguing against the separation agreement, he made a strong case in favor of
separation. The court found his line of attack totally without foundation and
Casimir lost his appeal. In February 1836 the court upheld its first decision.
Far from being discouraged, Casimir took his appeal to a higher court in
Bourges, which meant that the details would become public.

Thinking it best not to be seen too often in the company of Michel de
Bourges, Sand sought to spend time with others. Charles Didier, a Swiss
writer whom George Sand had met in 1833, often served as Sand's new confidant. She spent so much time with him that gossip was inevitable. Liszt
wrote from Geneva to ask if the rumors were true, and Michel became irate
when he heard them in Bourges. From Didier's diary we know that he suffered from the great attraction he felt for Sand. Although they probably
shared a few intimate moments, there was never any profound love between
Sand and the Swiss writer.[14]

Several public hearings were conducted in Bourges, bringing all the details of the Dudevant household out into the public.[15] The public trial
began on 25 July 1836. George Sand had thirteen witnesses to speak on
her behalf; Casimir had four. Casimir's attorney used the same grievances
and arguments he had used in his previous appeal, which Michel de

Bourges easily demolished. The judges were equally divided, five against five. The public denounced the stalemate so vociferously in George Sand's support that Casimir gave in and accepted the original agreement. George Sand returned to Nohant with Solange. She wrote to her mother, "Finally I'm free!" (*Corres.*, 3:501).

Liszt

Shortly after the trial, George Sand took her children to visit Liszt in Geneva. Liszt and Sand had been friends since 1834 and shared a common bond in music. Liszt's musical genius corresponded to her romantic ideals. He was doubtless attracted to her because she embodied a combination of aristocratic background and democratic ideas. He found in her the same love and pursuit of knowledge that he lived.

Theirs was a friendship based on respect and shared ideals. It was Sand's novels that had inspired Liszt and Marie d'Agoult. They had both read *Indiana* and *Lélia* and were known to have lovingly disputed which of the two had first read *Leone Leoni*. Nonetheless, rumors about Liszt and Sand ran rampant. Sand explains in her *Journal intime* that she might have loved him, for he possessed the admirable qualities that she sought in a man. But she simply did not love him. In the words of her famous analogy, "I would very much regret to learn that I liked spinach, for if I liked it I would eat it, but as it is, I can't stand it" (*OA*, 2:959).

At the time of Sand's visit to Geneva, Liszt had just finished a commemorative piece dedicated to la Malibran, who had just died in a horseback riding accident. While he put the final touches on his *Rondo fantastique*, which he dedicated to Sand, George listened from a supine position under the piano. She was inspired that night to write a short story, "Le Contrebandier," based on the Liszt piano piece.[16]

Liszt and Marie came for a long visit at Nohant in the summer of 1837, during which they witnessed the end of the dying relationship with Michel de Bourges. Sand described her deep disappointment with the affair in *Entretiens journaliers avec le Docteur Piffoël;* owing to the introspective, diarylike style, this account rings truer than the version in her autobiography. These passages are rich in thoughts on love, relationships, men, and the inevitable disillusion of an ended affair and the doubt that she will ever learn to conduct her private life better.[17]

When the affair with Michel was finished, the famous actor Victor Bocage came to Nohant to entice Sand to write a play for him. He was quite obviously courting Sand, as Marie d'Agoult notes in her *Mémoires*, and Barry agrees that Sand probably allowed his flattery to work, perhaps even at the same time as she was being entertained by Félicien Mallefille.[18] Mallefille, a friend of Liszt and Marie, showed up at Nohant in July. He was a playwright and flattered Sand's weakness for young intellectuals. To the great chagrin of Didier, who visited Nohant that summer, Mallefille soon became Sand's new lover and Maurice's new tutor.

In August of 1837 Sand's mother lost the long battle with a lingering disease. As Sand was comforting her mother in her final days, she learned that Casimir had kidnapped Solange and had taken her to his family's home in Guillery (near Bordeaux). George had to obtain a judicial order and police assistance to get her daughter back.

Sand was able to devote some time to her writing in 1838. Despite crippling pain due to rheumatism, she managed to finish *L'Uscoque* (The Corsair), although sometimes only by dictating to Mallefille. She immediately started a new novel, *Spiridion*.

Balzac, visiting in a nearby town, wrote to ask permission to call on Sand at Nohant. The two authors had known each other in their younger days in Paris in the early 1830s. They had, however, become somewhat estranged because of Sand's split with Sandeau, whom Balzac had counseled and promoted. Sand welcomed the chance to renew their friendship. Balzac stayed at Nohant for a week in late February 1838, during which time they discussed their ideas on literature, marriage, and freedom. Balzac must have sensed the strained relations between the Berrichon "lioness" and Marie d'Agoult. He used this information and intuition in a novel entitled *Béatrix* (1844).[19]

Chopin

New financial problems took Sand back to Paris, where she was kindly put up by Carlotta Marliani. In this house Sand met several interesting people, including Victor Hugo, Charles Nodier, and Frédéric Chopin. Sand had met Chopin before and was already smitten by him. She had asked Marie and Liszt to bring the composer and his poet friend Mickiewicz to Nohant with them the previous year. Chopin, traditional in many ways, had been somewhat frightened by the overt aggressiveness of the Berrichon author and had declined the invitation. When they met again in Paris, Chopin was less put off by the behavior of "the lioness."[20]

Sand took this occasion to write a long letter to Chopin's friend, Count Albert Grzymala. She wrote frankly about her situation with Mallefille and inquired about Chopin's amorous exploits. We do not have Grzymala's reply, but Sand lost no time in pursuing her courtship. By early June Sand returned to Paris and molded the tender beginnings of the nine-year affair.

Despite Chopin's moral and religious misgivings at entering into an affair with a woman who was separated from her husband and was the mother of two children, he allowed himself to be seduced, and the romantic couple spent the winter in Majorca. Their first accommodations proved to be ill equipped for the damp weather of that winter. Chopin's coughing became a serious worry to Sand and to the local population, who were convinced he was harboring some terrible, contagious disease. Sand managed to find them an abandoned charterhouse at Valldemosa, overlooking the sea. The Arabic mosaics and remote location of the monastery gave the couple the fantastic and romantic surroundings they desired. Chopin's Pleyel piano soon arrived, and he set to work.

In the two short months the couple spent at Valldemosa, Sand completed revisions on *Lélia* and finished *Spiridion*.[21] Chopin composed a number of ballads and preludes, two polonaises, and the third scherzo. This represents a considerable amount of work, especially considering how ill he was. By mid-February, Chopin was feeling completely cut off from civilization, his coughing fits were becoming more and more severe, and Sand was so exhausted with trying to play mother, housekeeper, nursemaid, and author, that they decided to leave the Spanish island for France.

Sand could no longer hide the truth of Chopin's consumption from herself. Once in France, his recovery was rapid and satisfactory. During their stay in Marseilles, Sand worked more than she had in Majorca. In five weeks she produced the *Essai sur le drame fantastique* (Essay on fantastic drama) and a novel in dialogue form, *Gabriel*.

By summer 1839, Chopin and Sand were installed at Nohant like a long-married couple. Despite the calm surroundings in the Berry, that summer was rather hectic for George Sand. She discovered that the repairs on the Hôtel de Narbonne were much more expensive than the original estimates, and she still owed Casimir some money by the terms of their agreement. To make ends meet it was imperative that she write. She exchanged heated letters with Bulloz trying to get him to honor their contract and print her essay on Goethe and *Les Sept Cordes de la lyre,* which he found much too "phantasmagorical" for his readers (*Corres.,* 4:701).

As for Chopin, this summer brought him the energy to complete several of his finest works: the Sonata in B-flat Minor, a nocturne, and three mazurkas. Despite his dislike for the countryside, he was able to bury himself in his work at Nohant, something he could ill afford to do in Paris, where he would be constantly committed to giving lessons and recitals.

Chopin needed the financial security of life in Paris, however, so they returned in October. Although George may have preferred to stay at Nohant and continue playing host to her many guests, she too found that her expenses were less in Paris. They established two separate residences, Chopin in the rue Tronchet, and George and the children in the rue Pigalle. During the day Chopin gave lessons while George, rising at midday after having written until quite late, would attend to domestic chores. Dinner en famille would follow.

Sand dashed off a short story, "Pauline," and then set to work on the project for the Théâtre Français that Buloz was pushing her to do. His recent appointment to the Royal Commission afforded her an opportunity to see a play mounted there. She produced her play, *Cosima,* which ran into several difficulties. Marie Dorval, in the title role, did not think much of the script. The play was finally staged and produced at the end of April 1840. It was very badly received and ran for only seven performances. This was a great emotional and financial blow to Sand.

Sand embarked on a new area of interest in her writing at this time: socialism. The preceding summer she had written an unpublished article in support of Barbès after his imprisonment. She was becoming interested in promoting social change through her work. This was as much a delayed reaction to Michel de Bourges's influence as an independent awakening to the current political climate. She made contact with Agricol Perdiguier, whose recent book, *Le Livre du compagnonnage,* spoke of reform during the period of industrial unrest France was experiencing. Late in the summer of 1840 Sand began her own novel exploring the same issue, *Le Compagnon du tour de France* (The Journeyman on the Tour of France).

Sand began to associate with other socialist reformers and rustic poets. Given his aristocratic tastes, Chopin did not appreciate these new colleagues, who would call frequently at the rue Pigalle. But Sand did meet one new friend of whom Chopin approved:. Pauline Viardot, the sister of Maria Garcia Malibran. Pauline's husband, Louis Viardot, had abandoned his job in the theater to promote his wife's singing career. Sand and Chopin eagerly watched and encouraged her progress.

The relationship with the Viardots turned out to be directly beneficial to Sand. Louis Viardot helped Pierre Leroux found *La Revue indépendante.* Sand contributed, first, *Horace,* then two articles, and finally *Consuelo* to this newspaper. Despite Sand's popularity, the newspaper could not attract enough regular subscribers to sustain it. Leroux eventually abandoned his responsibility, leaving uncorrected proofs and unfinished business. The *Revue* folded, but Sand rounded up a group of friends of the Opposition, and with their financial support created *L'Eclaireur de l'Indre,* which Pierre Leroux edited in Boussac. Even Chopin was prevailed upon to contribute fifty francs.

The publication of *Horace* marked the end of Sand's moribund relationship with Marie d'Agoult. There had always been an underlying tension between the two women, mostly due to Marie's jealousy at the effect George Sand had on Liszt.[22] Sand learned from Lamennais and from Carlotta Marliani of disparaging remarks Marie had made about her. *Horace,* however, struck the final blow to their relationship. The character of the Vicomtesse de Chailly is a thinly veiled caricature of Marie, depicting her vanity and her slow wit, which Sand referred to as "artificial intelligence." After this turn of events the two women never spoke again.[23]

Sand's new female friend, the talented mezzo-soprano Pauline Viardot, took on the role of confidante. Sand had "saved" Pauline from marrying Musset and introduced her to Louis Viardot, whom the singer married in 1840. The two women were totally devoted to each other.[24] Pauline found herself virtually barred from any Paris stage during the 1841–42 season because of rivalries. This situation gave Sand an idea for a novella. With Chopin's reflections on music in general, and on Slavic music in particular, and with Leroux's socialist-historical commentaries in his *Encyclopédie nouvelle,* Sand soon developed a colossal plot that would cover over a thousand pages in two books—*Consuelo* and its sequel, *La Comtesse de Rudolstadt.* This is doubtless Sand's most enterprising and serious composition.

The summer of 1844 brought a tragedy to the Sand-Chopin household: the death of Chopin's father. Chopin was already depressed because of chronic coughing and the weakness it had caused him. The news of his father's death sent him into a deeper depression. He locked himself in his room for forty-eight hours and would see no one. At the same time, Chopin's sister and her husband made a trip to France, and George Sand was quick to invite them to Nohant, where they arrived in early August. Given these circumstances and the added strain of an advanced deadline, Sand still managed to finish *Jeanne* and begin her next novel, *Le Meunier d'Angibault* (The Miller of Angibault).

About a year later, Augustine Brault, a distant cousin of Sophie, came into the lives of the family at Nohant. Her family was poor and her mother, hoping for a fine marriage, encouraged Augustine to "befriend" Maurice Sand, but Maurice's sentiments were for Pauline Viardot. Augustine's mother was greatly displeased at the failed plan and beat her for it. When George found out about this, she took Augustine in as an adoptive daughter at Nohant, virtually replacing Solange. But, Augustine's presence at Nohant would later cause many difficulties.

This is perhaps the beginning of the complex rivalries that plagued the last months of Chopin and Sand's companionship. Returning to Paris was imperative for Chopin's sense of well-being, whereas Maurice much preferred to remain at Nohant. The next summer's events provided a new source of competition for the two men. Maurice invited another pupil of Eugène Delacroix, Eugène Lambert, for a visit at Nohant. His presence along with that of other guests meant that all extra beds at Nohant were occupied. When Chopin wished to invite his compatriot and friend Newakowski to Nohant, he was told there was no room. Chopin accused Sand of showing favoritism toward Maurice, and flew into a jealous rage.

Solange fueled the disagreement. She was jealous of both Augustine and her mother, and at age sixteen, in 1844, she took pleasure in teasing and flirting. As Chopin had more affinities with Solange than with Maurice, apparently her charms did not go unnoticed by Chopin. Eager to vent her jealousy of her Brault cousin, Solange told Chopin that Maurice was Augustine's lover. Chopin attacked Maurice on moral causes, and Maurice threatened to leave Nohant. George Sand refused to hear talk of his leaving.

Chopin left for Paris in November 1846, not realizing he would never see Nohant again. For a while he and Sand exchanged friendly letters, but he grew cool toward her when he discovered that plans for Solange's marriage with the aristocrat Preaulx had been broken off so that she could marry an irresponsible sculptor, Auguste Clésinger, and that George Sand had reluctantly given her permission for the match without first consulting with Chopin. Casimir readily agreed to the marriage.

Shortly after Solange's honeymoon, she quarreled with her husband and fled his volatile temper. Once back at Nohant, she discovered Sand's intent to marry off Augustine with a handsome dowry to the painter Théodore Rousseau. Solange could not accept that her mother's money would go to Augustine, so she concocted a complex scheme to embroil not only Augustine with her fiancé, but also her mother with her lover of nine years. The jealous lies she told everyone succeeded in breaking off relations all around.

The last time Sand and Chopin saw each other was by chance, on the steps to Carlotta Marliani's house, at which time Chopin informed Sand of the birth of Solange's child in the spring of 1848.[25] Chopin died, in Paris, eighteen months later.

Revolution and the Republic

Victor Borie, a young actor, soon replaced Chopin as Sand's love interest. Solange was outraged and spread the news in disapproving terms to anyone who would listen. In the meantime, debts had piled up and Sand was having difficulty publishing her novel "Célio Floriani."[26] With the encouragement of Maurice and others, she undertook the writing of her memoirs. This was to be her next ambitious work. She finally managed to establish a workable contract with the help of her friend and editor, Pierre-Jules Hetzel.

February 1848 found Sand at Nohant, buried in accounts of her father's life during the Napoleonic conquests. At the same time, Maurice was in Paris, and when rioting broke out, he took a stand and helped to build barricades. Sand was constantly concerned for his safety. By the end of February she decided to go to Paris to see for herself what was happening. Her correspondence with her son during this period is a most valuable historical document because of the frequency with which they wrote and because of their efforts to explain and rectify the accounts given in newspapers.[27]

Sand felt a need to participate in the provisional government, especially as she had little confidence in Lamartine's leadership abilities. She immediately began to publish short, idealistic tracts, manifestoes, and open letters to the people and to the middle classes. She started a newspaper with Borie and Louis Viardot, *La Cause du peuple,* but Paris could not support another liberal opinion paper, and it folded after just three weeks.

At the height of this enthusiasm, Pauline Viardot composed a new "Marseillaise" to words by Dupont, and George Sand wrote a stage play commemorating the republic and the people. This drama, *Le roi attend*, was produced in Paris, and the proletariat, who were given free tickets, received the spectacle very well.

Sand's feminism was by this time legendary. Yet she refused to run for the Assembly, saying that in nineteenth-century society, women are still subjugated to the whims of their husbands by dint of their marriage contract, and that the social status of women needed to be resolved before any political freedom could be attempted.

Nonetheless, George Sand continued to fulfill her unofficial role as minister of propaganda, the muse of the republic.[28] Perhaps her most famous and certainly most effective article during this time took the form of an attack on reactionaries. In the sixteenth *Bulletin de la République* Sand pronounced a conviction in the Marxist notion of revolution, which many held as the cause of the next day's rioting.

The elections of 23 April brought back a moderate Assembly. Sand's "prediction" in the sixteenth *Bulletin* came about on 15 May during a march for a free Poland, a cause that Lamartine had refused to support. The march soon turned into a display of the power of the people. The National Guard tried to disperse the crowd, but pandemonium reigned. Sand realized that her ideal of a new social order no longer had a chance.

Berry was not left unscathed by the events of February–May 1848. George Sand returned to find her reputation at a new low in La Châtre, where she was blamed for the May riots as well as communist espionage with Russia. Meanwhile her personal life was being lambasted by Augustine's father, in his libelous pamphlet *Une Contemporaine: biographie et intrigues de George Sand* (A Contemporary woman: the life and escapades of George Sand). Sand was in the process of taking court action when more bloody riots broke out in Paris.

The June riots discouraged Sand more than ever from believing in the possibility of a peaceful republic. She could not safely go to Paris, nor did she want to. Publishing had suffered as great a blow as had everything else in this time of social turmoil. Risking the printing of Sand's memoirs was not wise, so the first volume was set aside and she undertook a different project, *La Petite Fadette*. It was hard to get even this little novel published, and Sand was obliged to accept a paltry sum for the manuscript.

In the remaining months of 1848, George Sand saw Prince Louis-Napoléon Bonaparte rise in importance in national politics until, in the December elections, he was chosen as president. Sand commented on this to Pauline Viardot, "They think Napoléon isn't dead and that, by voting for his nephew, they are voting for him" (*Corres.,* 8:732).

The end of 1848 had dealt a heavy blow to her sociopolitical ideals, but it had also brought the death of three friends. Sand's half-brother, Hippolyte Chatiron, died of alcohol poisoning at age fifty on Christmas day, 1848. Five months later, Marie Dorval died. Five months after that, Chopin died. Solange went to Nohant to inform her mother of Chopin's death to keep her from reading about it in the papers. Sand was deeply upset by Chopin's death and could not work for several days. In late 1850 she lost two more friends, Carlotta Marliani and Balzac. At this point Sand had fewer and fewer reasons to go to the capital.

Victor Borie was a good companion and a satisfactory lover, but when Sand discovered how generously he helped himself to her money, she encouraged him to strike out on his own. Although he did undertake the editorship of a liberal newspaper, the first issue was too proletariat in its politics; the newspaper was seized and Borie condemned to a year in prison. He fled Berry, first to Paris, then to Brussels. This was a perfect opportunity for Sand to break with him. Borie eventually returned to Paris and served several months in prison. He was then once again welcomed, as a friend, at Nohant.

Not far behind Borie was the German liberal pianist, Hermann Müller-Strübing. He and Sand pleased each other immensely at first, but after a month his role was reduced to companion, pianist, and translator of the first volume of Sand's memoirs into German. His place was almost immediately taken by Alexandre Manceau, a young engraver, thirteen years Sand's junior. The soft-spoken Manceau soon took over an important role in the household. As the theater at Nohant was reestablished, Manceau saw to it that rehearsals were conducted in an orderly and professional manner, taking every opportunity to criticize.[29] He also took over most of the business of running Nohant. Maurice was not pleased with this arrangement, but for the moment he could not intervene.

The success of Sand's play *François le Champi* (Francis the Waif) at the Odéon (1849), with Pierre Bocage in the title role, gave a much needed boost to her career. Again thanks to Bocage, her next play, *Claudie* (1851), was a success at the Porte-Saint-Martin theater. *Le Mariage de Victorine* (Victorine's Wedding) would have continued successfully at the Gymnase theater later that year had Louis-Napoléon not chosen that moment to make his coup d'état.

Two days after Napoléon's take-over, Sand returned to Nohant. There were arbitrary arrests, and most of Sand's friends had taken refuge either in England or in Belgium. At the rumor that she, too, might be arrested, Sand decided to approach the president of the Republic directly. "I am not Mme de Staël," she wrote in January 1852, and succeeded, through some well-placed connections, in getting an audience.[30] She obtained from Napoléon a promise to release her friends and most of the Berrichons who were imprisoned. By the end of these dealings, Sand decided that she was through with politics.

The Manceau Years

The big theater at Nohant was being revived, thanks to Manceau's insistent support. Meanwhile, the "little theater" reserved for Maurice's marionettes, stood idle. With a little encouragement, both theaters were once again active, and the entire household was employed in costume and scenery production.

Behind the house at Nohant there was another family project, the construction of a grotto and a little chalet, soon to be called the Trianon. This was a favorite place of George Sand's granddaughter, Jeanne-Gabrielle Clésinger, born in May 1849. Solange had brought her daughter to Nohant in January 1852. Nini, as she was called, and grandmother got along very well.

Meanwhile, Clésinger took advantage of his wife's absence to resume his debauchery. When she heard of his activities, Solange, not to be done out of any fun or revenge, adopted a similar behavior. Leaving Nini at Nohant, the couple led separate, dissolute lives; legal separation was imminent. Then, in May 1854, Clésinger burst into Solange's apartments and removed a packet of incriminating letters to her suitor. The separation could, then, be effected on his terms.

Custody of Nini remained a problem. She was to be placed with George Sand, but as the judge expected his decision to be appealed, he ordered Nini be kept in a Paris boardinghouse pending final judgment. Solange was allowed to visit Nini only in the home. Clésinger occasionally took her for carriage rides, but he was not careful to dress her warmly against the winter weather. In January 1855 Jeanne-Gabrielle Clésinger died of scarlet fever.

George Sand was devastated by the news. Everything at Nohant, especially the Trianon and the gardens, reminded her of her granddaughter. Manceau thought she would do well with a change of scenery and organized a trip to Italy. They left Nohant in March of 1855 and traveled to Marseilles, Genoa, Rome, and Florence. Sand was disappointed with papal Rome, which she considered a theocratic tyranny worse than the current regime in France. She wove her impressions into a narrative, *La Daniella* (1857).

La Daniella found favor with no one. Its blatant anticlerical tone and condemnation not only of papal Rome, but also of the Italian people, was criticized by Catholics and liberals alike. The scandal took such force that *La Presse,* the newspaper that was serializing the novel, was seized.

To escape the controversy, Sand and Manceau traveled to the Creuse in June 1857. They stopped in a small village on the river Gargilesse where the panorama captivated them both. Manceau ended up purchasing the small hut where they stayed, and this became their refuge for much of the rest of Manceau's life. Sand wrote many of her works in this cottage.

One of the books she finished at Gargilesse was *Elle et Lui* (*She and He*), a fictionalized version of her relationship with Musset, who had died in March 1857. The novel lacked subtlety and Buloz hesitated to print it. When he did, it was badly received, especially by Paul de Musset, Alfred's overprotective brother.

Sainte-Beuve encouraged the Académie to grant Sand their twenty-thousand-franc prize. When this grant was voted down, the emperor offered her the identical sum from his pocket, which the author declined. The empress asked that the Académie at least offer her a chair. From an anonymous author there appeared about this time a pamphlet, *Les Femmes à l'Académie* (Women in the Académie), with a hypothetical description of Sand's reception into the hallowed halls. Sand riposted with a witty pamphlet, *Pourquoi les femmes à l'Académie?* (Why women in the Académie?), wherein she explained that the "overly mature" men of the Académie were not receptive to change and that she herself was unwilling to become a member of this "vestige of a past era."[31]

Undaunted, Sand continued to work, producing *Le Marquis de Villemer* in 1858 and, after her bout with typhoid fever in the autumn of 1860, *Valvèdre,* touted by several as her best work from this period.[32] By the spring of 1861, George Sand was ready for another vacation. She and Manceau went to the Riviera with Maurice, who left them to join Prince Jérome Bonaparte on a steamship cruise to Algeria, Spain, and eventually to America.

After their return in July, Sand and Manceau welcomed Alexandre Dumas fils to Nohant. His relationship with Sand had begun several years beforehand, through his father. In Poland Dumas fils happened upon George Sand's letters to Chopin. He wrote to his father of the news; Dumas père passed this information on to Sand, who requested the immediate return of the letters. Dumas fils was able to obtain the letters, which he sent to her along with copies he had made. Sand immediately burned this correspondence to protect Solange's reputation (*Corres.,* 10:442–43).

Dumas fils and Sand admired each other. Their relationship remained Platonic: he called her "maman" and she called him "my son"; they collaborated on a number of dramatic enterprises. When Dumas next came to Nohant with several friends, he brought along the fat Charles Marchal, who stayed on for a month after Dumas and the others had left. This young painter was Sand's last lover.

In May 1862 Maurice, aged thirty-eight, married Marcelina Calamatta, aged twenty. George Sand had known Lina since she was a child because she was the daughter of her friend Luigi Calamatta, the famous engraver. The marriage pleased Sand all the more because Lina adored her and willingly took the place of a lost daughter in Sand's life. Lina is said to have uttered her admiration in these terms: "I married him because I loved her."[33] On Bastille Day of the following year, Lina gave birth to a son, Marc-Antoine.

During this period Sand had devoted her energies almost entirely to theater. She wrote many plays, not all of them box office successes. But it was a novel that made Sand the heroine of the Paris liberal youth. In *Mademoiselle la Quintinie* (1863) she took up the anticlerical standard again, but this time with moral conviction and a solid plot. She then transformed the novel *Le*

Marquis de Villemer into a stage play, with some help from Dumas fils. The play, performed in February 1864, was a great success.

It was at this time that Maurice began to desire the power he felt his familial and professional position commanded. He inquired of his mother whether he or Manceau was the master at Nohant. George Sand assured him that he was the rightful heir of Nohant. Pleased at her support, Maurice then asked her to inform Manceau that he should leave. Once again, Sand allowed her son to dictate her personal life. She told Manceau that evening that he was free to leave Nohant. Ironically, Maurice and Lina soon after accepted Casimir's offer to set them up at Guillery.

Sad to depart after fifteen years at Nohant, Manceau left for Paris the next week, early December 1863. Sand joined him in his small apartment in early January, and the next week they attended the premiere of his verse play, *Une Journée à Dresde,* which was well received. Sand was soon in rehearsals for the stage version of *Le Marquis de Villemer.* When it opened in 1864, with the emperor and empress in attendance, it was a theatrical and political triumph for Sand.

Sand intended to stay with Manceau in Paris, but the apartment was much too small for the two of them. They found a cottage in Palaiseau, a suburb south of Paris. To make the transition to the new house easier, Sand sold almost all of the paintings and drawings given to her by Delacroix, who had recently died. They moved to Palaiseau in June, and Sand kept a small studio in Paris.

Due to limited space in the Palaiseau cottage, several manuscripts that Sand deemed no longer useful were destroyed in the fireplace, including the famous "Engelwald," which she had not published for political reasons. She also destroyed unpublished fragments of *Mauprat, Cosima,* and a few other pieces.[34]

She was very distraught at the death of her grandson at Guillery. She also realized she would have to nurse Manceau, now quite ill, to the end. She took a sudden trip to Gargilesse with Charles Marchal in September 1864. She and Marchal had previously corresponded, specifically concerning her role in securing the Légion d'honneur for Marchal. Manceau did not seem to be upset by this trip and awaited Sand's return to Paris.

Manceau's illness was growing steadily worse. By January 1865 he was coughing up blood, and it was obvious that the end was near. Manceau's doctor had prescribed oxygen, which he took when he had trouble breathing. Sand and Manceau undertook a collaborative effort and completed a novel, *Bonheur* (Happiness), in early May 1865. Shortly afterwards he was too weak to write, and they made no entries in their common agenda after June. In August Manceau died, leaving all his property and engraving materials to Maurice. Sand lay on the bed beside his body for several hours after his death trying to come to peace with herself.

Sand stayed at Palaiseau after Manceau's death. In January 1866 Sand's desire for another grandchild was satisfied when Lina Sand gave birth to a baby girl, Aurore. Three weeks after the birth of her granddaughter, Sand returned to Palaiseau and began seeing Marchal very often. She was at work on her new novel, *Le Dernier amour* (Last Love). The title clearly indicates the direction of her thoughts at the time.

Curiously, though Marchal was the greatest source of inspiration for *Le Dernier amour,* Sand dedicated it to Flaubert. Sand and Flaubert first met in 1857 at a dinner among several literati. In 1863 Sand wrote him a warm letter praising *Salammbô,* which was not well received by the public or critics. He greatly appreciated this gesture. Flaubert had not liked many of Sand's early works; only *Jacques* stood out in his mind, largely because of the theme of "free love." But at the premiere of *Le Marquis de Villemer* in 1864 he was so moved that he wept openly.

After Manceau's death, Sand contacted Flaubert again and spent a few days with him at Croisset in August 1866. She enjoyed her visit with the younger novelist so much that she returned in November for a week's stay. He read fragments of his *Tentation de Saint Antoine* to her, and as he was working on *L'Education sentimentale* at the time, he plied her with questions on the events of 1848.

Although they had widely differing opinions on literature, Sand and Flaubert were able to discuss their ideas openly. Neither ever brought the other over to his camp, but these discussions enabled them to clarify their own thoughts on literature. Flaubert called her his "chère Maître," an interesting nickname because not only does it demonstrate his esteem for her literary prowess, but it also illustrates the mixture of genders that he perceived as essential in her character. ("Chère" is feminine, "Maître" is masculine.) Flaubert requested a portrait of Sand. She sent him two, which he kept near his writing desk.

At about this time Juliette Lambert LaMessine, a young woman forty years Sand's junior, published a political tract, *Idées anti-Proudhoniennes,* defending the concepts of George Sand and Marie d'Agoult that Proudhon had ridiculed in an earlier publication. George Sand was doubly mistrusting of Juliette: first, Sand never really liked or trusted other women authors, and second, Juliette had already been swept up by the Paris salon of Marie d'Agoult. Nevertheless, the two women corresponded and George Sand sent her a copy of *Monsieur Sylvestre,* which Juliette critiqued.

Juliette declared her intention to marry Edmond Adam after the death of her husband, from whom she had been separated. Marie berated her for adopting such a blatantly bourgeois course of action. Only when Marie had scorned Juliette did George Sand agree to meet the young woman. Their friendship was guaranteed from the moment of their first meeting. Sand accepted Juliette's invitation to spend some time at her Riviera villa near Cannes in October 1867. There she met Edmond Plauchut who joined them from Nice to complete the party. Plauchut, who was Maurice's age, seemed to have taken Marchal's place in Sand's heart. Lina, who had stayed at Nohant because of her pregnancy, gave birth to another girl, Gabrielle, in March 1868.

In the autumn of 1868, Flaubert published the work he had been preparing for five years, *L'Education sentimentale*. Neither popular nor critical reception was very favorable. Many journalist-critics refused to write articles on it. George Sand wrote a laudatory review of the novel for *La Liberté*, which the editor, Emile de Girardin, refused to print.

George Sand urged Flaubert to spend the Christmas holidays with her and her family in Nohant that year. He accepted the invitation, but he proved to be as difficult a guest as Gautier had been: he did not appreciate the marionette theater and only wanted to sit and discuss literature with Sand. At their encouragement, he read them passages from his next novel, *La Tentation de Saint Antoine*, but he was still visibly shaken by the failure of *L'Education*.

Early in 1870 Sand went to Paris for rehearsals of what was to be her last play, *L'Autre* (The other), which was produced later that month at the Odéon, starring Sarah Bernhardt. Also in February 1870, *La Revue des Deux Mondes* began to serialize Sand's latest novel, *Malgrétout* (In Spite of Everything). Shortly after that *Césarine Dietrich* appeared.

At the same time, circumstances leading up to the Franco-Prussian War, although of major concern in the capital, did not affect Sand and her world at Nohant very much. She considered the Foreign Affairs Ministry to be petty and naïve in its games with Bismarck. The declaration of war surprised and saddened her and her guests, most of whom returned to Paris the next day. Because of a smallpox epidemic, George Sand and her family withdrew to the hills of the Creuse for six weeks. During this time, there was very little news of the situation in Paris.

Two balloons, called "Armand Barbès" and "George Sand," carried Gambetta and several Americans out of a besieged Paris. Sand was honored by this gesture, but her sympathies did not lie with the political movement. She had little feeling for the reactionary assembly at Versailles and even less for the fanatic Parisians who were seeking a communist utopia. Although George Sand remained a communist throughout this period and to her death, she was a spiritual believer but not a military activist.

After the Commune, friends once again came to Nohant. Sand was still hard at work, producing her *Contes d'une grand-mère* as well as several more novels.[35] By mid-May 1876 Sand's chronic colic took a turn for the worse when she developed gastric complications. Doctors and specialists were brought from the region as well as from Paris to consult and treat her. Laxatives were prescribed and two minor operations were performed on her intestines, but with little relief. Finally, in early June 1876, uttering the words "Laissez verdure" (Leave the greenery), George Sand died.

Solange was summoned from Paris just in time to see her mother before she died. That day she assumed her mother's position at the head of the table. She claimed to have found a note, which has yet to be uncovered, saying George Sand wanted a religious burial. Both Lina and Maurice doubted this desire, but Maurice, who had the deciding voice in the matter, concluded that it would be better for the people of Nohant to bury their mother with Catholic rites. A religious service was conducted in the chapel at Nohant, attended by many literati and politicians. George Sand was buried in the garden at Nohant.

Chapter Two
Writing and Independence

Already at the age of three or four, Aurore Dupin practiced narrative techniques, retelling and rearranging at whim the stories of Greek mythology and the saints' lives her mother read to her. Her mother found this creative activity tiresome but could not discourage Aurore from performing for her family.[1] Aurore's literary beginnings included her own mythology, which consisted of stories she dedicated to Corambé, the deity she had invented. It has been argued that the diversity of elements in Corambé stems from the conflict Aurore felt between the vivid imagination of her mother and the Voltairian rigor of her grandmother.[2] The suffering and emptiness she felt at the absence of her father encouraged her to create a mythological ideal, which served as both surrogate parent and god.

Aurore's urge to create evinced the need to express her dreams and desires. her father's premature death supplies a plausible reason for this need, as does the absence of her mother. Corambé's words, which she called a "book" or "song," demonstrated the warmth of a father coupled with the tone of a mother's consolation (*OA*, 1:812–813; 819–21). The anguish that characterized Aurore's younger years, filtered through the deity, surfaced as a need to write.

Early Writings and Collaboration

Aurore began to write after her marriage, largely in response to the requests of Jane Bazouin, a close friend from Sand's convent years. She first jotted down a sketchy account of her trip to Spain. Though she was only four years old at the time of this trip, she seems to have remembered quite a few details. *Voyage en Espagne* (1829), however, does not display the stylistic powers Sand evidenced in her correspondence of this period.[3]

In *Voyage en Auvergne* (1829, written two years after the actual trip), Aurore's literary musings began to take shape (*OA*, 2:497–527). She ostensibly picked up the pen to vent an ill-defined uneasiness. Hoping a writing cure might help, she wondered to whom she should write? To her mother? to Zoé? to Jane? No one would like her in this mood, so she abandoned the idea.

The device of questions and false starts demonstrates a preoccupation with structure and point of view.

Aurore not only wanted and needed to write, she was already beginning to conceive a narrative voice, distinct from her own and from the one she used in correspondence. *Voyage en Auvergne* was her first attempt, other than the correspondence with Aurélien de Sèze, to establish in writing her independence from both her husband and her status as a wife. Aurore was attempting to break out of the stifling sphere of the model nineteenth-century, aristocratic woman.

Aurore's first novel, "La Marraine," came again at Jane Bazouin's behest, as evidenced by a letter that heads the manuscript. In this letter, which M. Lubin includes in Sand's correspondence, Aurore professes to having no literary talent except for a recipe for plum pudding and a laundress's bill (*Corres.*, 1:561–64). Yet, she also speaks of form and the problem of coherence in any literary undertaking, thus displaying the modest beginnings of a concern for literary structure.[4]

Another version of what M. Lubin calls the "lettre-préface" appears in the short piece "Histoire du rêveur."[5] This short story, badly written and poorly constructed, does show glimpses of Sand's future talent for the fantastic and the use of the mysteries of music. It is the tale of a young Frenchman suffering from "mal du siècle" who decides to emulate Empedocles by throwing himself into the crater of Mount Etna. "Tricket" is the name of one of the narrators. Given Aurore's excellent knowledge of English, which she learned at the convent, there is no doubt that the name comes from the story of the cricket inserted within the text.

Aurore did undertake early on a full-length novel, *Aimée* (1830), but as no one liked it, she burned the manuscript and began other projects.[6] She began to collaborate with her lover, Jules Sandeau, and together they produced a very short piece, "La Prima donna," for *La Revue de Paris* (April 1831), signed "J. Sand." The pen name for the writing duet, a truncated version of Sandeau's name, was Delatouche's idea.

"La Prima donna" is the story of an opera singer who marries a nobleman. Raised to a new station in life, Gina must give up the stage; this loss marks the end of her will to live. She finds some energy again only when her husband agrees, against his better judgment, to allow her to sing on stage again. Gina dies singing the appropriately tragic role of Juliette.

Aurore and Sandeau produced a second story one month later, "La Fille d'Albano," signed simply "J. S."[7] The emotional fabric is more involved and subtler than that of their first piece. Once again the fate of a woman artist occupies the center of the story. Laurence, an Andalusian artist, is about to

marry a French aristocrat. Her brother reminds her of her talent and her dedication to art, thus persuading her to escape a marriage that will stifle her creative abilities. Here, as well as in "Histoire d'un rêveur" and "La Prima
donna," there are qualities of the artist, especially of the woman artist, that recall Aurore Dudevant's own predicament and that will later serve to flesh out
the title character of *Consuelo*.

Aurore and Sandeau ghost-wrote a novel at Delatouche's request, *Le
Commissionnaire,* and then undertook the last work on which they would collaborate, the full-length novel *Rose et Blanche.* As the title predicts, the work
puts together two very different but oddly complementary heroines, an
actress/singer and a nun. Two equally different men stand opposite the
female characters, neither one very likeable and together in many ways the
prototype for the typical Sand hero: the weak, young man unable to make decisions, easily swayed and not always very ethical.[8] Rose, certainly the most
interesting character, escapes the selfish grasp of her mother who tries to sell
her into prostitution. Horace, selfish in his own way, places her in a convent
with her friend Blanche. He ends up falling in love with her but does not
marry her because of class differences. Rose learns to appreciate what the convent has to offer an orphan. She also first realizes the sublime ecstasy of music
during a religious ceremony there. Later she will leave the convent to explore
the honored place of music on the stage with la Pasta as her idol, which provides a strong contrast with her stage experiences as a young girl under the tutelage of her mother. Rose refuses, however, to compromise her concept of art
because of the whims of style. She dies alone and sad, whereas Blanche has
left the convent and has married Horace.

Curiously, neither author claimed this work for his own nor included it in
his collected works. Many details, including the use of musical imagery and
the recurrence of like characterizations in later novels by George Sand, point
to the probability that Aurore wrote the majority of the book.[9] Though it has
been advanced that *Rose et Blanche* demonstrates a strong tendency toward
realism,[10] the thematics establish the basis for the idealized world that would
come to characterize George Sand's oeuvre.

Literary Independence

Only two months after the successful publication of *Rose et Blanche,*
Aurore began work alone on a new novel, *Indiana.*[11] Delatouche wished to
retain "Sand" for commercial reasons. It was agreed that Jules Sandeau would
henceforth take up his own full name, and Aurore would use the truncated
version with another first name. She decided on "Georges" because of the

Berrichon resonances it had for her. When *Indiana* appeared in May 1832, it carried the name "G. Sand."[12] George Sand, an independent and promising writer, had been born.

Indiana is often held to be the quintessential Sand novel because it deplores the fate of women in marriage. In contrast to other works of fiction by women at this time, to which Sainte-Beuve referred as "*romans intimes*," *Indiana* displays three-dimensional characters cleverly revealed in an omniscient third-person point of view.[13]

The nineteen-year-old Indiana grows uninspired by life with her elderly husband and her dull English cousin, Ralph. The dashing Raymon de Ramière, who has already seduced Indiana's Creole maid, Noun, now sets about conquering Indiana, who is far from disinterested. Noun, pregnant with Raymon's child, learns that Raymon is abandoning her. She despairs at his attempts to seduce her mistress and drowns herself. Indiana also attempts suicide, though she never abandons herself to Raymon's wiles. Followed by Ralph, she retreats to the Isle of Bourbon (Réunion). She plans to jump off a cliff; to prove his eternal devotion to his cousin, Ralph intends to do the same.

A second conclusion, now considered the traditional ending, saves them so that they can live together in a Rousseauistic existence on the island, where Indiana finally recognizes in Ralph the object of her love.[14] The addition of the epilogue has plagued critics of Sand for some time. It seems to jar with the narrative flow, yet it also serves as a coherent closure device. No satisfactory explanation for the epilogue has yet been reached.[15]

Indiana was a great public and critical success when it appeared in May 1832. Critics declared it a faithful portrayal of the sensibilities of the era and an open declaration of war on the Napoleonic Code. Some even made favorable comparisons to *Le Rouge et le Noir* and *Notre-Dame de Paris*, both of which had appeared recently.[16]

After setting her first novel in Paris, Sand used her knowledge and love of the Berry to create the geographical situation of *Valentine*. Also a love story that attacks societal strictures of class and marriage, this second novel presents a relationship that is more poetic than that of *Indiana*. Bénédict is a gentle man of modest origins but imbued with a natural knowledge; Valentine is an aristocrat, but simple and sensitive.

The scene of their first encounter, one of the most famous in the novel, exhibits Sand's attitude toward cross-class relationships. Valentine has come to a village fête where Bénédict invites her to dance the bourrée. Tradition commands that the dance begin with an exchange of kisses between partners. The tenseness of the situation is well rendered by the stern expression of Valentine's mother and the exhortations of the amused villagers; a long trill on the bagpipes, the musical signal for the kiss, underlines the social import of the act. Valentine and Bénédict soon realize their love and its impossibility, more because Valentine is married than because of the class difference.

Another cross-class relationship provides the love interest in a later novel, *Tamaris* (1862). The narrator is a doctor who never gives his name; his class origins remain a mystery, but his social status clearly puts him in the upper-middle-class bracket. The woman calls herself Mme Martin, but she is, in fact, the widowed Marquise d'Elmeval. After many a pretext to convene over some problem or other of her son, the marquise and the narrator finally recognize their feelings. Unlike Bénédict and Valentine, they do marry and the novel ends well. In many ways, despite the similarity, *Tamaris* presents the mirror image of *Valentine,* in both social context and commentary.

Sand published a short story in the *Revue de Paris* in the summer of 1832, about the time she began writing *Valentine.* "Melchior" is the ironic retelling, in a maritime setting, of the Romeo and Juliet story. Sand's quizzical twist has the hero lose all memory of his misfortune, except for once a year when the recollection drives him berserk; then he returns to "normal behavior." This "normal behavior," says Sand, is the point at which he is actually craziest.

About the same time, Sand began another story, "Pauline," which she set aside until late 1839.[17] This sad tale of two female friends who become enemies introduces several Sandian themes: the antithesis of Paris and the provinces, or of Parisians and provincials, although Sand never exploits this theme as much as Balzac does; the opposition of the actress and the innocent maiden; the young woman grown bitter at having spent her youth caring for her sick mother; and the egocentric, jealous man who comes between two friends.

Before the end of 1832, George Sand produced yet another piece of writing, this time a short story published in *La Revue de Paris* in early December: "La Marquise."[18] By means of a frame story and double narrators, a device she had already used in earlier tales, Sand examines the love of an upper-class widow for an actor. The structure of the relationship resembles that of *Rose et Blanche,* but with a reversal of genders. Beyond the now familiar Sandian theme of crossing class boundaries, "La Marquise" presents another interesting notion, that of illusion and the stage.[19]

In 1833 Sand produced "Cora" and "Garnier," which have been called the worst examples of hack-writing in Sand's career.[20] Another short story, "Lavinia, une vieille histoire" ("Lavinia, An Old Tale"), appeared in *Les Heures du soir* in March 1833. Here Sand portrays the abandoned woman who, ten years after an affair, requests the return of her portrait and love letters because Lionel, the cruel man whom she loves, is planning to marry. Lionel realizes, alas too late, the quality of the woman he has foolishly let go and tries to persuade her to take him back. It is finally the misused woman who has the upper hand and rejects him, though it is to her own chagrin, for she still loves him deeply.[21]

In the same vein, but completely opposed to the romantic ethos, *Valvèdre* (1861) links a young poet type, Francis Valigny, with the wife of his best friend's teacher and mentor, Alida de Valvèdre. While rumors of her infidelities are unfounded, Alida does return Francis's love, largely out of the boredom in which her preoccupied scientist husband leaves her. Alida and Francis are aided and abetted by the cunning, vengeful, unsuccessful suitor of Alida, Moserwald, a rich Jewish merchant. Sand exploits several stereotypes: a scientist more interested in his work than human relationships; a bored wife who toys with distraction and finds herself caught in her own game; a rich Jew with a mean and dishonest character. The most striking trait of the novel remains its defiant criticism of the romantic ideal, especially as seen in the cult of morbid introspection.

Lélia

George and Jules took separate apartments in early 1833, at Sand's expense, and by March their breakup was final. Sand's ill-fated and brief affair with Mérimée occurred at about the same time. She had also just discovered that she was being discriminated against on the marketplace: the *Revue de Paris* was paying its male contributors more than her.[22] It is no wonder that she vented her antipatriarchal feelings in the novel she was writing at the time. *Lélia*, published in late July 1833, is a confused repository of ill feelings, an attempt to define unhappiness with men, disappointment with herself, and disenchantment with society, with religion, and indeed with life in general.

Lélia marks a turning point in Sand's literary production. It started as a short story entitled "Trenmor," centering around an ex-gambler who had repented. A problematic relationship between two young lovers, Lélia and Sténio, makes up a minor subplot. Sand acted on Buloz's criticism that this story line would profit from greater development, and accordingly concentrated on the unhappy antiheroine.[23]

Lélia is an allegorical novel about an unwitting "femme fatale" who cannot find an acceptable justification for satisfying her desires. Lélia is tormented by her inability to define her inadequacies and her unwillingness to seek viable solutions for her loneliness. She suffers from a compounded case of "mal du siècle" and stubbornness.[24]

Lélia, who loves and is loved by the young poet Sténio, has lost all respect for men, love, and God. She denies her love for Sténio, but leads him on at the same time. Trenmor, a repentent criminal, inspires Sténio's jealousy. To escape her situation Lélia flees to a convent, where Magnus saves her from an accident and falls in love with her. Sténio is again jealous. Circumstances put Lélia in contact with her long-lost sister, Pulchérie, who tries to tell Lélia that she has alienated everyone with her philosophical queries, and also tries to persuade Lélia to adopt hedonism as the only positive way of life. In an effort to convince her sister of this, Pulchérie seduces Sténio in Lélia's presence without his ever being aware of the switch. When later he does find out the truth, he cries out against Lélia and turns to debauchery. Once again Lélia chooses the convent; this time she takes vows and attains a high position instructing novices. The cardinal falls in love with her. Sténio, disguised as a nun, enters the convent and disrupts Lélia's lecture, and then tries to seduce one of the novices in her charge, but Lélia herself surprises him. Then, in her cell, she finally confesses the reasons for her past behavior. Sténio, despondent at losing someone he only now truly appreciates, drowns himself. Magnus, who failed to answer Sténio's calls for help, holds himself guilty for Sténio's death, and escapes to a monastary where he accuses Lélia of plotting a political scheme. The Cardinal escapes by taking poison, but Lélia is called up before the Inquisition and is sent away to a charterhouse. There Trenmor witnesses her death and buries her opposite Sténio.

According to Gustave Planche, Lélia personifies Doubt, Trenmor Expiation and Stoicism, Sténio Poetry and Gullibility, Magnus Superstition and Repressed Desire, and Pulchérie the Senses. This oversimplification presents as many problems as solutions, but it does bear witness to the enormous metaphysical reaches Sand had hoped for in her novel as well as the use of types and the preachy nature of the narration.[25] The construct of types and metaphysical monologues makes this novel a sort of distorted allegory rather than a myth, as has been suggested.[26] The similarity between *Lélia* and *La Peau de chagrin* has been noted,[27] but there is more to be understood from the mixture of gambling, debauchery, and sexual dissatisfaction: whereas Pulchérie is willing to take a risk and is not punished for it by the narrator,[28] Lélia cannot allow herself a simple venture and thus does not reap any joy.

The style of this innovative novel enhances the theme of metaphysical quandary. The mystical and illusive nature of the heroine recalls the style Nerval used to describe *Les Filles du feu*. While Sand would certainly deny any tendencies toward obscurantism, she allows Lélia to suffer the throes of religious doubt without offering an easy solution. The second *Lélia* (1839) brings the character's searchings to a more felicitous end, for Sand makes her an abbess in this version.[29]

Lélia has been the subject of much critical attention. She has been called "une sorte d'Oberman féminisé" (a kind of female Obermann), a female Byronic hero(ine), and "a woman who denies love."[30] Most critics, especially men, have castigated Lélia for not finding sexual fulfillment. André Maurois went so far as to posit the so-called frigidity of this character as a public avowal of impotence on the part of the author. We must not, however, confuse a lack of sexual fulfillment with a failure to experience such satisfaction. P. Reboul speaks of a similar "impotence" in the eponymic character of "La Marquise" (*Lélia*, xli–xlii), which is not only an oversimplification but a misinterpretation of human sexuality.[31]

Lélia could have marked a turning point for Sand as well as for the structure of the nineteenth-century novel. She dreamt of a new genre, a "nonvisible novel" that would "not seek to amuse and entertain readers with an idle imagination, [but would] appeal little to the eye and constantly to the soul."[32] The novel's success—its first printing sold out quickly—owed more to notorious reviews than laudatory ones. George Sand was hurt by some of the attacks of her critics, whose inconsistencies she in turn condemned in her preface to the 1842 edition.[33] She would, nonetheless, abandon this new direction in narrative fiction. *Lélia* remains unique in Sand's oeuvre and without many analogues in the history of the French novel.

Sand was quite fond of *Lélia*. She called it her "best piece," the only work that interested her.[34] As early as October 1835, however, she also admitted that *Lélia* was rather obscure, even for her, and showed that it had been written under the influence of emotional suffering. Sand planned a total overhaul of her metaphysical novel. She had put so many of her intimate thoughts in it, thoughts that were no longer necessarily part of her current world view, that she was not sure how to present her new thoughts without detracting from what she considered her masterpiece.

The skepticism of the first version had to go. Two factors operated in George Sand's mind in this matter. First, she was no longer in the depths of despair that had shaken her most fundamental beliefs in 1833; second, she feared that a work of such scandalous and questionable morality would harm her legal case against her husband. It was imperative that she rewrite the novel to reinstate her faith in humanity and in God, if not in the Church.

George Sand was obviously having trouble with her rewriting, which she undertook in 1836. In a letter to Abbé Lamennais she said, "I want to complete a book that I filled with all my bitterness and pain and that I now want to rewrite with the ray of hope that has appeared to me" (*Corres.*, 3:595). She goes on to say that the abbé had agreed to help her in the new direction her life and her writing were taking and that she would like his advice to ensure a clear, tidy ending for her novel.

Her new direction certainly comes from having met Lamennais, Pierre Leroux, Franz Liszt, and Michel de Bourges. New ideas, not yet solidly acquired, gleaned from discussions with these lively minds, were to take on a new form in a story already set down. The process, however, was difficult and slow.

Sand finished the second *Lélia* only in early 1839 while at Majorca. The manuscript was sent to Buloz from Barcelona on 15 February 1839.[35] Sand extracted several passages from the original out of modesty and decency. The doctrine of doubt had ceded its place to a doctrine of progress. The character of Trenmor seems to have lost most of its prescriptive charm. Sand spoke frankly in the second *Lélia* on her ideas of love and maternity. These pleasures find a new form, albeit slightly forced, in the second version of *Lélia*.

Independent Women

Late in 1833 Sand published in the *Revue des Deux Mondes* a short story called "Metella," a fascinating tale about the intricacies of a waning yet jealous love pitted against the trials of an idealistic love, the whole complicated by the prejudice of age differences. The story, told in two parts, sets up two distinct triangles among the characters. Although the title character is constant to both parts and consistent in her fear of growing old, there is relatively little unity between the two sections.

Sand and Musset left for Italy at the end of 1833. Sand's work during her stay in Italy, mostly in Venice, includes *Le Secrétaire intime* (Private secretary), *André, Leone Leoni, Jacques,* and the first two *Lettres d'un voyageur*. Venice, as well as the situation with Musset, served as much of the inspiration for these works (I discuss the Italian influence in the next chapter), but *André* and *Jacques* take place in France (Berry for the former, and Touraine and Dauphiné for the latter) and seem to have little to do, at least on the surface, with the exotic setting in which they came to light.

André started out as a novella and became a full-length novel, published in 1835. Once again the reader recognizes the typical Sandian universe of unhappy love and cross-class marriage. André, the listless son of a country squire, the Marquis de Morland, falls in love with Geneviève, an "*artisane*" (a Berrichon variant of "grisette") who makes artificial flowers.

Geneviève's naïveté leads her into compromising situations because she remains unaware of the growing relationship between her and André. André satisfies Geneviève's thirst for knowledge in botany and other sciences, but his inability to face his father with his desire to marry a peasant girl both disappoints and hurts her. Geneviève's circumstances reach a nadir when she becomes pregnant and the couple is forced to beg André's father for shelter in order to survive. Geneviève falls at the marquis's hand and thereafter feels no movement from within her womb. She dies in childbirth, and the baby is stillborn. André remains ill for a year, but relations are improved between him and his father.

Jacques, an epistolary novel written in 1834, depicts a similar situation from a man's point of view. Jacques has fallen in love with and proposed to Fernande, a girl half his age. At thirty-five he can offer her money, position, devotion, and the fruit of his experience. But as connubial bliss turns to frustration and boredom, it is not surprising that Fernande should allow herself to be seduced by Octave, a young, handsome man closer to her own age. Octave is, in fact, the ex-lover of Sylvia, Jacques's half-sister. Fernande is also Sylvia's half-sister. The near-incestuous relationships reflect the closeness of the epistolary ties more than that of the romantic bonds.

Sylvia and Jacques have much in common, as do Fernande and Octave. The hidden story, one that Sand preferred to leave untested and unresolved, questions the familial bond between Sylvia and Jacques and the possibility of the intimate relationship they would like to have enjoyed. Sand profited from a cliché—"We aren't made for each other"[36]—but she renewed the commonplace by requiring a rearrangement of partners through the dissolution of marriage and the hint of incestuous desires.

Musset can be seen, in a way, as the model for Jacques. He, too, came to accept Pagello as George Sand's new lover, at least to a certain degree in the beginning, and left Venice so that they might continue their lives together. Jacques assembles all that was positive and generous in Musset's attitude, leaving aside the jealous outbursts and the vengeful attacks.[37] But in a more complex way, Jacques also resembles Metella in his fear of growing old.[38] Metella worried about the superficial, traditionally feminine concerns of aging, but her real fear resides in doubting her ability to keep her man. Jacques suffers from the identical problem, for although he knows from the outset that he far surpasses Fernande in experience, he fails to foresee that as she gains experience, she will develop her own individuality. Like Jacques, Metalla loses her lover to a younger rival. But in both instances the man leaves because he is unable to cope with competition, whether he is the competitor or the object of envy.

The divergence of two people's development recalls the characters

Geneviève and André. André tutors Geneviève in botany, but her sensitivity aids her intelligence and she soon surpasses André's too factual knowledge. Geneviève is superior to André in moral stamina and clear thinking. The final situation at the marquis's château proves to André that he has failed to learn from Geneviève the most important lesson of his life: self-esteem, which engenders generous love.

Superiority unites the two characters Geneviève and Sylvia (*Jacques*), for Sylvia, throughout the novel, remains kinder, more moral, and more generous than Octave, even more so than Fernande. The next novel wherein the woman's superiority over man is the primary theme is *Mauprat* (1837).[39] In this work, Edmée de Mauprat loves her cousin, Bernard, but cannot accept such a poorly educated and uncultured creature because of her own self-esteem. She undertakes a rigorous training program to bring Bernard up to her own standards. Her program involves moral as well as intellectual issues. Finally, through much work on Bernard's part and a complex psychological breakthrough on Edmée's part, the two can be united, although Edmée is ever the superior one.

Mauprat also takes place in Berry and introduces the moral fiber and stubbornness of its people. Edmée, from the lesser branch of the Mauprat family, is abducted and almost raped by her cousins of the upper branch. The youngest cousin, Bernard, defends her, though he is not at first entirely without jealous desires. He makes her promise that if he saves her, she will be his. She agrees, but Bernard soon falls in love with Edmée and submits to her plans for his moral and intellectual rehabilitation. An odd, solitary philosopher, Patience, wanders through the woods and appears whenever Edmée needs support or advice. Many obstacles block Edmée's passage to a position of power, including an ugly trial, which is reminiscent of Sand's trials for legal separation from Casimir. The courtroom scene pits Edmée against the reputation of the upper branch of the Mauprats, that is, woman against the legal establishment. Edmée defends herself against all odds and finally wins honor, home, and happiness.

The aspects of the Napoleonic Code concerning a woman's forced and total submission to her husband find an important place in this work.[40] The theme is not new with *Mauprat* and, in fact, can be detected as early as *Indiana*. The woman's supremacy in *Mauprat,* as we have noted, is most clearly shown in an intellectual light, but also entails a moral and social superiority. Financial and hierarchical status, however, are also on Edmée's side, because she controls the estate of her father, for all intents and purposes, and, indeed, by the end of the novel, she is in complete legal control of her family's legacy.[41]

There is a certain progression in the strength and superiority of women from Geneviève to Sylvia to Edmée. The narrator's attitude toward her characters does not always encourage the reader to follow this progression with approbation. Sylvia, for example, is presented in a suspicious light—she could be Jacques's hidden mistress—and her situation hardly improves when Jacques invites her to share his home with his new wife of less than a year. Sylvia is also responsible for introducing Octave into the picture, and she does little to arrest his growing interest in Fernande. Sylvia does ellicit some compassion when her relationship to Fernande and her mother is divulged, and she does remain completely supportive of Jacques in his suffering, though to what end is unclear. While she is the ideal of a strong woman, she does not necessarily fit the bill on a moral level; neither does Fernande, for that matter. This deficiency demonstrates the degree to which this novel was attacked on moral grounds.

The progression of female characters from weak to strong is clear. Geneviève, although strong and independent, loses both these qualities when she becomes inextricably linked with André. Sylvia is careful to remain independent, which may well cost her in terms of emotional satisfaction, but she maintains an honest approach to love, even when Jacques suggests another suitor for her. Edmée is, from the outset, strong and upright. Her principal fault is lacking the capacity for emotional expression, which she learns. In this way, her bildung parallels Bernard's socialization process.

Sand's development from a fledgling to an established writer bears witness to several important aspects of George Sand's career and personality. Gaining independence for a woman, according to Sand, is a slow and arduous task because of the inadequate education of women. We may read "education" here as both formal learning and upbringing. George Sand attempted, through her rich and varied portrayal of strong women, to present French women with a goal, not an unrealistic ideal, but a pragmatic approach to coping in the world.

Sand's own independence did not come easily. The key to her emergence as an individual was writing. Nor did writing come to her easily, as we have seen. Her Berrichon determination, encouragement from a few people around her, and a surprisingly short apprenticeship saw her to a successful beginning.

Sand's most common thematic area in these early works is women's freedom: freedom from one's husband, from social class, from social conventions, from economic and political exigencies. But freedom is soon lost again if she who earns it is incapable of managing it. The women from George Sand's early works who desire freedom—Indiana, Valentine, Lélia,

Geneviève, Sylvia, Edmée—designate a clear progression of individuals who are increasingly ready to comprehend independence and the attendant power. Sand learned the value of independence early on, partly from her grandmother's teaching and partly as a result of her feelings of abandonment by her father and her mother. As she began to write, she gained control over her own life and finally understood the power, and the dangers, of independence.

Chapter Three
Travel and Writing

George Sand takes her place alongside Chateaubriand, Byron, Lamartine and Flaubert in her fondness for travel, although she stays closer to Stendhal insomuch as her wanderings, apart from the short sojourn in Majorca, took her no farther from her native land than Italy. The relationship between travel and writing constitutes one of the fundamentals of the romantic spirit. Travel, as an escape from one's plights, is psychological as well as geographical and cultural. Later authors, notably Nerval and Rimbaud, would forgo the pretext of physical displacement in their travel literature. Sand aligned herself with the early romantics' principle of wandering in pursuit of the truth. The elements of Sand's travel experience that offer an insight into her spirit of wandering are the early travelogues, the famous *Lettres d'un voyageur,* and the influence of Italy on Sand's writing.

The Travelogues

Sand's earliest travelogue recounts some details of the trip she took to the Pyrenees with Casimir in the summer of 1825. The only extant record of the journal makes up part of *Histoire de ma vie* (part 4, chapters 10 and 11). At this time Sand thought she might be consumptive and considered this trip a treatment, but feared she might never return. She wrote in short, melancholy sentences, referring to herself in the third person.

Thanks to the encouragement of her convent friend Jane Bazouin, Sand set down on paper some memories of her earliest trips. *Voyage en Espagne* (1829) recounts the journey the five-year-old Aurore made with her mother in 1808 to Madrid, where her father was in the service of Murat. Her recollections, which would become more detailed twenty-five years later in her legitimate autobiography, comprise only the memory of a few sensations. At the same time, Sand wrote down her memories of a recent trip to take the waters at Mont d'Or. *Voyage au Mont d'Or,* later called *Voyage en Auvergne,* not only gives more precise and interesting details than the Spanish memoirs, but it also offers some insightful glimpses into Sand's desire to write and the connection she makes between traveling and writing. Some of the more intuitive

39

remarks in this text describe other people at the spa. Sand reports a sample dialogue, showing her inclinations for dramatic writing. She paints the "actors" as superficial, opinionated, and sometimes downright stupid. She becomes a much more active participant through her pen than through actual social intercourse. In the beginning of the text, Sand decides the only way to banish her feelings of disquietude is to write. She ends up writing to her mother a bilious letter that she never posts. She also plans out several chapters of her autobiography but does not succeed in lifting her spirits. She concludes that her trip has failed its purpose: "Such is man: he travels to calm his restlessness and nothing satisfies him" (*OA*, 2:512). Neither traveling nor writing can cure her anxieties.

In *Un Hiver à Majorque,* a decade later, Sand describes a world virtually unknown to her compatriots. She provides objective information concerning the history, geography, climate, cuisine, and regional costumes of Majorca. To this she adds her own anecdotes that illustrate or supplement the factual data and entertain the reader with digressions. Like *Voyage en Auvergne, Majorque* also presents many of Sand's ponderings on life and writing. Personal details make the text more like a journal in many ways and provide a most interesting perspective of Sand's development as an author.

The notion of travel itself arises often in *Un Hiver à Majorque*. Sand asks why one travels, what one hopes to find elsewhere that cannot be found at home. Apart from the danger and expense, the many disillusive attempts ought to cure the obsession with travel, yet we start again, "because these days, we don't feel good anywhere, and travel is one of the most pleasant and deceptive manifestations of the ideal" (*OA*, 2:1052), an escape from "le monde officiel" (the legitimate world). The search for happiness rather than truth is the real goal of travel. Sand defines this special happiness as "contact, relationships, and friendly exchanges with others" (*OA*, 2:1053), a sort of duty to make meaningful contacts that would bring satisfaction. Yet, she continues, most of us only travel in search of mystery and isolation in an effort to escape the company of others. Sand's purpose in writing her travelogue is to warn her readers of the dangers of imagined escape.

Escapism nonetheless constitutes the core of Sand's Majorcan text. First, the trip itself was Chopin's scheme to avoid the gaze of society and family. The text, too, comprises an interesting set of evasions. Sand glibly shifts from discussions on Majorcan flora to literary inventions loosely based on physical surroundings or historical events. These digressions contain a sense of historical fiction that Sand will develop later, notably in *Consuelo* (1842–44), *Les Dames vertes* (1857; The green ladies), *L'Homme de neige* (1858; The snowman), *Les Beaux Messieurs de Bois-Doré* (1862; The handsome sires of Bois-

Doré), *Cadio* (1867), and *Nanon* (1872). Sand also makes good use of local dialect, which she incorporates into the discourse of foreign travel; she exploits this device in her Italian texts as well as in the case of *L'Homme de neige,* which takes place in Sweden. This is also the period in which she begins to conceive her rustic series, wherein she will make liberal use of Berrichon dialect. Sand also links *Un Hiver à Majorque* with her own Berry in descriptions of landscape that remind her of her native province.

One more instance of escapism in *Un Hiver à Marjorque* stands out: the absence of Chopin's name. Sand alludes to him as either "one of us" or "the other," and often, especially toward the end of the narrative, as "the sick one." From this moment on, Sand assumed a role that was more maternal than amorous. It would seem obvious that the failure to use Chopin's name explicitly in this text belies her desire, as early as 1841, to hide from the reality of Chopin's physical weakness, or, in fact, to be rid of him altogether. By rejecting his name, a form of castration, and recognizing his frailty, a symbol of impotence, Sand unveils her dissatisfaction and, at the same time, her sense of loyalty and duty. In this sense, psychological escapism parallels the psychological journey that is an integral part of the exoticism of travel.

Les Lettres d'un voyageur

Les Lettres d'un voyageur is a rich yet strangely difficult text. Sand admits she tried to hide under a narrator of her own invention, an older uncle, a traveler who would share his vast experience with the addressees and the readers.[1] Sand's approach induces several alternative readings of the text, and in several instances the themes of family stability and social condemnation, couched in a masculine discourse, ring false. The genres that commingle in this text usually complement each other, though sometimes the mixture detracts from the unity of the piece. Those letters that retain the characteristics of true correspondence (4, 5, 6, 7, 9), often digress into the style of a diary, which is not entirely outside the realm of personal letter writing. Others more closely resemble an open letter to the editor (8, 12) or sometimes professional letters rather than friendly ones (11). Still others recall the style of travelogues (1, 2, 3, 10), nominally the second most important trait of the collection according to the title.

The twelve letters constituting this text were written between March 1834 and November 1836. The first three letters address Venice and the surrounding area, the sights and mores of the inhabitants, as well as the relationship of art to nature, and the privileged position of travel in regard to these concerns. All three were directed to Musset, though he remains unnamed.

This omission did not prevent all of Paris from knowing exactly what famous poet was being evoked (*OA*, 2:638). Musset gave his approval for the letters to appear in print. Buloz was just as encouraging about the project, asserting that Sand was making great strides in poetic creation.[2]

Letters 4 and 5 provide insight into Sand's despair during the months preceding the separation trials. She freely discusses suicide, and at the same time encourages her friends not to be swayed by her own morose reaction to the world. Letter 9 also delivers invectives against society at large. This letter dates from the time of Sand's trial. It is interesting to note that in Letter 12, originally written at about the same time, Sand defends her ideas of marriage.

Letter 6 marks a turning point in Sand's life. It describes her responses, both political and artistic, to Michel de Bourges. The position of this letter at the center of the collection further bears out its importance in Sand's progression toward artistic rebellion. Letter 8 also shows strong political reaction, this time against the former Minister of Foreign Affairs Tallyrand. Her vituperations lack any subtlety and resemble a personal attack more than an objective commentary. Sainte-Beuve decried the criticism as the ideal of ugliness.[3]

Letters 7, 10, and 11 discuss music. The first letter, addressed to Liszt, speaks mostly of solitude. Sand also stumbles upon a volume of Lavater on phrenology and derives great interest in applying this science to people around her and to the physiognomy of her fictional characters. Letter 10 discusses Sand's trip to visit Liszt and Marie d'Agoult in the area of Geneva. This trip follows her legal success in the separation trial with Casimir, which explains the levity of tone here. She describes the countryside and the wonderful effects of wine and travel on the soul. Letter 11, addressed to Meyerbeer, discusses music, specifically his opera *Les Huguenots*. Sand's comments cover the relation of music to literature, to the public, and to the critics (see chapter 6).

The Nature of the Travelogue   Sand interspersed the travel theme throughout the letters, though it is concentrated in the first three, which are about Venice. Specifically Sand discusses the goal of traveling. While most travelers publish their *récits de voyage* to be informative and witty, Sand uses travel, and thus writing about travel, as a pretext for the more important issue of searching for her own identity (*OA*, 2:636).

Traveling teaches us the art of observation. One starts with generalizations and ends up with subtle comparisons that expose the basic truths of stereotypes. Sand devotes quite a large section to the dress and mores of Venetian men and women, sometimes comparing the coquettish nature of these women to the snobbish classism of Parisian women. Just as travel reflects life, she says, so does the art of observation parallel the science of life (Letter 10, *OA*, 2:899–900).

The simple desire to see other, different places represents perhaps the most obvious reason for traveling. Not only does Sand give us detailed descriptions of the Tyrolian countryside (which, incidentally, she did not visit during the travels with Pagello, as her letter would have us believe), of Venice, and some of the surrounding islands, but she compares them to the Alps and the Pyrenees, rendering her travelogue more accessible to French readers and linking this trip with others in her own past. In describing Venice, Sand does not content herself with a torpid portrait of common sights and activities; she delights in depicting festivals and takes the opportunity to comment on the Venetian penchant for gaiety and a seemingly carefree life.

Sand depicts the Veneto as a refreshing and purifying place. Her descriptions use adjectives that evoke coolness, whiteness, calm, and rejuvenation. Yet, at the end of the Venetian letters she chances to contemplate home and the possible desire to return to France: "Oh my homeland! a puzzling name of which I have never thought and which still only offers me an inscrutable meaning! Is, then, the memory of former suffering which you evoke sweeter than the present feeling of joy? Could I forget you if I wanted to? And why is it that I don't want to?" (*OA*, 2:734–35). Not surprisingly, the next letter is written at Nohant, just after her return from Venice.

The tedium of society offers one of the best reasons for traveling. Thus Sand develops her conception of dream as travel. Although not original with Sand, she takes pleasure in the sensation of leaving reality behind and looking forward to adventures in the unknown. In Letter 1 she neglects her current situation with Pagello by revelling in romanticized memories of the past (*OA*, 2:669). No doubt she regrets such a sudden break with Musset. Later in the same letter, Sand recounts a dream that led her on a trip around the world (*OA*, 2:688–91). A vocabulary of solitude and rejuvenation demonstrates to what degree Sand wishes to remove herself from unwanted social obligations.

Another dream puts the author amidst a group of kind people. It is the calm and soothing society of these musicians peacefully floating along in a bark that guides her through that dream and the narrative. She recommends to anyone of bad humor that he take to himself at the water's edge and await the calm brought by the Venetian air, which always carries with it strains of music (*OA*, 2:673–74).

Travel and Reflection   Traveling and writing enjoy a special bond for Sand. She frequently refers to writing while on trips or in her writing about trips and always gives special attention to the poetic link between the physical and emotional displacement of traveling and the act of writing.

M. Lubin points out the liberty of innovation Sand assured herself by choosing the mixed-genre style of the *Lettres* (*OA*, 2:636). Sand freely shifts in and out of a formal mode of writing. She often makes self-conscious references to the ostensible genre of the text. She begins her letter to Charles Didier by stating she will fulfill her promise to give him a sort of travelogue (Letter 10, *OA*, 2:881). A similar convention begins the Letter 11 to Meyerbeer (*OA*, 2:917). In these and several other cases, the pretext of the travel diary provides a superficial unity amongst the various letters.

Discussion stemming from the observation of foreign people and customs, however, succeeds better in drawing a tie between travel and reflection, and thus between travel and writing. Such exploration of ideas often moves from the other to the self and links the narrator to her surroundings, both abroad and in her dear "vallée noire" (the "black valley," as Sand calls her area of Berry). Many of these discussions involve art, specifically literature and music.

Under attack from Michel de Bourges, Sand defends art as she sees it. Letter 6 may well be taken as Sand's apologia of art and the artist. As Michel invokes Plato's desire to rid the Republic of artists, Sand riposte that the effective usefulness of the artist is to give sainted emotions and mystical enthusiasm to those who work by the sweat of their brow. Usefulness, says Sand, does not have to be described in terms of social action, but it should involve a conscientious effort to raise humanity to a higher level of reflection and to allow for dreams of a better future.

How does this "ars poetica" relate to travel? Sand continues to demonstrate throughout this text how a foreign context can bring a fresh perspective to one's world view. The lucidity of thought and perspective that travel affords almost always gives rise to a desire to write. Only by the act of writing can Sand organize her mind and her emotions. At this stage the writing usually resembles a pseudoautobiography, but soon she realizes the romantic and novelistic possibilities inherent in the form. George Sand is not necessarily original in directly connecting travel with writing, but we can appreciate the development of the creative act of writing through this close association.

Music and Suicide   Starting with the first letter, Sand draws parallels between nature and music. The Tyrolian countryside reminds the narrator of Beethoven symphonies. In Letter 11, to Meyerbeer, Sand quotes Liszt on the link between music and the written word: to insist on a highly conventional coda in an aria is akin to the superficial ending in letters of which the French are so fond. The comparison gains in irony due to the context of correspondence in which it is couched here.

The most frequent evocations of music in relation to travel appear in the letters on Venice. Here Sand advances her notion that music is an integral part of the Venetian landscape. In the aforementioned dream from Letter 2, not only are there mysterious people singing, presumably some sort of bacchanal, but Beppa, the narrator's interlocutor, sings a gentle children's song. Sand gives us the lyrics to this folk song, in Venetian dialect (*OA*, 2:698–90), and expresses the tendency for the music to rock her into and out of the dream mode, a movement similar to that of the water on which she and her group of friends float aimlessly.

A few pages further on Sand evokes the vocal bravura of caged nightingales. The song of these prisoners enchants the narrator with its ability to brighten the dull life of urbanites who would rather be in the country. No doubt Sand was feeling oppressed at times by the physical limits of Venice. Yet, the song of the birds blends in with the night life of the city, because when a serenader ambles by, the plumed singers respect the human's song and then try to outdo him with songs of their own.

The song of the gondoliers finds its requisite place in Sand's descriptions of Venice. Such commentary can be found in any guidebook of Venice, painting the quaint tunes as part of the splendor of the landscape. Instead of praising their lilting melodies wafting across the gentle waters of the lagoon, however, Sand analyzes the vocal qualities of these men whom she would rather hear than trained opera stars. Their "art," lacking in formal musical training, combines with the movement of the water and the changes in ambience in accordance with the time of the day. A single tenor usually begins, joined on the second verse by fellow gondoliers. The choir swells and diminishes following a tacit artistry that belongs only to these men, despite efforts of classical musicians to note it down (*OA*, 2:695–97).

Sand brings the musical commentary back to the context of the tour guide by adding that Venice, with the acoustics of the canals and the absence of horse and carriage noises, provides an environment particularly conducive to music. Here the music truly belongs to the city and forms a part of the total picture. Later Sand describes how a spontaneous concert arose one morning in the lagoon and earned the respect and mutual admiration of all the gondoliers and passengers present. The scene appears rather unlikely, because she puts oboes, violins, and harps aboard the boats. But the musical rhythms and harmonies Sand evokes exhibit her love of Venetian music.

Another important topic of the *Lettres* is suicide. Sand addresses her complaints on life to Jules Néraud and François Rollinat (Letters 4 and 5), all the while urging them not to become despondent on her behalf. She admits having contemplated suicide and shares her thoughts on the meaning of such an act. Her primordial reason for not seriously entertaining suicide is her children.

Sand admired Mme de Staël, and at this time she had just read her *Réflexions sur le suicide*. In principle, Staël's essay intends to dissuade the reader from the temptation of suicide, no matter how attractive a solution it might seem. Sand realizes, however, that she is less fortunate than Mme de Staël, and thus that her own life has much less worth than that of the author of *Corinne*. Her own attraction to suicide, which she admits she put into the character of Lélia and tried to rectify in the character of Jacques, had returned. Finally, she says that if she does not commit suicide, it will be because she lacks the courage.

Both letters, which include the most negative thoughts of the whole text, were written at Nohant. What, if any, is the relationship between suicide and travel? That Sand was not on a trip when she wrote these missives falsifies their inclusion in the collection of a traveler's letters. She attempts to maintain the notion of travel by referring to her correspondents' trips; yet the overwhelming coincidence of her own immobility and the depression of two recent failures in love does not lack significance. Like Lélia, George Sand cannot yet entirely accept the changes that are operating in her personal life, which she approaches as much practically as morally. Using the same technique she had employed in *Auvergne*, she looks for a solution, or at least some solace, in writing. She distances herself from undue influences in a way she does not when writing in Venice, and sets to examining her problems from what she sees as a more objective point of view. She merely gives vent to her pessimism, an understandable reaction to the circumstances she experienced in 1835 and 1836. These musings constitute a psychological and emotional voyage in themselves. They also belie a very real desire to leave the present situation, to leave Casimir, of course, but also to leave Nohant. Writing down these desires helps to vent the frustration, thus giving her the courage to pursue the legal settlement to which she felt she was entitled.

In *Lettres d'un voyageur* Sand combines a typical romantic hero's lyrical outpouring with a dramatic and realistic context. A similar need for introspection amidst historical turmoil would lead Sand, much later, to write down her queries in a sort of travelogue during the Franco-Prussian War. Because of a smallpox epidemic, Sand takes her grandchildren and flees into the healthful countryside of the Creuse valley. At the same time, the Prussian forces are advancing and up-to-the-minute news of their position is hard to come by. At a loss for meaningful dialogue based on fact, Sand turns to her notebook and scribbles daily musings in her *Journal d'un voyageur pendant la guerre* (Diary of a wartime traveler) (1871). Again she vacillates between travelogue—descriptions of the rugged Creuse countryside—and her own fears, doubts, and reassessments of political theory. Much of this text presents valuable material for redefining Sand's personal values as she grows older and more isolated from Parisian society.

Italy

Travel abroad almost always meant Italy for George Sand. Since her days at the convent, where she mastered Italian and ventured into the literature of Dante and Ariosto, she had always dreamed of visiting the land of exoticism and history. She eventually took that voyage with Musset.

Italy remains the most influential factor of Sand's travel experience. She produced some of her best work of the transitional period between *Lélia* and *La Comtesse de Rudolstadt* while in Venice. Many of the later novels also owe a clear debt to observations made during the Italian sojourn. In this instance, both the act of traveling and the result of travel prove interesting. The Venetian novels, born of dedication and hard work, parallel the turmoil in Sand's personal life. The works that develop from this period testify to the mixture of travel, observation, and heightened emotions that characterized these months.

Venice provides the main setting for the short novel *Le Secrétaire intime*. None of the description, however, evokes even a vague image of the canaled city, aside from two general references to waterways and one mention of a gondola. Sand wrote *Le Secrétaire intime* in November and December of 1833, just before her departure for Italy with Musset. It is not surprising that there is little detail of Venice, of which the novel offers only an anticipatory depiction. A stereotypical portrayal of Italians in the novel betrays a standard French prejudice toward their cisalpine neighbors. This commentary is also present in "Mattea," composed at about the same time, and would become more pronounced in *Leone Leoni* and *La Daniella*. Princess Quintilia, whose very name suggests her Latin heritage, embodies the strong and often volatile emotions of the stereotypical Italian, although she tempers these faults with tolerance, a sense of equality, and the strength of a noble woman who well knows how to protect her reputation while still en-

joying a full personal life. The hero of *Secrétaire*, Louis comte de Saint-
Julien, the only Frenchman amongst the principal characters, also displays
an a priori basis for his judgments.

Through circuitous explanations and mistaken identities, Saint-Julien
discovers that, after the death of her first aged husband whom she never
saw, the princess married the proxy husband of that arranged marriage.
This young and proud husband refuses to accept Quintilia's title; he leaves
the princess's domain and is assumed dead. He surfaces years later and returns to Venice under various assumed names; he and the princess see each
other on the sly, thus adding to the intrigue. Having supposedly learned
tolerance, Saint-Julien returns to his mother, whose unfaithfulness to his
father he has now learned to accept. A strange yet amusing passage of the
novel, which Sand published separately, carries the title "Le Bal
entomologique" and describes a costume ball where everyone dresses as his
favorite insect.[4]

Another short story, "Mattea" (1835), follows in the Venetian series.[5]
"Mattea" evokes the Orientalism of Venice that her compatriots found so enticing. Even though little more than St. Mark's Square enjoys a detailed description in this text, Sand's depictions of the city exploit and satisfy the
French reader's preconceptions of Venice.

A Venetian and a Turk, both fabric merchants, trade silk cargoes across the
Adriatic, thus providing a rich backdrop for the use of exotic costumes and
conventions.[6] But this setting, which represents Europe's gateway to the East,
also furnishes the raw material for religious and political intolerance, the
principal theme of the story. Sand introduces us to the Venetians' prejudices
against Turks, implicitly inviting us to examine our own xenophobia. She
also levies ample criticism on the overly strict upbringing of girls. Still the
heroine ends up happily married to her exploiter, with whom she has two
children. She is also reconciled with her father after her mother's death.
Sand's statements on the liberation of women do not always bring her arguments to a satisfying conclusion. The love story is, nonetheless, very romantic
and shows Sand's expert manipulation of "effets de réel." The palpable presence of Venice serves as a successful vehicle for these themes, recalling *Les
Lettres persanes*, though on a smaller scale.

L'Uscoque, a similar tale that combines the exoticism of Venetian, Turkish,
and Arabic flavors, came in 1837. This Venetian tale freely draws from
Byron, to whom references abound in the text. The corsair, Orio Soranzo, is
irresistibly handsome and marries a woman intended for another. His exploits with pirates in the Adriatic soon become more important for him than
his wife, and he goes mad. He kills his wife and her former fiancé, Count

Ezzelino. But upon meeting the count's sister, Argiria, he is fascinated by the degree to which she resembles her dead brother. Guilt and madness drive him to entertain killing her too, but he is too much in love with her. Latent homosexuality also surfaces in Orio's relationship with his Arab mistress, Naam, whom he commands to dress in masculine garb. She is the only one to have any influence over him. When Naam dies, a traveling merchant tells of the funeral and of the spiteful stories that had once circulated that Naam was a woman.[7]

Leone Leoni (1834) constitutes one of Sand's most famous, and for some critics, infamous works of Italian influence. The contrast between the Venice of this novel and that of previous ones affirms Sand's adeptness at realistic, albeit romanticized, description. She also hones her technique of putting description to the service of tone and characterization. Sand presents her readers with a quintessentially romantic love story.[8] The resemblances with *Manon Lescaut* are far from coincidence; Sand had just reread the Prévost novel before leaving for Italy and was determined to rewrite it from a different perspective.[9] It provides an excellent example of Sand's fondness for convoluted intrigue.

Leoni, an addicted gambler, arranges to marry Juliette, the daughter of a rich Belgian jeweler. Unable to prove his financial stability to Juliette's father, Leoni all but kidnaps Juliette. He secretly sells the jewels garnered from the fancy evening dress Juliette was wearing the night they fled. They live well beyond their means, and Leoni leaves Juliette to join another rich mistress in Milan. Juliette follows him there and agrees to live as his sister in the palace of his new mistress, who is quite ill and soon befriends Juliette. The mistress dies, leaving the house and great wealth to Leoni and Juliette. Juliette then learns her father has died and her mother is sick and dying; she returns to her mother's side in Brussels. While she is away, scandal arises surrounding the death of the mistress, and Leoni is incarcerated. Juliette, whose mother has since died, liquidates all the assets of her inheritance to bail out Leoni and to pay his debts. Leoni, however, tries to sell her to another man; when she discovers this, she jumps out the window and is saved by Aleo, who is willing to marry her and restore her to a socially acceptable position. Juliette is still in love with Leoni, however, and when she spies him some time later on a nearby gondola, she leaps from the arms of Aleo to ride off with Leoni once again. Aleo plots to assassinate Leoni, but instead mistakenly kills Leoni's cohort, a French marquis.

Leone Leoni received some bitter attacks because of its slanderous depiction of Italians. The Italian Leoni embodies all the stereotypes of the swindler and the unfaithful lover;[10] but just as dishonest is the French marquis, who is equally ruthless in his dealings with Leoni and Juliette. He even double-crosses his "business associate," which forces Leoni to do likewise, but only to protect himself from the marquis. Moreover, the marquis turns to assassination, a level to which Leoni never stoops.

La Dernière Aldini (1837; The last of the Aldini women) offers a good dose of Italian folklore. Lélio, the hero, is an authentic singing gondolier. He charms Venetian ladies and manages to be hired into palace service for a female admirer who pays for his musical training. In the second part of the novel, in Naples, he meets and falls in love with another woman who turns out to be the daughter of the first. Many evocations of Venetian songs and a sprinkling of dialect make this novel an enjoyable addition to the "nouvelles vénitiennes."

L'Orco (1838; The ogre) describes a masked woman who seduces a man at a ball during carnival. The woman's identity remains a secret, but she probably incarnates the humiliation of Venice's submission to Austrian domination.[11] The sole Venetian landmark in the story is the Arsenal, which Sand visited at night. She also incorporated a wealth of the city's history, especially maritime history.[12]

A decade later Sand wrote a novel about social classes with an Italian setting, *Le Piccinino* (1847; The good little boy). The Sicilian stereotype of dishonesty abounds here. A shifty Sicilian, nicknamed "The Adventurous Judge," is the illegitimate son of Prince de Castro Reale, who in old age becomes the chief of the bandits. The prince's legitimate son, Duke de Castro Reale, marries Agatha de Palmarosa, whom he seduced by force. Their son Michel must be taken away to safeguard him from Agatha's parents. Michel is raised by a commoner who sends him to Rome to train as an artist. When he returns to Sicily, he suffers from a strange attraction to his mother, Agatha, who appears ageless. He comes close to death in many stereotypical Sicilian misadventures. Eventually all mistaken identities are cleared up and Michel remains pure, though less naive.

Many years after Sand's trip to Venice with Musset, another Italian voyage made a strong impression on George Sand—the one she made in 1855 with Manceau and Maurice after the death of her granddaughter, Jeanne Clésinger. This time the route led her from Genoa to Rome and Florence. Her reactions to Rome and to the state of affairs of the Italians show much more political awareness than in earlier years. Still bitter at the outcome of the 1848 revolt in France, angry at the loss of her granddaughter, and fighting against the dogma of the Church, Sand found that the Italy of 1855, and especially Rome, was filled with hypocrisy and vulgarity. *La Daniella* (1857) is peopled with condemnatory stereotypes, mostly Italians but also English.

The work is the longest of this period and received some of the strongest attacks levied against Sand since *Lélia*.

Written in a pseudoepistolary style typical of Sand, the novel presents itself as a travelogue. On the first page of the introduction the narrator tells the reader that he will transcribe "a novel and a trip, or a trip during a novel, or a novel during a trip. . . . It's the story written by itself."[13] The narrative technique, reminiscent of that used in the other travel novels we have discussed, shifts between the modes of personal thoughts and general description of landscape, architecture, and regional, or in this case, national manners. Sand inserts metanarrative formulae to remind us that her story takes place on a trip and ought to be understood as coming from a foreigner's point of view. The traveler promises a detailed account of his observations in a kind of contract: "a detailed account of my trip, of my impressions, whatever they may be, and even of my escapades, if I have any. This for the duration of a year, without a break of more than a week" (*La Daniella*, 1:20).

Once again Sand links the importance of writing to traveling as a means of sorting out one's problems. But to explain why so little description of landscape or architecture interrupts long passages of plot development, the narrator interjects: "We have removed several chapters from Jean Valreg's diary. . . . His travel impressions were encroaching upon his life's story."[14] The conclusion, which takes the reader outside the generic form, announces "Here ends Jean Valreg's diary," and wraps up loose ends of the plot that Valreg could not have foreseen. This novel, though not one of Sand's most enthralling, communicates some of the excitement of Gothic style and constitutes another in the series of novels that combines travel and writing. The most salient quality of the novel resides in Sand's use of the Gothic techniques of suspense, mistaken identities, and several subterranean passages in which many a harrowing moment takes place. In this aspect, Sand follows Ann Radcliffe's view of Italianism and the exotic intrigue of *The Italian*.

Jean Valreg does not fail to use some of the usual pejorative clichés in describing the Italians he observes; these remarks usually concern the class of servants, whom he judges faithful when he appreciates them and deceitful when he does not. Rather than a sign of anti-Italianism, Sand demonstrates here her gift of irony, as Valreg falls in love with and marries an Italian servant girl, Daniella. Once the hint of a lasting love is established, the stereotypical comments disappear for the most part. And as for the anticlerical commentary, a principal source of criticism for the novel, it is certainly a major theme of the novel, but it is scarcely more blatant here than in several of Sand's other novels.[15]

Several of Sand's other novels take place in Italy, such as *Les Maîtres mosaïstes* (The master mosaic workers), *Lucrezia Floriani, La Dernière Aldini,* to name three. Poli declares that Sand's descriptions of Venice are perhaps the most precise in *Consuelo.*[16] These works are treated in more depth in later chapters. A word must be said here about two novels written in Venice, but which take place in France: *André* and *Jacques.* There is little indication that Sand was homesick during her stay in Venice, except perhaps the strange ending to Letter 3 of *Lettres d'un voyageur.* The preface to *André* also suggests a certain nostalgia for her homeland.[17] This may account, in part, for her transferring a newly mastered technique of integrating realistic description into plot and characterization from the novels set in Italy to a novel set in provincial France.

Even though an ill-furnished argument could attempt to identify Fernande's adultery with Sand's, the remainder of the social context of *Jacques* does not justify such a comparison.[18] Nor does Sand's newly begun career correspond to Geneviève's long-established trade in *André.* There is perhaps nothing extraordinary in that during an emotion-filled period in Venice, Sand withdrew to write two novels that take place in her own country, one in Creuse (just south of Berry) and the other mostly in Savoy. Italians, ironically, rather appreciated *André,* which enjoys the distinction, along with *La Petite Fadette,* of being the Sand work most frequently translated into Italian. *Jacques,* censured because of its nondenunciatory treatment of adultery and suicide, remained unknown to the Italian public.[19]

Historical fiction, though not Sand's most typical genre, does satisfy another need to escape. Travel through time instead of travel through space adds a different yet similar dimension to the fashion of the exotic. Sand's most exotic historical fiction is probably *Les Beaux Messieurs de Bois-Doré* (1857). The text gives adequate costume description and name-dropping of prominent seventeenth-century figures to situate the reader in a comfortably removed setting. Also set in the seventeenth century and written in the same year, *Les Dames vertes* completes a sense of manners for the time period.

Consuelo (1842–44) moves us up to the eighteenth century. Most of the plot occurs around 1750 and includes political and especially cultural markers to help pinpoint the action. A large portion of the politico-religious theme stems from the history of Church Reform in fifteenth-century Bohemia. Although Sand covers the major events necessary to her reader in *Consuelo,* she shares the rest of her research in *Jean Zyska* (1843).

The French Revolution offered Sand yet another era of fascination; she wrote three pieces concerning this period. As early as 1847, she began writing "Monsieur Rousset." She planned to create a novel of manners describing the beliefs of Berrichon countrymen during the Revolution. She never finished the novel, but a fragment was published in 1851. She intended to include it in her later revolutionary novel, *Nanon,* but finally she added the segment as a chapter of *Simon* in the complete works.[20] *Nanon* (1872) portrays the problems of a strong and intelligent, lower-class woman and an illiterate, neglected aristocrat during the Reign of Terror. (See chapter 5 for a more precise treatment of the feminist theme in this novel.) A novel in dialogue form also takes place during the postrevolutionary period, *Cadio* (1867). The plot is set in Vendée in 1793 and describes the strife of political and religious adherences within a family. In the introduction, Sand details some thoughts on the genre of historical fiction. First, she says, there is always another perspective to any historical event. Second, this historical novel tells the story of revolutionary psychology without bothering with historical persons. She reserves the freedom to ignore famous people and even various events.[21]

Sand's travel literature fulfilled many expectations of the nineteenth-century reader. As both travelogue and prose fiction, this writing satisfied her desire for exoticism. Sand causes writing to flow from the experience of traveling, or rather, she crystallizes the importance of the voyage in writing. From a metaliterary perspective this aspect of her travel writings, though perhaps not original with Sand, remains one of the most fascinating facets of this group of works.

Chapter Four

Nohant and Berry

Far removed from Italy and the Italians, yet still farther separated from Paris and the Parisians, Sand's own Berry and her beloved Berrichons provide the cadre and the focus for many of Sand's best-known works. In an unreserved display of exoticism within the Hexagon—as important an element of the romantic movement as travel to far-off lands—Sand portrays her native province in all its savagery and subtlety. Her descriptions of the physical and social aspects of Berry and the conscious exposition of local traditions and customs help to acquaint the reading public with a part of France they would otherwise never know, bringing to French literature what the Brontë sisters and Thomas Hardy brought to English literature.

Sand has always been known for her rustic novels, though only recently has the literary value of these works been examined. Sand effected some innovations in this genre, specifically in the area of regional language and socialist discourse. Just about the time Balzac was amusing his readers with the characteristic German deformation of French sounds in *Le Cousin Pons,* Sand brought to Parisian readers an awareness of dialects and the beauty of an idiom totally removed from literary French.

Using agrarian people as protagonists begs the comparison with another Balzac novel, *Les Paysans.* Balzac had already ventured to portray the manners of countryfolk in *Le Médecin de campagne* (1833) and *Le Curé de village* (1841), but the author of these treatises made no attempt to discover the world view of the farming population;[1] only in *Les Paysans* did he delve into the agricultural community from a humanist perspective. He found this society rather closed to him, however, and the results of his analyses disappointed both him and his public. The first part of *Les Paysans* appeared in 1844 (the full version was published only posthumously, in 1854), and critics decried a lack of sincerity in the depiction of the plight of tenant farmers who were at odds with their new feudal lords, the bourgeoisie.

George Sand naturally reacted against the unsympathetic treatment of country people by Balzac. She had always been familiar with the farmers of the "vallée noire," thus Balzac's lack of sensitivity both shocked and inspired her. Her own writings about country folk give Virgilian praise to farmers and posit their important role in the future of the new France. She had already written *Jeanne* (1844) and felt a need to portray other aspects of the folk she called "the real French people."[2] The continuation of these plans was delayed somewhat by the events of February and June 1848, but Sand would eventually pick up the pen to defend and portray her countrymen.

George Sand's "Berry novels" fall under two categories: those she specifically grouped under the rubric of "rustic novels" (*les romans champêtres*)[3] and all others that make important use of a Berrichon setting.

Les Romans champêtres

Traditionally categorized as *les romans champêtres* are *La Mare au diable* (1846; The Devil's Pool), *François le champi* (1848; François the Waif), and *La Petite Fadette* (1849; Little Fadette). Other novels, notably *Jeanne* (1844) and *Les Maîtres sonneurs* (1853; The master bag-pipers), are considered "rustic" as well, although Sand did not designate them as such. These five titles form the core of George Sand's rustic novels.

Jeanne, George Sand writes in the 1852 preface, "is the first attempt of what would later lead me to write *La Mare au diable, François le champi,* and *La Petite Fadette.*"[4] The first mention of a series of rustic novels, however, came in the 1851 preface to *La Mare au diable*: "When I began, with *La Mare au diable,* a series of rustic novels, which I planned to bring together under the title of *Veillées du Chanvreur* (The Hemp-Dresser's Tales), I had no system and no pretense of literary revolution."[5] In this short preface Sand identifies the "*roman de moeurs rustiques*" (novel of rustic manners) as an age-old genre that she borrowed for the simple purpose of presenting nature in its simplest and most beautiful form.[6] She had already articulated this goal in the foreword to *François le champi,* all the while trying to imitate the hemp-dresser's storytelling style, which would become the format for the rustic novels—that of recounting a story that has been handed down from one person to the next, from generation to generation. The importance of the oral tradition accounts for the emphasis on spoken language, which I shall discuss further on.

Jeanne, with all the historical and symbolic resonances of the eponymous character's name, paints the figure of a beautiful and simple peasant girl, coveted by three men: an English nobleman, a French nobleman, and a French bourgeois. Like Chateaubriand's Amélie, Jeanne swore to her mother on her deathbed that she would never marry, a promise she kept steadfastly. The social commentary is fairly predictable: the French bourgeois, Léon, is vulgar and insults Jeanne with his persistent attempts at seduction; the

French nobleman, Guillaume, tries to repress his love for Jeanne, ostensibly out of respect for her and for Arthur, the Englishman, his best friend, who has declared his love for Jeanne. All three fail in their attempts, even Arthur, despite the characteristically direct approach that Sand often assigns English people. Jeanne dies very young, presumably because this is the only way she can keep her promise to her mother.[7]

In *La Mare au diable,* Germain, a man in his mid-thirties, agrees to remarry for the sake of his children three years after the death of his wife. At the same time, Marie, a young girl of fifteen, leaves home to earn a small wage as a shepherdess. They accompany each other on the way to their new lives, and both meet with disappointment and disillusion. Despite the age difference, they become devoted to each other and marry happily. An appendix to the novel, called *Les Noces de campagne* (The Country Wedding), gives a detailed account of Germain and Marie's wedding, although this is quite obviously a description of Berrichon weddings in general. The amount of historical and sociological observance has frequently been cited as proof of Sand's desire to document Berrichon life.

François le champi tells the story of a foundling, beginning with Madeleine rescuing him at age six and continuing until their marriage. Madeleine's wicked first husband, Blanchet, forbids her to waste bread and time on the urchin, so she must send him away. Later, when Blanchet dies, François returns to help Madeleine through her illness and the financial and legal difficulties she inherits from her husband. Once he has solved all her woes through honest cleverness and money from his own mysterious inheritance, they marry. As François is younger than Madeleine and she raises him as though he were her own son, there is a strong suspicion of incest, which elicited quite a scandal when the novel first appeared. Even though Sand made every effort to eschew the topic in her narrative, the theme of the older woman and the young boy, not an uncommon one for Sand, shines through rather clearly.

La Petite Fadette examines the case of another outsider, Fadette, the granddaughter of a sorceress. Fadette, who is accustomed to being shunned, falls in love with Landry, to the amusement of his friends and to the great chagrin of his twin brother, Sylvinet. Landry tries to extricate himself from the oath that binds him to Fadette because of a favor she did him, accomplished through seemingly magical powers; but he soon finds her attractive and falls in love with her. They survive the vicissitudes of the reactions of the family and the community, not to mention those of the jealous twin, and eventually celebrate their wedding.

Les Maîtres sonneurs brings together four childhood friends and an outsider who pass through various triangles, finally forming two couples, Brulette-Huriel and Thérence-Tiennet, and a self-exiled outcast, Joset, who is one of the original four. Joset discovers his gift for music and determines to become a master bagpiper in the tradition of the region. Overzealous practicing, pride, and ambition cause Joset to separate himself from his friends, family, and love interest. He fails to enter the "confrérie" ("guild") of bagpipers for political reasons, and, incapable of explaining his individual aesthetics, he alienates everyone and exiles himself, which eventually leads to his death.

Country customs, habits, and beliefs, then, constitute the identifying force of the rustic novels. George Sand aims to examine the sociological makeup of the Berrichon people and to exalt them as the picture of goodness and as fundamentally French. Her use of realism is only moderate and her sense of socialistic progress is rather conservative,[8] often clashing with her overtly socialist writings of the same period. Her romanticized style at once reduces the verisimilitude of the picture and homogenizes the characters so that they could hail from any province of France.[9]

Authentic geographical place names, however, set the cadre solidly in the Berry. *Jeanne* uses to advantage the famous "pierres jaumâtres" outside of Toulx;[10] *Le Mare au diable* takes place in St. Chartier, *François* in Cormouer, and *Fadette* in La Cosse; *Les Maîtres sonneurs* contrasts the Bourbonnais with the Berry in topographic terms with symbolic overtones. These references, along with exact geographical descriptions, have allowed critics to affirm the presence of precise locations in these novels. The location and disposition of the mysterious pond in the middle of the woods in *La Mare au diable* are instrumental in evoking the change of mood and intention of the characters. Similar arrangements of hills and streams in *François* and *Fadette* place the action in a location that becomes even more unmistakably the Berry. It has been said that while Sand uses actual place names, in *Fadette* she put them together in such a haphazard manner that the true topography is not respected. *Mauprat, Jeanne,* and *Le Meunier d'Angibault,* however, show remarkable adherence to the actual arrangement of the sites.[11]

Perhaps the most authentic aspect of Sand's Berry is the depiction of regional dress and traditions, which portrays a believable people.[12] The traditional praise of the agrarian laborer, which recalls the origins of the pastoral genre in Virgil, offers soothing pictures of sturdy men and women hard at work in the fields. Hard work typifies the heroes of *François* and *Fadette* as well, a quality always stressed and often contrasted with the indolence of others.

An equally customary opposition, this time more reminiscent of

Rousseau, pits country life against the evils of the city. Normally Berry would vie with Paris in this antithesis, but Sand usually puts the country location at odds with a Berrichon town. This creates a contrast of Georgian good and civilized evil within the confines of the province. There are no references to Paris in any of these novels, which underscores the isolation and exoticism of the province. This is a central element of Sand's rustic genre.

The Berrichon town provides a suitable setting for town fêtes with events that interrupt the otherwise routine and ordinary lives of the characters involved in farming or raising animals. We witness the dancing and music of the festival of St. Androche in *Fadette,* and the ritualistic wedding parades and dancing in *La Mare au diable.* Sand gives much attention to the rituals of conquering and seduction.[13] Similar descriptions of wedding customs will constitute a substantial passage at the end of *Les Maîtres sonneurs.* The narrator conspicuously excludes the description of the wedding at the end of *François,* explaining that the account would be too long. I believe, rather, that such a description would detract from the private tone of the work. This rustic novel differs from the other two in its intimate setting: there are no town fêtes or public gatherings, and a wedding celebration would detract from the importance of the central relationship.

Customs often spring from superstitions, which abound in the rustic novels. Sand invented nothing in the area of Berrichon beliefs.[14] She made a careful study of regional legends, which she published as articles at about the same time as she published the series of rustic novels. Gathered and published together under the title *Promenades autour d'un village,*[15] these articles illustrate Sand's close observations of Berrichon manners and customs, superstitions, and attractions. Perhaps the most interesting remark in these pages is Sand's analysis of how Christianity had to join with age-old pagan rituals and traditions to gather the people to the new religion.[16]

In the second portion of Sand's treatise on Berrichon customs, "Les Visions de la nuit dans les campagnes" (Nocturnal visions in the country), she describes several nocturnal manifestations of spirits, good and evil, or good until provoked to vengeance. Sand herself admits to never having experienced such hallucinations, but she assures us that she believes they exist in the collective mind of these folk and that these beliefs evince the power of an upbringing rich in the traditions of an ancient civilization.

Sorcery naturally plays an important role in Sand's rustic novels. The title *La Mare au diable* hints at the role of superstition in this work. The famous devil's pool is named only once, but, again, the native Berrichon employs both pagan and Christian rituals and symbols to ensure a sage solution to problems. The admixture of superstition and Church ritual remains characteristic of Berrichon sorcery in Sand's rustic novels. *La Petite Fadette* depicts the story of an outsider, Little Fadette, who is kept apart from "proper" society because of her grandmother's unexplained magical powers and practice of herbal medicine (reminiscent of Sand's own dabbling in medicine). The heroine has learned many of her grandmother's "tricks." The first tme she uses her "powers," Landry, who will subsequently fall in love with Fadette, requests the girl's help in finding his twin. When Sylvinet turns up safe and sound, Landry thanks God, "without thinking to ask His forgiveness for having used the devil's knowledge in order to get this good fortune."[17] Later, when Fadette works what seems to be a miracle on Sylvinet, whose state of psychological exhaustion has induced a dangerously high fever, the narrator explains that Fadette's so-called magic comprised more religion than deviltry.[18]

The absence of any mention of superstition in *François le champi* may seem odd at first glance. We do find it, though, in the form of a general prejudice and fear of foundlings. Abandoned children, it is said, bring only sadness and trouble. They are always idiots and surely children of the devil. François constantly looks, in vain, however, for an explanation for this commonly held belief. The first indication of the waif's Christian upbringing comes in the form of the written word: he learns to read from the Gospel and the Saints' Lives. This and his kind, honest demeanor prove that his morals do not come under the control of Satan. Thus the lesson of accepting the outsider becomes clear, as it does in *Fadette*.

An implicit link exists between superstition and religion in *Mauprat* (1837) in the character of Patience, an old sage who lives in the forest and who is good friends with the country priest. *Jeanne* proposes an explicit marriage of superstition and religion. Jeanne is usually careful to avoid any pagan explanation that would go counter to Church teaching, but she also concocts some rather extravagant rationalizations. The most poignant example of this tendency concerns her promise of chastity. The country priest tries to explain to her that because she took the oath and renewed it on the pagan "pierre jomâtre," it no longer holds and could in fact be annulled by the Church in Rome. But for Jeanne, her oath to her mother and her fear of the vengeance of the local spirits are much stronger than any pope.

Sand's treatment of language constitutes perhaps the most original aspect of the rustic novels.[19] In the foreword to *François le champi* the narrator/ author states her desire to imitate the language of her Berrichon characters so that the true color of their personalities would not be lost. Still, the typical Parisian reader would not comprehend the language of these Berrichons and would require a translation into a simple idiom. Thus Sand instituted a style

of colloquial writing that mimicked peasant speech, slipping in regional vocabulary items to give an air of an authentic linguistic environment. The insertion of dialectal words and phrases is often false, however, and breaks the
flow of the narrative. Sand is frequently obliged to give a paraphrase in standard French. Still, her technique of restating actual regional idiosyncracies
differs from Balzac's amusing use of deformed French.[20]

The linguistic system of the rustic group progresses throughout the three
novels. *Mauprat* uses regional dialect only sparingly, unlike the analogous
Wuthering Heights, where whole speeches are in regional English.[21] *Jeanne*
uses Berrichon vocabulary in a gratuitous manner, always followed by a translation in French in parentheses. The reader becomes accustomed to the inter-
ruptions, but the device remains artificial. The use of italics puts the dialectal
phrases on the same level as Sir Arthur's mistakes in French;[22] Sand is careful
to correct this misunderstanding in future instances of dialect. The attempt
to improve the incorporation of regional speech in *La Mare au diable* creates
a strain of forced innovation, producing an obstacle that sharply contrasts
with the simplicity of the story. The narrator comments on this problem in
the foreword to *François le champi* and predicts a smoother use of Berrichon
dialect in this instance. The inclusion of the idiom does improve, not because
it merges seamlessly with standard French, but because this time the device is
less stilted, more natural. Intermittent interventions by the narrator recall the
storytelling frame of the novel; moving in and out of this structure thus corresponds to, and parallels, the mixing of linguistic registers.

A greater pool of Berrichon dialectal words and expressions come into the
dialogue in *Le Meunier d'Angibault* (1845). Frequent footnotes explain
these phrases, but there are also numerous intranarrative devices that divulge
the meanings. Sand improves this technique in *Le Péché de Monsieur Antoine*
(1845). No footnotes intrude on the narrative; rather expressions are explained naturally as the non-Berrichon characters learn their meanings along
with the reader. *La Petite Fadette* displays the most blatant and clever use of
Berrichon vocabulary, but here there is less pretense of a literary invention
and the reader can simply get on with the business of adopting a new linguistic subgroup that helps to define the characters of this novel. *Les Maîtres sonneurs* offers the greatest and best use of Berrichon dialect. Here the characters
display their personalities simply and frankly through their language.

Of Sand's original plan to assemble three novels about Berrichon life
under the title of *Veillées du chanvreur,* there remains only a memory. But the
very concept of characters and stories belonging to a portion of France other
than Paris, forgotten or ignored in time and space, helps the rustic works
hang together. The term of "veillées" appears only in *Maîtres sonneurs,* where

it supplies the unifying factor of form. The author explains its use in the dedication, stating, "*[Je vais] raconter ce que racontaient les paysans à la veillée,
dans ma jeunesse, quand j'avais le temps de les écouter. . . . Elle [l'histoire] me
fut dite . . . en plusieurs soirées de* breyage; *c'est ainsi . . . qu'on appelle les
heures assez avancées de la nuit où l'on broie le chanvre, et où chacun alors
apportait sa chronique*" ([I'm going] to tell you what the farmers told me during those evening gatherings, during my youth when I had the time to listen. . . . I was told this story . . . over several evenings of *brakage*; . . . this is
the term for the late hours of the night when one brakes hemp, and when
everybody tells their news).[23]

Thirty-two "veillées," the chapter divisions of the story, constitute the
novel. Sand's formal use of the term lends a concrete interpretation of the
concept of evening gatherings. Along with the reference to a country setting,
where yarns were spun along with hemp, here the term also recalls the time
represented in the recounting of the story, thus a conscious reference to its
literariness and to its orality. Such a temporal and cultural symbol serves to
unify the work and to situate it concisely and significantly in a network of
themes and tone.

The rustic novels have often been called Sand's third period of literary production, marking a supposed desire to retract from the public eye and to concentrate on the less complicated issues of daily life. These novels have also
often been too easily dismissed as easy reading for adolescents. It is important
to consider that Sand realized, in her musings about the importance of the
large population of French farmers in the political scheme of her day, that she
and most others knew very little about the peasant mind and thus very little
about another important aspect of the human condition. In an approach that
is far more honest and less pretentious than Balzac's in "Scènes de la vie de
campagne," Sand attempted to put down her observations of basic human
problems as they manifested themselves in a country context. Therefore there
is still much to be learned from this cycle of rustic novels.

Berry in Other Works

Although George Sand's intention was to group only three novels under
the rubric of rustic novels, several other works fall into a similar category. A
few novels do take place in other provinces, for instance *Mademoiselle
Merquem* is situated in Normandy, and *Tamaris* is set on the Riviera. But
because Sand desired to make the center of France known to the Parisian
reading public, and because the inhabitants of "la Vallée Noire" were the

people Sand knew best, she was spurred on in her use of Berrichon customs in her fiction.

Valentine, Sand's second novel, provides the foray into Berry. In this work she gives a graphic description of the terrain, several place names, and much detail of local customs. The famous scene of the bourrée, where Valentine and Bénédict first meet and kiss, provides a picturesque view of country fêtes and dance traditions. A limited use of local vocabulary sprinkled throughout the narrative and in Bénédict's speech hints at the serious presentation of a non-Parisian idiom.

André, too, takes place in Berry. This novel, written in Venice, betrays Sand's momentary homesickness for her native province. The references in *André* often denote a generic province, not necessarily Berry, and only minimal description of the topography intrudes in the narrative. *Le Meunier d'Angibault,* which is concurrent with the beginnings of the rustic series, presents Berrichon customs, habits, and manners. The country aspect of the plot is of prime importance here, because Sand is discussing the socialist theories as they apply to farmers who are the mainstay and hope of the France of the future. *Le Compagnon du tour de France* (1840) falls into a similar, ancillary rubric wherein the provincial/country aspect functions in service of the socialist theme.

Simon (1836) is set in Marche, the hilly region to the south of Berry, part of modern Creuse. This is the first novel to expand the provincial area that Sand explores in her fictional world. Later on she will exploit Bourbonnais, making comparative commentary on the psychological effect of topography on behavior. The contrast between Berrichon and Bourbonnais people is central to the plot and tone of *Les Maîtres sonneurs. Mauprat* (1837) describes the rugged terrain of Berry, paralleling the unrefined and stubborn nature of Berrichon people.

Mont-Revêche (1852) takes place in a hilly region, probably Creuse. The terrain is of some importance to the setting, but precise place names are few. *La Ville noire* (The Black city) (1860) has approximatly the same topography, perhaps with more precipices and torrents, which also suggests Creuse. The second half of *Le Marquis de Villemer* (1860) also takes place in Creuse. Sand exploits the marquis's Creusois background to paint provincial customs and character traits that distinguish these people from the hypocritical Parisians and from the hypocrisy the marquis must adopt while in the capital. *Adriani* (1854) is situated in Ardèche. The importance of the province here is its distance from Paris.

Le Journal d'un voyageur pendant la guerre (1871) takes us through various sections of Creuse as George Sand and her children attempt to escape the smallpox epidemic. At the same time, she describes the sensation of a divided country and especially the frustration of lacking current, firsthand news. Much of the description of Creuse resembles the travelogue style Sand used in her early literary endeavors.

Nanon (1872) again crosses Berry with Creuse. This novel, which depicts revolutionary France, attempts to provide a view of the period from the provincial perspective. The Berrichons are far removed from the Revolution, and the pervading tone reflects more nationalism than regionalism.[24]

About the same time as *les romans champêtres* had found a solid place in Sand's tradition, she began to find a certain success on the Paris stage. What better and more innovative concept to bring to the theater than the largely unknown world of Berry. *François le champi* was transformed into a stage production (1849), with much emphasis on the realistic representation of Berrichon costume, speech, and music. *Claudie* (1851) was Sand's next great theatrical success. Here Berrichon festival customs, more sober than Parisian conventions, played a large part in the production.[25] *Le Pressoir* and *Mauprat* soon followed, in 1853, and *La Petite Fadette* in 1869, at the Opéra-Comique, put in verse by Michel Carré and with a full musical score by T. Semet.

The treatment of Berrichon dialect on the stage required a solution different from that found for the rustic novels, for authorial interventions giving linguistic commentary would have taxed the public. Sand did manage to find a functional solution by using expressions and rhythms that mimicked Berrichon dialect. Some examples include: "*Vous n'avez point de fiance envers moi*," or, "*J'y vas, j'y cours, not' maîtresse, j'allume une clarté*" (You don't give me no credence. I'm a-goin', I'm a-runnin', m'am, I'll be lightin' a taper). Théophile Gautier, in particular, found the result successful and realistic.[26]

George Sand's rustic novels, as well as the incidentally Berrichon novels, herald many aspects of the romantic novel of her generation. Obvious inheritors of the ideals of Rousseau, these works go beyond the bucolic setting that portrays an idyllic social unity apart from civilization. Sand takes her characters into the yet unchartered waters of applied socialism at the very heart of France. Honest manual labor, especially farming, extols the forthrightness of the French people. It was these people who, according to George Sand, missed the opportunity to take charge during the 1848 revolt because no one in Paris bothered to inform them of the possibilities. Sand was determined to publicize their existence and their worth.

The rustic novels provide a perfect setting for socialistic and religious commentary. As the characters were refreshingly new to the Parisian reader, they were able to redirect the reader's thoughts. Instead of focusing condescending appreciation on the quaintness of such novels, the reader began to see current issues in a new light, all the more refreshing because he never expected to encounter such issues in the context of a provincial novel. A kind of initiation takes place for the reader, as well as for the characters, as he experiences an intellectual and contextual reinvigoration in the rustic novels. The reader learns that it is possible to integrate, in a common discourse, social and religious issues as well as rural and urban problems.[27]

The rustic novels, far from the placid praises of agrarian life so common in American novels and stories of this era, mirror the hopes of a generation of socialists who look to the general population for the future of France. Sand also extolled the artistic abilities of a simple folk. New art forms and unknown artists were brought to the attention of Paris cultural circles. This is the era of the proletarian poet and the country musician, endowed with the gift of improvisation and often using crude yet moving images of the earth and nature. Sand attempts, through her use of country folk, to advance a socialist definition for the future of France. This attempt is the rustic novel of George Sand, which goes beyond the antithesis of Paris and the provinces and manages to engage the reader in a whole set of social issues that look to the future of France from the ironically conservative point of view of the provinces.

Chapter Five
Ideologies

Socialist thought affected Sand's expression on nearly all important issues, especially society, religion, and feminism. Sand's works of fiction starting in 1840 offer embryonic statements of ideologies, though earlier texts bear witness to her interest in, and comprehension of, society's problems. Political tracts and literary criticism, as well as Sand's prose fiction, point to her concern for modern French society.

Social Injustice

Equality across Social Boundaries   George Sand had always felt a strong aversion to social inequities. She wrote about social injustice from the beginning of her career. In *Valentine* she not only comments on the possibility of mixed class relationships, but she also paints the peasant as an intelligent and artistically talented character. The novel attests Valentine and Bénédict's equality before God and even before a select few of their small community. Society in the larger sense, represented by Valentine's mother and to a lesser extent by her husband, perpetuates the inequities.

Le Secrétaire intime decries exploiting a socially advantageous marriage, that is, Princess Quintilia's marriage with Max Sparchi. Max refused to mount the social ladder by rejecting a noble title from his bride. This comment on class differences is much more interesting than the relationship between the princess and the hero.

The relationship described in *Jacques* has several social implications. First, Jacques is older, more wealthy, and of a higher social rank than Fernande. This gives him certain rights over her that he is careful not to abuse. Sand thus sets up the magnanimity of the hero. Yet, Fernande does feel her inferior status, which, despite her gratitude, she resents. This explains, in part, why she embarks on an intimate relationship with Octave, also of high birth. Sand does not so much excuse adultery on the basis of social inequities as she explains the dangers of inequality and its implications for the family structure.

In *André* Sand tackles head on the problem of mixing social classes in a relationship. As a result of André's bourgeois snobbery and his father's adamant refusal to admit a lower-class woman into the family, the lives of four people are destroyed: Geneviève, her baby, André, and his father.

Tévérino (1846) contrasts the ingenuity of the modest class with the ennui of the aristocracy. Léonce and Sabina G . . . take a trip, trying to invent some diversions for themselves. Tévérino, a smuggler's sister, and a curé serve to amuse them. At the same time, these lower-class people show natures vastly more interesting than these of the aristocrats, whom they satirize with their cunning and wit.[1]

Commentary on the class system is not limited to Sand's early production. Both *Monsieur Sylvestre* (1865) and *Confession d'une jeune fille* (1864; Confession of a young woman) laud the principle, albeit somewhat naïve, of not compromising the values of humanity for the sake of social rank. The latter example especially pits those who seek a higher status through money and deceit against the heroine and her entourage, who must brace temptation in the face of ruinous gossip and financial disaster.

Love does not always conquer the inequities of mixed social classes. *Tamaris* (1862) ends with a doctor marrying a marquise. This couple is paralleled by another of a more modest nature, a career sailor and a woman of French and Indian blood born out of wedlock. In clear contrast to the morals of the upper-class couple, they display the morals traditionally associated with lower classes. The socialist values in this novel recall the gestures of Restoration charity rather than militant socialist concern.

Sand does not discuss in these early novels a need to pull down social class markers, just the need to be able to cross them. Herein lies the criticism of Michel de Bourges when he first meets Sand in 1835. Against Michel's notions that relegated art to a place outside the Republic, Sand retorted in Letter 6 of *Les Lettres d'un voyageur* that art has a place in all matters, including politics. Despite her wish to defend art, we cannot read into this letter an apology of "art for art's sake." She uses a vocabulary that intensifies her nascent socialist inclinations. Yet she lashes out against what she sees as Michel's desire to impose a political thematics onto her art. Not only does she declare that she has already conceived socialist notions, perhaps yet unordered, but she retains the right to claim total responsibility for them, without the threat of accidental paternity from some outside source.

Social Reform and Socialist Theory   *Simon* (1836)—in which the title character displays much of Michel de Bourges's temperament, appearance, background, and profession—represents Sand's first conscious effort at socialist theory in literature. This modest novel takes place during the Restoration and spans the gamut of political allegiances from peasant republican to returning émigré. The attorney Parquet is the son of a worker. Simon, his godson, is also the son of a laborer and likewise studies law. Simon's father was killed by *"chouans"* during the aftermath of the Revolution. Count de Fougères, along with his daughter Fiamma, returns from Trieste, where he has spent his years of exile, and buys back the family estate in Marche. Simon and Fiamma fall in love.

Sand has constructed this type of ill-fated love before. In *Simon,* however, the social clash represents a greater issue because the historical setting of the narrative creates political tension, all main characters are republican by birth and station (Fougères is actually a secondary character), and, finally, because Fiamma's republican nature seems, at the outset, to originate in her Venetian heritage. But we find out in the final chapter that she is the illegitimate child of a bandit and her patrician mother. Everything her legal father has done to discredit her mother and to buy his way back into the aristocracy both in Marche and in Paris, disgusts her and leads her to disinherit herself.

Very little actual republican dialogue links the characters to a larger organization. The novel represents a postimperial Marche well removed from the undercurrents that were adrift in Paris; nothing marks the change from Louis XVIII to Charles X. Ironically, the most explicit discourse on republican activity takes place between Fiamma and her cousin, Asolo, a secondary character who tries to instill in her the desire to become Italy's Joan of Arc and to return to the Veneto as his bride.

Le Compagnon du tour de France (1840) stands as Sand's first successful insertion of socialist theories into narrative form, and is far superior to *Simon* in this respect. The tone and circumstances derive from Agricol Perdiguier's then recently published book, *Le Livre du compagnonnage,* a treatise on the guild system. Sand, while admitting the failings of the trade unions and the corruption that compromised their ideals, gives her hero, Pierre Huguenin, the character of the innocent socialist without pretense of reform.

The plot of *Le Compagnon* does not differ substantially from many of Sand's other novels where the standard love interest bridges class differences. Only the context of labor guilds and socialist discourse offers a new dimension. Both Pierre and Yseult de Villepreux, the heroine, speak of socialist ideals and utopian dreams. While Sand's text does not suggest a utopia, nonetheless, there are several passages that reveal profound idealism in Pierre Huguenin's perception of socialist theory.[2] Other characters, notably Count de Villepreux and Achille Lefort, use the spirit of Carbonarism to advance their own selfish ideas. Yseult's idealism, too, is attenuated by her elevated station in life and her lack of practical involvement; she does try to help establish a *"vente"* (a chapter), of Carbonarists in Villepreux; but she does not realize that both her father and Achille are playing out personal vengeance and/or exploitation fantansies, and using her as their pawn.

Sand equivocates on the theme of class struggle in this novel. First, Yseult holds high ideals for a socialist state, yet she stands aloof from those around her, refusing to dance at weekly gatherings. Moreover, the position of Count de Villepreux, pretending to hold Carbonarist sympathies yet in reality faithful to Orléanist sentiments, spreads a pallor of ambiguity over his class and his family. Add to that the questionable situation of Joséphine, bourgeoise by birth, who married hastily into the aristocracy; she begins the novel wishing to renege on her accession to the upper class, yet by the end she shuns the thought of marriage to a laborer.

In the case of both women, Sand's portrayal is disadvantageous to both socialist and feminist arguments. Joséphine, the bourgeoise, yields to the seductions of a handsome worker, though her desire to arrive far outweighs her wish to marry him. Yseult, noble by name as well as by birth, remains pure. Even when she does declare her love and proposes marriage to Pierre, she cannot carry out her plan because she has a duty to respect her grandfather's bidding that she not marry a commoner.

Sand fills the novel with passages that theorize on socialist models, especially on the problem of property. Communism and socialism find themselves compared, though with no preference. Pierre contemplates the perils of infinite divisions of land that would inevitably lead to war and corruption. The examples of corruption among the Carbonarists and between rival labor guilds provide Sand with ready-made lessons on the failure of such systems. And yet we do not have a sense of fatalism. Pierre Huguenin represents the type of Sandian hero whose sympathies we embrace even though they are rather idealistic.

The most rewarding aspect of socialist commentary in *Compagnon* resides in Pierre's doubts. He listens to Carbonarist propaganda and trade union fervor, and to his father's antiguild talk; still he tries to sort through his fears and dreams. His view is based in pessimism, and this is perhaps why he hesitates to join Achille Lefort and the ranks of the Carbonarists. Yet his speech against entering into competition with other trade unions stems from a profound need for progress and practical considerations of amelioration. The lackluster ending to the novel seems to compromise both his and Yseult's ideals, but in fact the two characters resolve to abandon neither ideals nor filial duty, both of which they hold as important principles.

Horace (1841) in many ways marks a departure for Sand from established world views, a departure from Buloz and *La Revue des Deux Mondes,* as well as from Pierre Leroux and Michel de Bourges. In this novel she gives free reign to her own synthesis of various socialist notions. Paul Arsène, a working-class provincial with a talent for art, rubs elbows unpretentiously with the bourgeois students who people the novel. Although he takes part in the St. Merri massacre alongside his middle-class compatriots, his presence serves as subtle proof that different classes can coexist peacefully.

Equality between social classes constitutes a large portion of the discourse of Théophile, the narrator in *Horace*. But in effect he is not really Arsène's equal, as he would have us believe. Arsène must forgo any dreams of becoming an artist because of financial exigencies, whereas Théophile can afford to continue his medical studies and support his mistress and still help pay some of Horace's debts. A more ironic depiction of social inequality emerges as Horace, a bourgeois, tries to join the ranks of provincial aristocrats, a group that is much more sectarian, Sand assures us, than Parisian nobility. His failure to arrive is symptomatic of the bourgeoisie's insufficient rise in social status after the 1830 revolt. Thus Horace becomes the romanticized version of a tragic "hero" who must leave a society where he sees he has no place. The novel ends on a hopeful note for him, however, because he starts his life and career over in Italy.

A secondary character, Laravinière, the president of the "bousingot" group, incarnates the socialist thoughts of the novel. As a mystic he recalls the role of Patience in *Mauprat* and presages that of Zdenko in *Consuelo*. He stays in the background, even though he is effectively involved with the main characters. Laravinière's proselytizing springs from Saint-Simonian teachings, but is very closely related to Pierre Leroux's interpretations. Like Leroux, Sand espouses the concept of syncretism and allows for combining seemingly divergent systems—political, economic, and moral. It is thus not unusual to find elements of Saint-Simon, Fourier, Enfantin, Leroux, and Babeuf in Laravinière's discourse.[3]

Consuelo (1842–43) and its sequel *La Comtesse de Rudolstadt* (1843–44) present a practical application of socialist ideals. Consuelo refuses the love of a noble because of his rank, even though she suspects in her heart it is a pure love. Albert's relationship with his lower-class right-hand man, Zdenko, though at times confusing, evinces a covert leveling of social classes both in terms of social rank and formal education. The most obvious application of socialist theory comes at the end of the long novel, when Consuelo and Albert roam the countryside, spreading the news of a freer society yet to come.[4]

In *Le Meunier d'Angibault* (1845) Sand concentrates on the evils of money. But contrary to the Balzacian ethos of inherent evil, the theme here distinguishes between dirty money and money used to procure good. Henri Lémor, the son of a merchant, despises money because of the tricks his father played on business associates in order to succeed. Henri bankrupts himself after his father's death by paying money back to these unfortunate people. He becomes a worker and sets out to join the working force of socialist France.

Henri's morals are, according to him, seriously compromised by his love for a widowed aristocrat, Marcelle de Blanchemont. As it is her money and not her class that repulses Henri, there is hope for their future together when Marcelle finds her husband has left her practically nothing. The Blanchemont farm has been under the supervision of M. Bricolin, who knows that Marcelle needs to liquidate it quickly and offers a low bid. Suspicious of this move, she accepts the aid of a kind neighbor, young Louis d'Angibault, a modest farmer who happens to be in love with Bricolin's daughter, Rose.

Louis and Henri become friends despite their opposing views on money. Louis is quite willing to find and use money to convince Bricolin he is worthy of his daughter's hand in marriage. Henri, on the other hand, will not accept even a windfall, since money carries and breeds evil, especially money that comes from the upper classes. Louis tries to convince Henri that because money from the aristocracy comes from the exploitation of the working class, the money in fact rightfully belongs to the workers. But Henri will not be so easily swayed: "No! Soiled money will soil the hand that accepts it!"[5]

Henri Lémor does not seem to have learned anything as a result of his ordeals. Sand presents him as an idealist who obsesses about principle without bothering to apply theory to practice. He continues to utter socialist platitudes: "Work is healthy for everyone; it stimulates joy and dulls pain, which might mean God invented it for everyone." And then: "How light will be our work and how beautiful our lives when everyone works for the good of everyone else."[6] At the end of the novel there is little indication that he has altered these ideas.

Louis, however, represents Sand's notion of the practical provincial who applies naturally acquired socialist ideas to his own life. Even though he does agree with Henri at the end of the book, saying "money is horrid," he still profits from Bricolin's greed and thus allows money to work for him. As for narrative action, Louis, the title character, does not play a bigger part than Marcelle or Bricolin, but his quiet manner of self-actualization adds a new slant to Sand's socialist notions in these pre-1848 days.

Le Péché de Monsieur Antoine (1845; Monsieur Antoine's sin) continues the tone and ideas of *Le Compagnon du tour de France*, although Sand now integrates socialist theory somewhat more smoothly into the narrative. Her ideas are no less vague and idealistic, however, and they lack the practical quality of *Le Meunier*. There is no doubt that the socialist discourse in *Compagnon* is far superior to that of subsequent novels, even though they promote the same notions.

In *Péché* we find the typical plot of cross-class love coupled with a mysterious birth and unknown identities. Also usual for novels of this type and written at this time—and here, Sand joins Balzac in a portrayal of the ironic financial upset between the classes—the bourgeois are wealthier than the nobles. Each one, therefore, acts according to the dictates of his own pride: for or against a noble family name, and for or against money.

The title of the novel does not betray Monsieur Antoine's noble name, for he is, in fact, Count Antoine de Châteaubrun. Having lost his money and estate during the Reign of Terror, he has managed to buy back the tumbling ruins of his family castle with the funds of his servant, Janille, with whom he has an ambiguous relationship. His daughter, Gilberte, typifies the Sandian heroine: beautiful but not coquettish, proud but not haughty, unconcerned with her title and unbothered by her modest financial situation. Emile Cardonnet, the son of an industrial entrepreneur in nearby Gargilesse, studies law and becomes acquainted with socialist theory, partly though his classmates, but mostly through an elderly marquis who lives near Châteaubrun.

Not unlike Dante and Beatrice, Emile shares his socialist readings with Gilberte, and given their common dream of equality, they fall in love. Prospects for their marriage are slim: Gilberte's adoptive mother Janille rebuffs Emile's proposal as it might give the impression that the family is looking to increase its fortune. On the other hand, M. Cardonnet, who adamantly opposes his son's liberal notions, tries to short-circuit the couple by agreeing to the financially disadvantageous marriage with Gilberte only if Emile will agree to abandon his socialist thinking forever.

Marquis Boisguilbault, the liberal-thinking neighbor, discloses his involvement with the Châteaubrun family: his wife, many years his junior and now deceased, was Gilberte's mother. Having learned to love Gilberte through Emile's eyes for her goodness, and having learned to love Emile for his intellectual inclinations, which the marquis wishes to encourage, the marquis arranges for everyone to accept the union of the young couple.

A local worker, Jean Jappeloup, who represents the proletariat's hatred of exploitative management, especially management by an outsider, helps Emile survey the area surrounding his father's mill. It becomes clear to Emile, after reading many scientific books and after listening to Jean's sagacious explanations, that his father's mill complex will soon fail. The sequence of these findings provides Sand the opportunity of pitting the practical knowledge of an indigen against the cold calculations of an outsider only interested in money. Thus the reader's desire to see the exploiter fail is satisfied. Unfortunately, this spur of the plot has no further development.

Despite the socialist ideals of Emile and the modest lack of pretention of Antoine and Gilberte, Marquis de Boisguilbault performs the strongest socialist acts in the novel. He wishes to have his estate converted after his death into a commune, to be directed by Emile and Gilberte, who will be the owners only if they are married. The commune will accommodate all those worthy of such a life; the grounds of the estate will be "*the garden of the commune,* that is its gynaeceum, its banquet and festival hall, its theater, and its church."[7]

Le Péché de Monsieur Antoine establishes a forum where George Sand plays out her desire for all classes of society to realize the need for reform. In keeping with Sand's idealistic world view, the natural intelligence of the simple people, as shown here in the character of Jean Jappeloup, combines with book learning. Those with money assume their responsibility toward the less fortunate and establish communes or similar institutions in which they share their fortune. The working class willingly consent to work so long as they receive respect and consideration, which demands a sense of justice and equality. Today we would call this view naïve, but in many ways it parallels the aspirations of the socialist thinkers of Sand's time and characterizes the peaceful attempts at social reform before the unrest of the late 1840s. *La Ville noire* (1860) presents similar ideas, reinforced by the topography of the setting, with a lower town, where the workers live, and an upper town, for the bourgeois. Socialist theory here, as in most of the later texts, is played out more subtly and in a less soapbox style.

Two early plays also herald the sort of social commentary that would characterize Sand's later dramatic production. In 1840 she published *Les Mississipiens,* a play about emigration and speculation that is set in the early eighteenth century. The hero, who changes his name to George Freeman after living eighteen years in America, returns to France to seek a satisfying emotional relationship. The materialistic and moral corruption of the Regency period has clear parallels for Restoration France.

Père Va-tout-seul (1844; Old man loner) is a dialogue about an octogenarian vagabond who refuses to be put in a beggars' home, which he equates with prison. A priest manages to raise the collective consciousness of the villagers to obtain a standing, rotating accommodation for the kindly beggar. Sand's plea for solidarity not only highlights problems in 1848, but also has implications for the 1990s.

Sand's political writing during the tumultuous days of 1848 took on a more practical aspect, usually in the form of open letters. She often wrote in *La Vraie République* but also in *La Cause du peuple,* a socialist paper founded by George Sand, which started, and ended, in April 1848. The articles and letters that Sand herself considered most important were reprinted in the volume *Questions politiques et sociales*.[8] Here are published her open letters, addressed to the people, to the middle class, and to the wealthy.

The two letters to the people, "Hier et aujourd'hui" ("Yesterday and Today") and "Aujourd'hui et Demain" ("Today and Tomorrow") appear shortly after the February revolt and insist on the people's need to communicate with the upper classes, to show they are not to be feared, and that they are willing to learn. The tone is somewhat patronizing but encouraging nonetheless, despite the rather idealistic discourse.

The letter to the middle class encourages its readers to continue to contemplate the duties of the bourgeoisie and to apply these duties to the people as in the period before the revolt. She advocates electing at least two citizens per department from the people's class: an urban worker and an agricultural worker. The letter to the rich, however, uses a stern tone to disentangle the misconception and fear of communism on the part of the aristocracy. She insists that socialists have not asked for the king's head: nothing like the anarchy of 1789 is present to frighten the rich. But, she warns them that if they do not comply, the poor have a much hardier constitution and will withstand hardship much better than they can. "Alas, no, the masses are not communist, and yet *France will be so before a hundred years pass*."[9]

About the same time, Sand published a long expository essay on socialism.[10] In four parts she traces the people's freedom from God to the system of universal suffrage. She warns against confusing the sophism of identity with the doctrine of equality; equality is a divine institution, exterior to any human contract. Thus progress represents the realm of man as he attempts to move toward God's truth; it is his duty to do so. The principal problem with the participation of the rich in the socialization of France is that of convincing the rich to sacrifice their financial dominion. Socialism does not propose to pillage or steal from the rich, rather to prohibit the wealth from multiplying and to see the money gradually sift down through all classes. This plea for cooperation represents one last cry to uphold the ideal so as not to drift back into the slavery of the past.[11]

The emphasis on a new religion as part of social reform brings us to a discussion of Sand's religious thought. Equality between classes, between the sexes, equality of opportunity as well as respect for everyone's choice, these questions necessarily claimed their importance in Sand's life and works. Her

religious beliefs strongly reflected her desires for a revision of societal structures, even in the nonfiction texts we have just seen.

Religion

Early Religious Sentiments   Sand remembers her religious
training largely in the form of her mother's recitation of meaningless prayers.
Her grandmother displayed a sort of Voltairian deism that young Aurore certainly assimilated. Sand states in her autobiography that although her grandmother taught her to be wary of the Church, Mme Dupin still succumbed to
the fear of scandal at the beginning of the Restoration and forced little
Aurore to make her first Holy Communion (*OA*, 1:840). The contradiction
in religious doctrine between Aurore's two mothers and the hypocrisy at
Nohant would color George Sand's view of religion.

Aurore's creation of Corambé remains the earliest indication of her
longing for an organized system of religion. The androgynous deity represents a mythology with monotheistic tendencies. The conflict between the
child's lively imagination and her grandmother's rejection of such fantastic ramblings may have been an important element in the birth of George
Sand the author.[12]

Sand's religious reflections shifted from Corambé to convent teachings.
At first Aurore paid little attention to religion classes, but there came a moment of epiphany, sometimes referred to as Sand's "conversion," when she
received a mystical message. In *Histoire de ma vie* she tells us she reread
parts of the Bible and the Saints' Lives, mostly out of boredom. One evening, strangely drawn to the chapel, she thought she heard a voice whisper
in her ear: "Tolle, lege!" Her reaction was modest: "I suffered under no mis-
guided illusion, nor did I believe it was a miracle. I was quite aware of the
sort of hallucination I'd fallen into and I was neither enraptured nor frightened. I sought neither to enhance the feeling nor to escape it. But I felt faith
taking hold of me, just as I had wished it, by the heart."[13] When her school-
ing at the convent came to a close, she inquired about entering the noviciat,
but was discouraged by her confessor.

So began a turning away from the Church, a slow process that kept Sand in
the intermediary position of a non-Protestant Christian who disagreed vio-
lently with the Vatican. Although she no longer believed absolute truth was
to be found in the Church any more than in any other religious form, she did
believe there could be more relative truth in Catholicism. And for that reason, she was not yet, at age seventeen, considering officially breaking from
the Church (*OA*, 1:1070).

First Literary Instances of Religious Thought   Apart from religious discussions in correspondence with convent friends, Sand's first evidence of pondering God and the universe can be found in *Voyage en Auvergne*. Next, *Rose et Blanche* unveils some of Sand's uneasiness with the Church. While the plot and tone of this novel were not entirely the creation of Sand herself, that much of the work takes place in a convent and that one of the main characters is a novice certainly points to a religious theme that Sand may have encouraged. The criticism of the Church as an institution, and especially the place of women in the Church, surfaces in the implicit comparison of the Church with prostitution. Rose's mother sells her into prostitution, a career for which she has been trained. To save her from such an unfortunate life, Henri takes her into his care. But when it becomes clear he can no longer keep her with him for reasons of propriety, he entrusts her to the care of his sister, who ships Rose off to a convent. There her life is confused, particularly when she begins to suspect the identity of her protectors.

Clearly the convent, as the refuge for lost girls, carries the stigma of a house of questionable motives, a house where girls who seem to have no other purpose are "sold" into the service of a masculine God. Blanche corroborates this distinction as she is a novice herself, yet she learns through her experience in the convent that she has been tricked out of a true understanding of life outside the cloister walls.

Sands early novels give little direct commentary on the Church. Critics in Sand's time, however, often felt she denigrated the Church's teachings by advancing immoral messages, but these matters concern moral issues and not organized religion. Even *Les Lettres d'un voyageur,* a text of some philosophical import, does not approach the question of religion directly. Sand does contemplate the wonders of Nature and God. She approaches a treatise on man's place vis-à-vis God in her discussions of the artist, and especially the musician. The only lengthy mention of religion per se in this text is Sand's defense of Lamennais (Letter 3). This section, entitled "L'Ennemi du pape" (The Pope's Enemy),[14] outlines what the Church has lost by excommunicating such a brilliant thinker. The passage offers a defense and support of religious tolerance much more than a discussion of religious ideas. Sand divulges a personal view of excommunication in the portrayal of the Cardinal in *Lélia*.

The short text "Mattea" does serve up a rather harsh view of dogma and the damaging effects it can have on the upbringing of a young girl. Mattea's mother leads a very austere life and imposes the same existence on her daughter, all in the name of the Church's teachings. Mattea's responds by trying to leave home by any means possible. Religious intolerance and the ills of overzealous adherence to dogma lie at the base of Mattea's discomfort and her desire to create for herself "une religion personnelle, pure, sincère, instinctive" (a personal, pure, sincere, and instinctual religion).

Lettres à Marcie also warns young women of the dangers of dogma. An ambiguity in this text belies Sand's hesitancy in this matter. While the male narrator cautions Marcie not to adhere too blindly to organized religion, he also tells her that she, being a woman, is in a good position to appreciate the pomp and circumstance of the liturgy. Sand's tendencies to draw away from and to go back to the Church have added many dimensions to her characters, especially her heroines.

The Search for a Religious System   Lélia is the first novel in which George Sand discusses religion explicitly. Here the struggle between abstinence and physical pleasure becomes a moral conflict that is couched in religious terms. Lélia's despondency finds no solace in prayer or in reflection. She withdraws from society more out of fear and confusion than out of an ascetic desire for solitude. Alone, she fails to gain a clearer understanding of her plight. Only after the death of Sténio does she believe that her ideal of chaste love will indeed bring her closer to God. Religion here links metaphysical and emotional ideals at the same time as it serves as a springboard for the exaltation of the imagination.

Reincarnation appears in an embryonic form in this novel. The notion of metempsychosis, which Sand probably learned from Saint-Simon or Enfantin and developed with the help of Pierre Leroux, encourages Lélia in her search for ideal love. This is most clearly shown in the chapter "Dans le désert" (In the desert). Love is the transcending force Lélia's metaphysical aspirations adopt. Disappointments in life have led Lélia, like Sand, to a point where emotional and spiritual love remains indivisible. Inversely, emotional and spiritual impotence, followed by physical impotence, accompanies religious doubts.[15]

In the 1839 version of Lélia Sand recasts the problem of love in more optimistic terms. Sténio still represents Eros and becomes bitter at Lélia's coldness. Lélia, on the other hand, does find a sense of calm in the convent this time. She becomes the high priestess of the Camaldules's monastery and derives a sense of mission and hope.

Trenmor's devotion to God also makes a subtle change from the stoicism of 1833 to a more refined sense of independence, which is not devoid of compassion. His guidance teaches both Lélia and Sténio the benefits of communion with God. In the second version, Sténio soon sets aside the jealousy that consumed him in 1833 and aspires to a more satisfied state of understanding; this, however, is not to be his destiny. That the source of Lélia's hope resides in God and not in Sténio drives the latter to deceit and suicide.

The most interesting addition to the 1839 version of *Lélia* comes in the completely new sixth part wherein George Sand displays what she has learned from Pierre Leroux in terms of a universal religion. Lélia hopes for a change within the dogma of the Church that would encourage progress in humanity.[16] In an ambiguous way, Sand espouses a search for a new religion that would grow from Catholicism rather than from anarchy. We will see her develop these ideas in *Spiridion*.[17]

The new Lélia finishes her life in hope, though she is accused by many of advancing strange and new doctrines that stray from dogma. The world of the convent is not yet ready for Lélia's, or for Sand's, new religion. This is the first exposé of a new religion in explicit terms, but it is closely followed by *Spiridion, Consuelo* and *Le Meunier d'Angibault*.[18]

Spiridion (1838–39) details a man's search for the true religion. Spiridion's quest, though much broader and radical than Sand's own, parallels her own religious wanderings. She began work on this novel shortly after she had revised plans for the second *Lélia*. Both works point to Sand's newfound hope, based primarily on the vision of a "new religion" and Leroux's trinity of belief, hope, and love. What sets the two religious novels apart is the frustration Spiridion and his disciples feel in their arduous search for truth, which stands in bittersweet contrast with the new Lélia's calm in the face of opposition and trial.

The premise of progress in *Spiridion* describes society as it outgrows one organized religion and rightly moves on to another. Spiridion, born and raised as a Jew, converts to Protestantism after reading Luther, and then to Catholicism through the teachings of Bossuet. Born Samuel Hébronius, he is baptized Pierre when he converts to Christianity; he takes the confirmation name of Spiridion, after the fourth-century Greek bishop, when he adopts Catholicism.

Spiridion becomes disillusioned with the lack of serious piety in his own monastery. He decides that Catholicism, too, has served its purpose and must now give way to a new religion. Because of the Inquisition's omnipresent eye, refuting the Church's teachings would be suicidal. Spiridion therefore continues to practice Catholicism outwardly. He examines his heart and the direction the Church should take, writes it all down, and confides it to a young monk in his charge, Fulgence, who buries the manuscript with Spiridion's body.

Fulgence never reads the manuscript, but just before his own death he passes the story on to a young monk, Alexis, who, just before his own death, relates the story to Angel, his disciple. Together they unearth the manuscript, after apparitions of Christ, Moses, David, Elijah, and Spiridion convince Alexis of the truth of his vision. The document has, by this time, gone unread for two generations and has thus become sacred in its own right. When Alexis reads the document, labeled *Hic est veritas!,* he is satisfied to discover that he has come to the same conclusions as Spiridion.

The text of the manuscript, almost certainly written in Sand's cell at So'n Vent in Majorca, is not very long. It constitutes the last fifteen pages of the novel, followed by a short commentary by Alexis, which carries little illumination Sand has not already given elsewhere in the novel. Influence from *The Imitation of Jesus Christ* and the Gospel of St. John are evident, as are the teachings of Leroux, Leibniz and Herder.[19]

The repeated apparitions of the dead Spiridion add an element of the Gothic. Moreover, whether the apparition is real or only the image kept in one's memory adds a fantastic twist to the religious theme.[20] It is important to note that Alexis did not work for Christ, but for the Holy Spirit. This part of the Trinity alone carries the possibility of reincarnation and supports Sand's idea that Christ's role was not an end but only one stage in the progress of religion.[21]

A final detail throws the ending of the novel into the political arena: as Alexis finishes his commentary on Spiridion's text, revolutionary soldiers burst into the room and kill him. Angel faints. What had seemed to portray only religious history now reinserts religion into a larger context. Just as Sand's hero moves to a higher religious plane, the prognosis for a similar political progression is portrayed as hopeful. The prefiguration of the Revolution can be seen in retrospect, but there is little in the text of the novel to suggest that such had been Sand's plan all along.

Like *Lélia, Spiridion* would know two versions. The second, published almost four years later, comprises several important modifications. First, the final scene sees the soldiers trampling on the Crucifix of a "sans-culotte" Christ, showing that the pre-1848 unrest is arousing Sand's interest. Second, the monks, who were Franciscan in the first version with a fair amount of Franciscan symbolism, have now become Benedictine. It has been suggested that the Benedictines better represented an intellectual order whose followers would be more prone to study.[22] Third, Angel unearths three manuscripts in the tomb of Spiridion: the Gospel of St. John, a gloss of the Scripture, and a final text on the supreme revelation. This final commentary, Spiridion's testament, interprets the second message of Christ as a proclamation of Christ as the end of one stage of religion. George Sand obviously views the Gospel of St. John not as an absolute truth, but as the preparation for the perfection that it heralds.[23] Fourth, while the first version stated that we are all Messiahs, the second version leaves out this thought.[24] We must be careful not to interpret this deletion as a change of heart but as an implicit message, which Sand would state explicitly in subsequent texts.

Sand's reform of the Church, through either the establishment of an "Eternal Gospel" or a synthesis of Bohemian Hussitism and Scottish Free-Masonry, harmonized well with the tenor of contemporary socialist doctrine.[25] Fraternal banquets, after the English model and as precursors to the political machinery of 1848, combined religious and social reform in ways similar to what Sand describes in *Consuelo, Jean Zyska,* and *Procope le Grand. Jean Zyska,* written between *Consuelo* and *La Comtesse de Rudolstadt* from the research Sand had accumulated for her masterpiece, is neither a history nor a novel, but a "simple account (*récit*) of true facts [*sic*] whose meaning and impact I sought more in my feeling than in erudition."[26] *Procope le Grand* underlines the far-reaching significance of the struggles during this pre-Luther era. Sand fails to bring a coherent sense of history to this account, but she does expose an obscure set of events that help to interpret the politico-religious significance of the character Zdenko in *Consuelo* and the whole segment of "les Invisibles" in *La Comtesse de Rudolstadt.*

Consuelo represents another aspect of Sand's religious message—the natural spirit of communion with God. Albert's ability to find a direct path to God through meditation corresponds to Consuelo's musical devotion. Together they perfect a musical form of communication they can share with others.

La Daniella carries the dubious distinction of being Sand's most virulent attack against the Church. Written in a period when her tolerance for institutions, political and religious, was ebbing, this novel indeed paints an uncomplimentary portrait of the clergy and of anyone adhering to the dogma of the Church.[27] Two characters, fra Cipriano and the narrator's uncle, represent the Church in an unfavorable light. Sand levies more attacks, however, on the stereotypical tendency of Italians to be subservient to the Church and to hide behind Catholic dogma in order to avoid having to reason for themselves.

Nanon, written fifteen years later, presents two sides of the clergy. The heroine's naïveté in matters of monks conflicts with the other characters' usual mockery of the clergy. At the same time, the monks at the local monastery present a stereotypical group of disgruntled men, bitter against society in general; this sentiment only worsens when they are "disowned" by the Republic under the Convention. One of them turns Jacobin and hunts the young novice, an aristocrat, desperate to put him and all his kin under the blade of the guillotine. Yet, one priest who remains after the monastery has been bought by a private citizen embodies all the qualities of a sympathetic cleric. He, too, is of noble birth and has been forgotten by his family. His ideas are rather liberal and he demonstrates that religious ideals can exist outside the structure of the Church.

Protestantism interested Sand as a possible alternative to Catholicism. Though Sand offers relatively little precise commentary on Protestantism in *Spiridion,* she would return to this matter in later texts. The early 1860s found her researching the advantages of a nonextremist version of Protestantism. Sand would have been quite happy to see her son Maurice marry into a Protestant family (Letter to Jules Boucoiran, *Corres.,* 16:35–36). As it turned out, Maurice and Lina married in a civil ceremony only, although they turned to Protestantism for the upbringing of their children. In 1863 their marriage was resanctified by a pastor and their child baptized in the Protestant faith.[28]

Sand put her hopes for an enlightened and free Protestantism in a novel, *Mademoiselle la Quintinie* (1863), which she wrote largely to counter Octave Feuillet's exaggerated religiosity in his novel *Sybille.* Sand tells the story of Lucie, a young girl born and raised Catholic. Lucie is an ardent believer, despite a lack of formal religious training. Her suitor, Emile, is from a Protestant family that refuses contact with Catholics. Emile takes great pains to explain, firmly yet precisely, his objections to the Roman Church. He finally succeeds in convincing his beloved of his point of view.

Written and published in a period of extreme orthodoxy strongly supported by a Spanish Catholic empress, *Mademoiselle la Quintinie* inspired at once many scornful and laudatory reactions. The very underpinnings of Catholicism suffer from a virulent ambush in this novel. Sand doubts the whole belief in hell, questions the usefulness of celibacy for priests, and attacks the institution of confession.

Another argument for Protestantism occurs in *Césarine Dietrich* (1870). The man Césarine loves admires her intellectual training and discipline, and attributes it to her Protestant heritage, citing her spiritual fathers' prowess in theological and intellectual contest. He recognizes in Césarine's heated devotion to her work her ancestors' passionate quest for liberty. Césarine's "passion" for her work is inspired not by any religious devotion, but by the possibility of asking her beloved for stylistic commentary on her writing.

Religious issues often spill over into matters of metaphysics and social theory. One work that exemplifies this problem is *Les Sept Cordes de la lyre,* a fantastic, mystical play about the meaning of love, God, and society. Written while Sand was trying to finish *Spiridion,* the similarity of themes shows the author's attempts to sort out the problems of a new religion in a new society. Hélène, the heroine and the only principal female of *Les Sept Cordes,* hears music from an ancient lyre that renders no sound for anyone else. Albertus, Hélène's guardian and a dedicated professor of philosophy, hears nothing at first, then painfully unpleasant noises offend his ears.

Albertus represents the arrogance of a man who thinks he can know everything through diligent study and logic. Too much intellectual activity has made him an atheist. When he begins to see, or rather to hear the truth, he regrets the time he has spent in study and the living he has missed. He learns of love for the first time in his life. And Hélène assures him that with faith and hope he will comprehend how love and art lead to God.[29]

Méphistophélès plays much the same role in *Les Sept Cordes* as he does in Goethe's *Faust.* He immediately sees the mysterious, magical, mystical lyre for what it represents—the power to know love and God. He plots to destroy it, but its power supercedes his own. Although Albertus inherited little from his predecessor Faust, he does fall victim to Méphistophélès's metamorphoses and arguments. And when Méphistophélès fails to entice Albertus to take an active role in his plot through preying on his intellectual curiosity, he attacks his dormant emotions with lies about Hélène. Thanks to Mésphistophélès, Albertus's affective element awakens.

This is not the only time George Sand uses the devil in her fiction. *Le Diable aux champs* (1851; The devil in the fields), a novel in dialogue form with metaliterary resonances, depicts puppets and animals as well as humans. The devil is, in fact, a puppet; but the commedia del l'arte troupe that uses him agrees that the devil is no longer fashionable and they hang him from a nearby tree.[30] At the same time, Ralph and Jacques, two farmers, discuss the nature of religion, disagreeing on whether doctrine interprets dogma or philosophy. One preaches the need for a new religion, to remove the false orthodoxy from Christianity and to return the passion to humanity. The other rejects the idea of a new religion, saying all religions stem from such distant origins that we cannot hope to distinguish them. The farmers do agree, however, that there is no need for eternal punishment, thus the devil does not exist. Evil, rather than a cause, is an effect, they say, and ignorance and superstition are the causes. As in the rustic novels, the typical superstitions that Sand uses enter into play and serve to distinguish the ignorant from the thinkers.

Feminism

Identifying Sand's Feminist Politics

> True genius, but true woman, dost deny
> The woman's nature with a manly scorn,
> And break away the gauds and armlets worn
> By weaker women in capitivity?
> Ah, vain denial!
>   ("To George Sand, a Recognition")

Elizabeth Barrett Browning, in the second of two sonnets dedicated to George Sand, identifies one problem of a woman writing under a male pseudonym. The theme of becoming "unsexed," which permeates both of these sonnets, stands at the center of Sand's feminism. Aurore Dupin, in fact, had little to do with the sequence of events leading to the birth of George Sand. When Aurore gave vent to the first overt, written expression of her independence in *Indiana,* her publisher wanted to retain a name already known to the reading public. Only a slight change, from J. Sand to G. Sand, heralded the new author's coming of age. But the unconventional spelling of her new Christian name (usually "George*s*" in French), the only part of her name that she actually chose, signals a desire to announce alterity. Sand lopped off the final "s" of her assumed first name just as the final syllable of her literary surname had been severed. Such an obvious emasculation, accentuated by the "feminine" sound of the mute-"e" ending, bears witness to the author's thinly veiled need to assert her true gender.

George Sand could have easily gained entry to the patriarchal literary tradition in France. She had already shown that she could imitate the Balzacian template. While it is true that *Indiana* uses a conventional male plot—what Gilbert and Gubar call the *Pamela* plot—[31] Sand soon breaks away from the masculine-dominated story structure. *Valentine,* her second novel, centers around a woman in virtually complete control of her destiny. Unlike Jane Eyre, Valentine already has financial and social security. Yet she still seeks to escape from subordination to both her husband and her class. Although the metaphors of slavery might be less blatant than those Brontë used for her heroine, Sand clearly illustrates her belief that all women are enslaved, regardless of their social class.

From this point forward, Sand's heroines undertake the struggle to rid themselves of the shackles of their male-dominated circumstances. The infamous Lélia represents a bold female type, unique in nineteenth-century

French literature. Her character does not demonstrate the self-esteem of Valentine, but she distinguishes herself by asking questions that no fictional woman had uttered before. Consumed with doubt, Lélia allows herself moral and metaphysical queries that border on cynicism and blasphemy. The frankness with which she ponders the conflict of love and passion led contemporary readers of the daring novel into realms not yet explored in fiction.[32] And after Sand recast her heroine in a more optimistic light, the "new" Lélia asks why women should not be allowed the same pleasures as men.

Edmée Mauprat, another woman who stands firm in the face of an unjust, indeed, barbarous patriarchy, rejects her cousins' debasing and subordinating definition of women. Edmée accedes to the position as head of household when her father falls ill, thus proving her right to power; she is not only a rightful, but also a capable heir. The importance she places on knowledge and reasoning makes Edmée the intellectual leader of the novel. Her struggle for independence succeeds because of her persistence, but also because of her love for Bernard and her ability to keep him working for her esteem. For Sand, love is always a fundamental factor in equality and mutual respect.

In the same year that *Mauprat* was published, another work, interesting for its implications for Sand's feminism, appeared serially in *Le Monde*. *Lettres à Marcie* (1837) is an unfinished series of letters that constitutes a one-sided correspondence from a man whose relationship to Marcie remains a mystery. The confusing and jumbled advice he gives Marcie represents the first explicit definition of Sand's position on women in mid-nineteenth-century France. On the one hand, Marcie should not allow the desires of men to determine what she might want for herself; being unmarried at age twenty-five need not carry any stigma. On the other hand, a woman defines herself, says the narrator, by family and home. The answer is not to be found, he tells her, in a convent where the strict, dogmatic adherence to formulae will reduce her powers of reasoning. Here the narrator tells Marcie that abstinence is worse than death, that marriage and motherhood are worthwhile pursuits. Yet he continues to encourage her to study and to earn the name of philosopher despite the tradition barring women from this appellation. Sand would maintain these conflicting notions throughout the 1840s and into the 1850s when the political climate waivered between reform and the status quo.

The plays *Cosima* (1839) and *Claudie* (1851) discuss the problem of women who are unhappy in marriage or in relationships with men. Cosima suffers from the boredom of a decent life that restricts her movement to the inside of her husband's house. Claudie, abandoned by a rake and now an unwed mother, eventually marries a kind and desirable man and is rein-

tegrated into society. Sand's message becomes stronger and more positive
with the years.

Women's handicap of inadequate education would remain a staple of
Sand's feminist ethos. In a note added to *Histoire de ma vie,* Sand declares
that all women, of all classes, cheat at games and are dishonest in matters that
concern themselves. This "instinct for duplicity," rather than originating in
some inherent need to deceive or to trick chance, comes from women's in-
complete moral education, she speculates. Women are taught honor only in
matters of decency and faithfulness. While these issues might interest men
only tangentially, would not women command respect for learning "men's"
honor in matters of gallantry and financial honesty? (*OA,* 1:667).

Women's education was the subject of one of Sand's earliest plays, *Gabriel*
(1839).[33] The central character, a young woman, has been raised as a boy for
reasons of inheritance in Renaissance Italy. She is told of the deception when
she turns seventeen, and sets out to meet her cousin, Astolphe, whom her
grandfather has tried to keep from inheriting the family title. Gabriel and
Astolphe gradually fall in love in an original manifestation of homoeroticism
devoid of any hint of homosexuality. Sand establishes a solid case for women
who are brought up with a so-called man's education being able to accom-
plish tasks, intellectual and political, as well as men can. The problem of
equality within a love relationship remains unresolved at the end of the play:
although Astolphe loves Gabrielle, he cannot relinquish his claim as the sole
male heir to the family title and inheritance. But Gabrielle refuses to abandon the freedom her masculine upbringing has afforded her, preferring death
to oppression.

In *Confession d'une jeune fille* (1864) George Sand puts the heroine in circumstances that recall her own upbringing. Lucienne de Valangis is raised by
her grandmother, without mother or father; she is also entirely educated by a
tutor who remains a dear friend of the family. Lucienne masters several foreign languages, ancient and modern, and is familiar with many philosophical
writings as well as works of literature. She sometimes sees her "masculine
training" as a hindrance and clearly a duality of reason and emotion renders
her a confused and inert character during much of the plot. Lucienne is far
from the strong woman Sand creates in Gabrielle.

The two characters closest to Lucienne incarnate traditional gender-based
roles. Frumence, the tutor, represents reason and logic, whereas Jennie, the
servant and confidante, spends most of her time trying to arrange everyone's
life according to their emotions, or more often according to her own perception of their emotions. Lucienne makes a strong case for feminism. She man-

ages to balance reason and emotion, and she bears up under social scorn and hypocrisy.

Marthe in *Horace* (1840) is a sort of unwitting Jane Eyre; she starts out unaware of why she continues to fall victim to the trappings of a patriarchal society. Her sole social training comes from novels and she is desperate to re-create a romantic destiny. Eugénie, Marthe's only friend as the proponent of Saint-Simonian feminist ideals in the novel represents a clear vision of feminism in her attempts to raise Marthe's consciousness. Marthe, who blindly accepts Horace's misogynistic world of pretense, finally applies the principles Eugénie has tried to teach her by leaving Horace. Only after regaining her self-esteem can she portray various roles on the stage and thereby come into her own as a woman and an artist.

Sand's next heroine, Consuelo, though less formally educated in the matter than Eugénie, also develops a natural sense of equality and avoids contact with those who do not share her ideals. Although Consuelo's accession to a position of respect is measured by comparison with men, whether the seer Albert de Rudolstadt or the political radicals of the masonic-like society of "les Invisibles," she establishes a place for women as the equals of men in the serious matters of art and politics. The feminist argument of this novel is attenuated, however, by the heroine's enervated position in the epilogue. Consuelo, having lost her voice, now serves merely as the interpreter of Albert's musical message to mankind.[34]

The heroine of *Lucrezia Floriani* represents a transitional figure. As an opera singer she suffers the ostracism and degradation of a woman of loose morals, a judgment that is accentuated because she is the unwed mother of four children. Rather than expose her children to the censoriousness of the world, she chooses to adopt a Rousseauistic manner of life in the country. While Lucrezia does not compromise her own self-esteem, she does accept society's judgment by leaving instead of forging a place of moral equality for her children. She does, however, show the fortitude of a financially and emotially stable woman when Prince Karol falls in love with her and tries to control her with sexual and social dominance. He wants to make her his mistress. He cannot marry her given his social rank; in fact, he is so repulsed by her situation he literally falls into a comatose fever once he recognizes he is in love with her. Despite Lucrezia's love for him, she refuses to endanger her independence.

The heroine of *La Daniella* wins her independence through marriage. Daniella, an orphan like Consuelo, gains partial independence as the personal servant and confidante of a rich and titled lady. When she is unwittingly thrown into rivalry with her mistress for the affections of Jean Valreg, the male protagonist, she leaves. Valreg's interest in Daniella puts them both in danger because Daniella's brother is insanely jealous. Here Sand once again draws on an Italian stereotype: the brother who, at all cost, must defend the honor of his sister. Daniella's brother exploits the time-honored right of the man to subordinate the women of the family in a pretext to vent his own machismo and to cover up his dishonest contraband dealings.

When the brother dies at the hand of a neighbor, Valreg's reputation remains unsullied and Daniella's future marriage is not compromised. Daniella can now accede to a position of independence, albeit as a married woman. But she has crossed social barriers through her virtue and goodness, thus gaining the full respect of Jean Valreg and becoming his equal.

An entirely different type of feminist is Nanon, in the novel by the same name (1871). Nanon perhaps best exemplifies Sand's ideal of a self-educated woman who assumes an important financial and political role. The novel takes place during the Revolution and depicts the distance in time and space between Berry and Creuse and the political events of Paris. The heroine is a peasant orphan who meets a novice, Emilien, who can hardly read. Together they learn to read, and Nanon soon becomes honored and respected by the entire village. Emilien, the son of an aristocrat who has rebuked his nobility, returns from the war and marries her. The transparence of this plot device renders it less convincing than the feminist argument of *Mauprat,* with which it must be compared.

Nanon puts herself in many situations that require abilities and skills for which women of her time were not usually trained. She conceives and executes an escape plan for Emilien. She establishes herself as proprietor and manager of a large tract of land. She instructs others in reading and writing, showing that she is not only a better student than Emilien but also a teacher capable of directing the intellectual development of others. She also conquers space in a way usually reserved for men: she learns to read and follow a map and sets out into the woods and plains of Berry and Creuse without ever getting lost. George Sand creates in Nanon her ideal woman. *Nanon* offers the pragmatic solution to the problem Jacques Laurent explains in *Isidora* (1845). His disapproval of the current state of women's education attacks society in general, which is illustrated by the female characters of the novel.

Marianne (1876) is Sand's last feminist novel. The heroine, though a simple country girl, less timid than the male protagonist would like to believe, states her case fairly plainly: she would like to know how to further her education while staying at home. Pierre, who is well educated and has worked as a tutor, promises to help select her reading material. Sand presents a mixed feminist message because Marianne defers to the man's experience and superior education.

George Sand created many models for feminists, but the only feminist character who has a model to emulate is Consuelo, who follows the steps her mother-in-law Wanda has shown her. This situation warrants futher examination. Sand's male characters sometimes display feminist sympathies; she rarely portrays an aggressive, insensitive masculine type, and the few she does create never have a sympathetic character. The feminist aspect of George Sand's fictional world is indisputable and has yet to be fully and fairly explored.

Marriage and Feminism Several critics have decried Sand's works as immoral, depicting them as attacks on the institution of marriage. Most of the direct assaults came early in Sand's career and thus assail the early novels of her oeuvre. Sand did not portray marriage itself as an evil; rather she criticized the institution as it was defined by the Napoleonic Code. Marriage remained uncontested by the majority of society, including women themselves, and Sand struggled throughout her career to reverse this apathy. She spoke out against "the abuses, the absurdities, the prejudices, and the vices of society." She did admit that she erred in saying "marriage" when she wished to criticize "married people" ("Lettre à M. Nisard," *OA*, 2:939).

Sand defended her early novels. The heroines of these works are driven by bitterness and seek consolation and/or escape. Only in *Jacques* did she admit to a problem with the implicit message in the role of adultery. The title character of *Jacques* speaks out firmly against marriage as "one of the most barbarian institutions society has ever established."[35] Fernande, the young woman in *Jacques,* innocently led to accept a father-figure as lover, learns too late that she does not love him. Her filial devotion does not fade in the wake of passion; it becomes better defined.

The matriarchal structure of the triangular relationship in "Metella" demands that the reader reexamine the questions of fidelity and the role of the mother-lover. Sand offers triangles that both intrigue and scandalize the reader. In this context the institution of marriage comes under the scrutiny of author and reader alike: to what extent is the institution of marriage to be understood as a mockery of women in the social and political arena?[36]

Despite the overbearing tone of despair, Sand's dream of marriage offers a spirit of truth, which eventually leads to the ideal, the absolute.[37] Yet, in all of these novels, the problem that causes the heroine to search for consolation outside the union occurs within the marriage. In later novels, the heroines display powers of reasoning coupled with the power to change the direction of their lives through a logical decision-making process.

In *Mademoiselle Merquem* the matters of age difference and reputation present no obstacle for the enamored couple. Because Merquem is older she holds the reins and controls the situation. Until she is satisfied that Armand understands the difference between pure and impure love, she cannot risk any vulnerability. A similar relationship exists between Anicée and Stéphen in *La Filleule* (1853; The goddaughter). An additional detail interests us here: Stéphen, who has dedicated his education to the soul of his deceased mother, takes her name as his legal surname instead of his father's.

The age difference in *Le Dernier amour* (1866) presents an interesting problem: Félicie Morgeron marries Sylvestre, fifteen years her senior, but is passionately in love with Tonino, her brother's godchild. She becomes Tonino's mistress, but she cannot conceal her jealousy when he marries a village girl. Sylvestre does not reveal that he has understood everything. When Félicie finally faces reality, she dies of shame and despair. This novel, written after *Monsieur Sylvestre* (1865), actually precedes it in narrative chronology. Sylvestre will concentrate, in this latter novel, on defining and obtaining happiness without marriage.

Class differences again plague the possibility of a love marriage in *Le Marquis de Villemer* (1860). Not only does the marquis's mother suffer from a status-conscious attitude, so does Caroline, the heroine. The situation is further complicated by the degree of nobility among aristocrats, for Caroline does carry a noble name, de Saint-Géneix. Yet, she is from the provinces and her family is poor. She has hired herself out as a private secretary, without embarrassment, in order to provide for herself and her sister's family. Her position vis-à-vis Urbain de Villemer could seem opportunistic to gossip-mongering outsiders. Caroline's fortitude stands her in good stead, and the marriage comes off without embarrassment on anyone's part. Jeanne, in *Ma Soeur Jeanne* (1874; My sister Jeanne), also controls the development of the relationship with Jean, who erroneously thinks he is her brother.

In these later novels, not only is the woman in control, but she also uses her position to avoid all pitfalls before allowing herself the pleasure of a decision. She is the active and no longer the passive member of the relationship. It is interesting to point out here that alone among all Sand's heroines, Césarine Dietrich does not "reform" as a result of love. She does not alter her selfish, egocentric character after she fails to control her life and the lives of those who surround her.[38]

Whereas Sand's heroines in the early novels are all married and are trying to escape an unsatisfactory situation, in her later novels they are able to make a choice based on human emotions and needs instead of financial strategies and societal conventions. The question of feminism is strengthened by the heroines' readiness to assume their individuality. Sand presents a less militant, a more foresighted approach to marriage in these novels. The heroines are definitely feminists; they represent the firm, individual decision to take their destinies into their own hands, and each one is rewarded for the courage and fortitude with which she conducts her life.

George Sand's Literary and Practical Feminism George Sand has been lauded as the first modern French feminist. While this claim is exaggerated, she does contribute to the liberation of the feminist novel. If Sand's forays into the traditional, male literary world mark her as a militant feminist, her relationships with women are complex and do not often provide strong proof of feminist politics. The conflict between Sand's mother and grandmother, the two principal women in her life, created a deep-rooted tension. Though the future George Sand learned much from both women, the atmosphere of competition and aggression that reigned between them is significant. It is not surprising that Sand did not have many satisfactory relationships with women.

Friendship between women in Sand's works provides some fruitful material. *Narcisse* (1858) develops the problems between Julia and Juliette when they fall in love with the same man. Similar situations arise in both *Constance Verrier* and *Isidora*.[39] Sand tells us in her memoirs that she does not really like women. She usually finds women superficial, and if they dare to show any semblance of intelligence, they quickly squelch it and hide again under the convention of the coquette. Sand managed to make enemies of most women she met.

George Sand's attitude toward militant feminism has often counted against her. She never saw eye to eye with Flora Tristan, who in turn had nothing good to say about Sand. Yet, in her novels Sand did offer feminist arguments and preached for a consciousness raising on the part of her *lectrices* (female readers). To reconcile this seeming contradiction, we must examine Sand's social and political reasons for disassociating herself from the militant feminist movement.

Sand's refusal to lobby for nomination as an Academician was a bitter disappointment to feminists. They had hoped she would become the first woman in the Académie and thus pave the road for women to hold revered positions in French society. And although Sand had no intention of advancing herself as a model for contemporary feminists, she suffered constant recruitment attempts. Beyond the half-hearted invitation for Sand to become the "Mère" of the Saint-Simonian movement, she was also the object of political pressure. It was a man, Ernest Legouvé, a member of the Club for the Emancipation of the People, who proposed George Sand as a candidate for the upcoming elections. Eugénie Niboyet, editor of the newly formed newspaper *La Voix des femmes,* seconded Sand's nomination (6 April 1848).

Sand responded to the suggestions of a nomination in *La Réforme* (9 April).[40] She writes that she did not plan nor had she ever intended to run for office, and that she was not associated with, and did not know, the women involved in this movement.

A more revealing document gives many details in this matter: a letter Sand wrote, but never finished or sent, to the leftist Central Committee. Sand explains her hesitation to give women the vote. She states the imperative of righting the educational wrong done to women. Because of civil and Church tradition, institutions run by men, women have been prevented from achieving more than but a portion of their capacity. Only when women of an entire generation have acquired an education equal to that of men can they hope to assume similar responsibilities. This, says Sand, must be the first reform: restoring women to their completeness. If women were to hold office among male deputies today, they would only represent half a man, the other half being the opinions of their husbands.[41] Note, however, what she says on the matter of progress in education: "Whatever progress is made in our education (I wouldn't want it the same as men's), woman will always be more an artist and a poet in her life, a man always in his work" (*Histoire de ma vie, OA,* 2:127).

In 1871 Sand replied to a woman's letter on universal suffrage by saying the main problem with the notion was the failure to take the future into consideration. First, the right to vote, she says, is a weapon for usurping power and is thus antithetical to the concept of a republic. Second, nothing is less sure than the intelligence of the voters. Third, the powers that be will take away the right to vote if they see fit anyway. The natural right falls to the elite of France: artists, scientists, economists, legislators. The attack in this letter is directed at the lower classes, but it automatically includes women among their ranks. This position, so radically different from Sand's position in the 1840s, can be explained, in part, as the result of a negative reaction to the acts of Parisians during the Commune.[42]

In spite of her equivocal stance, Sand opened the possibility for women to write fiction that diverged from the male-dominated genre. Hers is a female discourse that discusses the problems of women in society, in the home, in love, as well as women subjugated by men. The feminism of George Sand does not rank among that of Simone de Beauvoir or Christiane Rochefort, and it is certainly not in the realm of Hélène Cixous or Luce Irigaray. Yet, we must consider George Sand, the woman and the writer, a feminist of strong courage and fortitude, one who encouraged many other women to take up the pen and to dare to state their desires.

Chapter Six
Music and Art

In her memoirs George Sand describes the scene of her own birth during an evening's festivities when relatives danced and her father played the violin. "During the last eight-bar shuffle, my aunt Lucie went into my mother's room, only to turn around immediately and declare, 'Come quickly, Maurice; you have a daughter. She was born in music; she'll be happy'" (*OA*, 1:464). Music surrounded Aurore during her childhood. Under the wardship of her grandmother, she profited from a full tradition of eighteenth-century music, especially from the Italian tradition. And in keeping with an aristocratic upbringing, she learned to play the harp, the guitar, and the pianoforte.[1]

Just as Aurore found pleasure in listening to the simple melodies her mother sang, she also enjoyed spending long evenings by the fire, listening to the songs and the stories of country folk. Later she developed a deep appreciation for sacred music at the Augustinian convent in Paris.

Early adulthood left Aurore with little exposure to music. Her husband bought her a new piano to cheer her up after the birth of their first child, but she abandoned playing because it bored Casimir, indeed, it chased him from the house.[2] On her own in Paris, Aurore did take advantage of the musical events the capital had to offer; in only seven years, she had met the majority of great musicians and composers in Paris at the time, including Liszt, Meyerbeer, Maria Malibran, Pauline Viardot, Berlioz, and, of course, Chopin.

Liszt would remain one of Sand's most influential friends of the 1830s and 1840s. He served as the real-life referent for her portrait of the artist.[3] They shared similar dreams of bringing "classical" music to the people through a socialist conception of musical training. Liszt's plan would not only put music within the scope of the masses, but it would use music as a means of spreading socialist notions.[4]

Writing to Liszt in Letter 6 of *Lettres d'un voyageur,* Sand admits that she envies the collectivity of musicians, who are a more communal group than writers. She deems Liszt's muse more fertile and charming than hers, which partly represents Sand's estimation of music and partly a self-deprecating comment on her own worth as an artist. She also writes about Liszt in her diary, "When Franz plays the piano, it soothes me. All my suffering becomes poetic and all my instincts take wing."[5]

Sand dedicates another letter from *Lettres d'un voyageur* to Giacomo Meyerbeer (Letter 11, *OA*, 2:916–35). She lauds him as the most brilliant contemporary poet, with special praise going to *Robert le diable* and *Les Huguenots*. A few passages depart from this panegyric to reflect on musical structures and nuances. She also discusses the effects of public expectations of art, a matter of great importance to George Sand.

Chopin and Sand's relationship has been the subject of many books.[6] His music touched her profoundly. In *Histoire de ma vie* she says his genius was the deepest and the most replete with feeling and emotion of any that ever existed.[7] She compares him to Bach, Beethoven, and Weber, judging Chopin greater than all three combined, and equal to Mozart.

From a life filled with such musical surroundings and acquaintances sprang, not surprisingly, many instances of musical influence in Sand's writing. Several of her first literary achievements use music. "Histoire du rêveur" (1830), a badly structured story of questionable style, puts a musician atop Mt. Etna, trying to escape reality. Through the voice of a mysterious singer, he is transported to another world, where he is surrounded by beautiful voices and prays that he never return to the real world. He does wake up, however, and later falls under the spell of music. This time he does not return to the real world; he dies. We shall see a similar ethos in "Carl" (1843) and in a story written near the end of Sand's life, "L'Orgue du titan" (1873).

"La Prima donna" (1831), written in collaboration with Jules Sandeau,[8] is the story of a gifted soprano tricked into marrying a nobleman who subsequently will not allow her to appear on the stage. Her health wanes and it becomes clear that she needs music to sustain her life. Once the doctor convinces her husband she must be allowed to return to the stage, the prima donna, resplendent with life, performs to perfection the role of Zingarelli's Juliette. Ironically, in the death scene the actress dies along with the character she portrays.

When la Malibran, the famous soprano, was killed in a horseback riding accident in 1836, Liszt composed a piano fantasia as a eulogy. He based it on a popular folk tune, "El Contrabandista," written down by Malibran's father, Manuel Garcia; readers will recognize it from Hugo's *Bug-Jargal*. Sand, in turn, wrote a short story inspired by Liszt's music.[9] In "Le Contrebandier" (1837) Sand creates a half-way genre, combining elements of the story from the lyrics of the original song with musical commentary of Liszt's piece. The result is in an interesting experiment in narrative that bespeaks the romantic flair for fantasy.

Often music serves as a catalyst for an amorous relationship in Sand's novels, such as in the beginning of *Valentine,* in *La Dernière Aldini,* and in *Adriani.* "Mouny-Robin," a short text from 1841, gives a musical commentary similar to Balzac's *Gambetta,* though it deals more with the general issue of romanticism. And an entry in her *Sketches and Hints* deftly describes her emotional response to hearing Beethoven's Pastoral Symphony (*OA,* 2:610–14). Sand will continue to include musical symbols and metaphors in many of her works, often as a part of the main themology.[10]

Les Sept Cordes de la lyre

Les Sept Cordes de la lyre (1839; The Seven-stringed lyre), an excellent example of philosophical drama, uses music to comment on the place of aesthetics alongside philosophy. While the dialogue form suggests stage presentation, the structure more readily communicates the notion of a debate wherein the authorial voice, unlike that of the narrator in a novel, can espouse several points of view.[11]

This text constitutes Sand's first conscious attempt to collect her thoughts on the mystical-religious function of music and the role it can play in literature. The religious implications in *Spiridion,* which she was struggling to finish at the same time, take on a heightened intensity in this drama. The work pleased nearly no one, save perhaps Liszt. Yet, on a metaphysical plane it gave Sand a forum in which to express her nascent philosophy of aesthetics and her ideas on religious transcendence.[12]

The plot of *Les Sept Cordes* is highly convoluted. Hélène has been orphaned; she and her sole inheritance, a beautiful lyre, come under the tutelage of Albertus, a professor of philosophy. The lyre produces music only Hélène can "understand," and nearly causes her to lose her mind. The Spirit of the Lyre speaks to her about a marvellous life, yet all she sees on earth is heartbreak and misery. Finally Albertus, too, hears and begins to understand the music of the lyre, and regrets his monastic devotion to science. As the lyre's strings break one by one, Hélène moves closer to divine love, just as Albertus is falling in love with her. Meanwhile, Méphistophélès tries to exploit this love to his own ends. But Albertus remains faithful to his newfound ideal and accepts Hélène's death and her union with the Spirit of the Lyre as a sign of hope for a renewal of his own emotional being.

At the center of this drama lies the beautiful seven-stringed lyre that holds the key to the metaphysical questions that will surface during the course of the text. The lyre has not rendered a sound for many years and thus serves no practical purpose. The *dolce et utile* doctrine soon leads to Albertus's struggle with the dialectic of intellectual study and emotional expression. The dilemma reflects Rousseau's double-edged legacy of solitude.

The instrument is the main character of this *drame*. Its form gives the work a structure. The diverse materials of the strings provide the symbolic organization of Sand's ideology: gold (idealism and faith), silver (hope and contemplation), steel (man's inventions, laws, manners, and passions), and bronze (love). As Hélène gradually accedes to higher planes of understanding, the theme of progress emerges. The lyre is inhabited by the Spirit of the Lyre, that is to say, Music, and as such stands as an obstacle that prevents Méphistophélès from controlling Hélène, the heroine.

The key to Hélène's character lies in the musical metaphors in the text. She understands the music of the Lyre with no training and without plucking the strings.[13] Hélène's genealogy and her madness supply the focal point for the musical images. Hélène is an orphan; her father, Meinbaker, was an instrument maker and an earlier ancestor, Adelsfreit, constructed the famous lyre. Sand uses this family structure to suggest a possible genetic link to music.

In addition to a familiarity with instruments, Hélène also inherits madness, or what seems to the others to be madness. Adelsfreit dies the day he completes the lyre; he dies as a result of having finished his life's ambition. The instrument is passed down to Meinbaker, who never allows Hélène to touch it. When Méphistophélès asks her to sell it in payment of Albertus's debts, she admits that she has touched the lyre and has disobeyed her father's wishes. The horrible sound the lyre renders causes Hélène to faint and fall into a long and grave illness.

One of the philosophy students divulges the real significance of Hélène's "madness" to Albertus: "Oh master, Hélène isn't mad at all! She's inspired!" Albertus, who is now beginning to see the worth of music, responds positively to this revelation: "Yes, she's a poet; that's a kind of sublime madness that I'd like to have for a moment so as to understand her and to know exactly where inspiration ends and sickness begins."[14] Hélène's madness comes from the Lyre, is provoked and exacerbated by the Lyre; but it is also cured by the Lyre.

Sand uses music in this text as a metaphor for human emotion, the highest form of which is love. The music of the Spirit of the Lyre constitutes an amorous discourse, a sort of seduction. When the Spirit of the Lyre asks Hélène to choose him over Albertus, for whom she also feels a filial love, she says she reserves her true love for God and eternity. Only if the Lyre can show her a glimpse of God can she elect him over Albertus.

Hélène's most powerful musical plea comes when she strikes a note on the last string of the lyre. Hélène never sings during the play; she communicates only through the Lyre's music. The instrument houses the means of transmitting her expression to God. She then also loves the Lyre and the Spirit of the Lyre. The notion of a trinity appears in Hélène's prayers: the Lyre, which is the instrument or vehicle for the Spirit of the Lyre, which speaks for God.

Music as a divine language enters Sand's fictional world in the form of a lyre, a metaphor that strongly suggests Pierre Leroux's and Liszt's influence. Not many readers, including Buloz, her editor, appreciated the highly metaphysical terms in which she attempted to communicate an extremely human message. She would take up the metaphor of the instrument again, fifteen years later, this time more successfully, with the bagpipes in *Les Maîtres sonneurs*.

Consuelo

Undoubtedly a masterpiece in the genre of the musical novel, *Consuelo* and its sequel, *La Comtesse de Rudolstadt* (The countess of Rudolstadt), represent two years of creation and publication, from 1842 to 1844. The plot of the thousand-page novel spans more than thirty years (ca. 1743–75), the adult life of the heroine. The musical theme centers on the purging of embellishments. As music is the divine language, the purest and most unornamented form reaches God directly. The title character takes much of her moral and musical fiber from the real-life inspirations of Pauline Garcia-Viardot, from whom Sand learned a great deal about the preparation of a singer and the interpretation of a composer's music.

The story of the novel is complex. Consuelo, the orphaned daughter of a Spanish gypsy, is taken into a Venetian singing school-convent by the famous maestro, Porpora. Her astonishing talent brings her to the attention of many theater directors. She flees Venice because her childhood friend and fiancé, Anzoleto, has been unfaithful to her with the current star of the Venetian stage, Corilla. With the help of Porpora, Consuelo is hired as the private music tutor of the daughter of Bohemian aristocrats, the Rudolstadt family.

Albert de Rudolstadt, the erudite but strange son, mystifies her with his tales of Old Bohemia. He believes he is the mystical descendant of ancient revolutionaries. He calls her Consuelo, whereas no one there knows her by this name. (She had adopted the customary diminutive of her teacher's name, la Porporina.) He considers her at once a messianic figure and a talented woman. Albert falls in love with Consuelo and she eventually realizes that she, too, is in love, having been seduced by Albert's untrained but perfect musicianship. He pledges eternal love to her all the while promising to respect her limits.

Unsure of her love, Consuelo rejects Albert's proposal of marriage and sets out for Vienna, where Porpora has gone. During the 250-mile journey she takes on foot, she meets Haydn, who develops his musical talents with Consuelo as his tutor. Once in Vienna, Porpora hears of Albert's proposal and admonishes Consuelo for paying heed to such silliness, and reminds her that as Countess of Rudolstadt she would never again be able to mount the planks and sing.[15] Porpora obtains an appointment at Berlin and takes Consuelo with him. Scarcely has she arrived, when she is whisked away with urgency: Albert is dying and his aunt has consented to their marriage, hoping it will save her nephew's life. Consuelo agrees to marry him mostly out of pity.

Though she hides her title and her marriage because of a mutual agreement with Albert's aunt, Consuelo returns to Berlin to fulfill her contract with the opera of Frederick the Great of Prussia. The Prussian public applauds her musical and vocal prowess. Failing to demonstrate her appreciation to the king, however, she finds herself in prison. A masked intruder, who seems strangely familiar to Consuelo, rescues her and takes her to a far-off palace. She has been chosen to study the doctrines of the Invisibles, a radical political group similar to the Freemasons. Albert, who has not really died and who has been watching Consuelo since her departure from Bohemia, provides the necessary testimony to introduce Consuelo into the secret society. Consuelo is inducted as a member of the Invisibles and is reunited with her beloved Albert. Together they roam throughout Eastern Europe with their children, preaching, through music—even though Consuelo has lost her voice—the love of humanity.

George Sand set her masterful musical novel in the eighteenth century so as to play on the aesthetic arguments uppermost in the musical world at that time—the differences between Italian and German opera, between profane and sacred works, and the fading of the heavy ornamentation of baroque style—which constitute the famous "Querelle des Bouffons" of which Rousseau had written. These matters interested Sand not so much as points of musical history but because they are analogous to contemporary questions of simplifying style and demystifying art in statements about social and political change.

Many of the musical citations contribute meaning to the novel, mostly because the lyrics advance plot and/or characterizations. But we cannot ignore that the operatic form requires balancing poetry and music; the beauty of the words achieves its full impact only when heightened by the music. Moreover, Albert hardly hears the words when Consuelo sings. The music itself and the expression of Consuelo's voice alone stir his emotions. Sand has been careful to use both instrumental and vocal music here, as she does in "Le Contrebandier" (The smuggler) and *Les Sept Cordes de la lyre.*

Musical notation also functions on a symbolic level in *Consuelo.* Written music, an undecipherable barrier to the *non initié,* often makes of musicians an elite. Similarly, the cryptic code writing of the Freemasons separates outsiders from members. In both instances, writing systems represent a language and thus a world of meaning in concrete form. In Derridian terms, these systems of writing predate their human and oral manifestations. Sand makes astute use of that quality by combining the two sign systems at various stages of the narrative. She used a similar system in *Les Sept Cordes,* but in this case it is an oral code, from which Albertus is excluded because he does not yet know the secret to deciphering it.[16]

Sand reveals the complexity of the musician's training in *Consuelo* by depicting the various stages of artistic development in different characters. Consuelo, of course, demonstrates the most honest approach: she is constant and ever dedicated to showing that her art must be used solely in the service of God. She has retained Porpora's most central principle: the true artist must have conscience. Artistic conscience surfaces in the beginning of the novel and recurs as the leitmotiv throughout the book, contributing to both the heroine's moral constitution and to the theme of musicianship.

Anzoleto provides the portrait of the artist who is imbued with great talent but little discipline: "He sang with remarkable energy, originality, and verve. For one innovation, he could be excused ten clumsy figures."[17] We will see the inverse of Anzoleto in the character of Célio in *Le Château des Désertes;* Celio possesses a sharp technique but little emotional foundation. The eponymous character in *Adriani* will also testify to the artist's need to develop beyond mere technical training.

The public presents a problem unique to the performing artist. Consuelo rebukes Anzoleto's brash catering to the audience. She will refuse to practice the fioritura she knows the public theater crowd wants to hear. Yet, she soon learns that she cannot hold an audience and thus cannot share her music. Consuelo cannot reconcile the boastful pride that seems to come with the musical profession with her own humble character. Albert has told her, however, that she must share her gift. He can only express his religious-musical feelings in private; Consuelo can show him how to share them with the public. Albert then compares the theater with the temple. Consuelo gracefully takes the stance of an artist in dialogue with the public, though she never limits her goal to simple amusement.

Ironically, Consuelo does not spend much time in front of the public in *La*

Comtesse de Rudolstadt. Moreover, she loses her voice in this volume. But she has shown Albert how to speak to others through his violin, and she uses her musical sensibilities to interpret his music for those who cannot yet understand its message.

George Sand's arguments center at once on the use of improvisation of ornamentation, and on the question of the complexity or simplicity of style. She comments on musical change using eighteenth-century musical terminology, all the while reflecting early nineteenth-century musical theories. Combining two major stylistic transitions involves the reader in a musical discussion that is historically not entirely representative of the diegetic locus of the text. This deftly engineered mixture offers one explanation of how *Consuelo* is at once an historical novel and an *engagé* novel.

Le Château des Désertes

Near the end of Chopin's stay at Nohant, Sand wrote a short but worthy novel, *Lucrezia Floriani* (1846). A dramatic artist and an unwed mother of four, thus doubly scorned by society, Lucrezia leaves success behind and finds solace in reclusion and in the joys of maternal devotion. Prince Karol falls in love with Lucrezia, but he cannot reconcile his love with his aristocratic nature. Unable to resolve the dilemma, he falls ill and Lucrezia cares for him along with her children. Even though she loves Karol, Lucrezia eventually refuses his devotion and dies.

Most critics have said, not always with objectivity, that the inspiration for Prince Karol, if not his exact portrait, was Chopin. George Sand clearly denies this and Georges Lubin, the emminent editor of Sand's correspondence, adamantly supports this point of view.[18] Another critic has pointed out that the character Lucrezia was drawn from the life and ideals of Marie Dorval, who had a quiet disdain of social conventions in spite of her reputation.[19]

Le Château des Désertes continues the lives of Lucrezia's children.[20] Célio, the eldest son, wishes to avenge his mother against the public's moral condemnation, but he fails in his own debut in Vienna. He leaves town immediately and sets up a theatrical workshop with his brothers and sisters and Cécilia, his childhood playmate. They develop a method that concentrates on the expression of emotion from within the actor. Reminiscent of the commedia del l'arte, the technique requires the troupe to sit down together to combine their interpretations of the work to be performed, here the Don Juan legend as told by Molière, Mozart, and Hoffmann.

Through this method Célio discovers that he must first find the emotion to be portrayed in order to create a convincing musical-dramatic expression.

A process of maturation ensues, paralleled by the development of a love plot. He thus grows emotionally and psychologically at the same time as he shows himself worthy of Cécilia's love. In this way Célio repeats and surpasses Anzoleto.

The role of the public and the artist's relationship with the public constitutes an important theme in *Le Château des Désertes*. Because of his poor reception in Vienna, Célio considers the public an ignorant group bound by convention. In self-defense, he blames the insipid public for his lackluster performance. In retrospect, Célio will regard his botched debut with more honesty, but he still hesitates on the issue of giving the public what it wants. Is such a gesture a betrayal of one's aesthetic principles? And at what point does the meaningless attempt to please insult the public?[21]

Art and artifice must, according to Sand, work together if theater is to be successful. The very nature of art constitutes less a realistic copy of a real phenomenon than a fictive pretext of reality for the purpose of a philosophic discussion or, especially in the case of music, for the purpose of eliciting emotions. The audience, as the recipient of the artist's message, completes the artistic exchange. Célio rejects the quotidien taste of his public, but his impertinence soon loses the sympathy of the reader. He only regains respect through slow and gradual emotional and psychological growth, and then proves himself worthy of his public.

Music, an integral factor of theater in *Le Château des Désertes*, remains a mainstay of Sand's dramatic conception. In this novel, music functions as a vehicle for emotions and as an indicator of emotional maturity. The aesthetic discussion here concerns the artist's relationship with the public and condemns the artist who refuses open communication. Is this not yet another statement of Sand's disapproval of Chopin's romantic solitude? By undertaking this complicated matter, *Le Château des Désertes* stands as an important musical novel in Sand's oeuvre.

Les Maîtres sonneurs

In *Les Maîtres sonneurs* (1853; The master bagpipers) music provides a "place" for the hero, Joset, to hide. The antithesis of traditional folk music and Joset's individual musical style parallels the larger social issue of conformism and tolerance. Sand's condemnation of intolerance will, however, find its equal in the total destruction of the egoistical, and egotistical, antihero.

Striving to develop his talent in preparation for a competition as master bagpiper, Joset roams the countryside in search of proper training. His apprenticeship mimics the journeyman's travels. His journey takes him from his native Berry to nearby Bourbonnais, thus providing Sand the opportunity to comment on the differences between these two regions in musical terms as well as in social and geographic terms. In the eighteenth "veillée," Sand expounds her theory of musical and emotional expression linked to geographic factors: the plains of Berry, symbolized by a major mode, produce joy, light, and activity, while the hills and forests of Bourbonnais, symbolized by a minor mode, give melancholy, shadows, and reverie.

Joset's exile represents a key theme in the novel. His is not the case of typical romantic solitude; he does not seek private contemplation; rather he wishes to escape social interaction because he has always felt different and inadequate. As a child, Joset was slow-witted and the other children shunned him. They called him *"l'ébervigé,"* "the stunned one" in Berrichon dialect. He always went off by himself to avoid further ridicule. Brulette, his childhood friend and the object of his adolescent love, refuses to pity him and claims he keeps to himself for selfish reasons.

Music becomes his solace and his refuge. Determined to develop self-expression through music, largely to convince Brulette of his love for her, he leaves the less musical Berry to search for a teacher in Bourbonnais. Joset finds a master bagpiper who is willing to instruct him. Le Grand Bûcheux (The Great Woodsman) represents wisdom and strength as well as music and emotional sensitivity. His son, Huriel, also a woodsman and a master bagpiper, falls in love with Brulette, who returns his love. Joset's jealousy becomes confused with his monomaniacal devotion to music. Eventually he tries to communicate his love to Brulette in the only way he can: through music. Brulette hears and understands the message, but Joset still has not proven to her that he is acting out of anything but selfishness. A particularly well-drawn passage shows Joset playing a familiar tune in such angry tones that it is obvious that his so-called love for Brulette remains turned inward, twisted with jealousy.[22]

One of the most innovative aspects of *Les Maîtres sonneurs* concerns Joset's initiation. This formal device, with the traditional elements of study, death, and rebirth, takes Joset through his musical training and competition. Though he succeeds in being accepted as a master bagpiper, he fails to become one of the brotherhood. Using an antibildungsroman construct, Sand puts Joset through an elaborate training process during which he would normally grow and mature, yet he regresses. Music becomes more and more a refuge for him as his already limited social skills fade into resentment and anger. Joset dies young and alone, probably by his own hand.

Sand gives a mixed message regarding musical expression in this novel.

On the one hand, Joset's powers of improvisation, like those of Zdenko in *Consuelo,* are laudable and surpass those of the interpreter. Yet, Joset's innovations carry him adrift of the established folk tradition and serve as another form of exile. His excessiveness in personal composition only reinforces his selfishness.

We must be careful not to interpret this as a sign of Sand's conservatism in musical composition; rather Sand is taking a stand against being different for the sake of originality. Sand thus condemns, in musical terms, the theory of art for art's sake. Joset, with his self-interested artistic expression, a trait often attributed to Chopin, constitutes Sand's best-drawn antihero. The novel presents a deep appreciation for the power, both good and bad, of music.

Adriani

Music as an honest expression of emotion puts *Adriani* (1854) on a par with *Le Château des Désertes.* Instead of a young singer lacking experience in life, the hero of *Adriani* is a middle-aged singer who is jaded to the celebrity of success on the stage. He enjoys a fine reputation as an opera singer. But the exigencies of his faithful fans have encroached too much on his private life. Feeling stifled, he leaves Paris to travel and to reflect on his profession. By chance he overhears a beautiful voice singing a Rossini aria at a neighboring house. Laure de Monteluz, recently widowed, seeks no companion but finds herself irresistibly drawn to Adriani's voice, too. The gondelier's aria from *Otello* brings both protagonists out of their private reflections to commiserate in their suffering: "*Nessun maggior dolore / che ricordarsi del tempo felice / nella miseria*" (There is no greater pain than to remember happy times in the midst of suffering).[23]

Adriani comes to think, later in the novel, that he has lost Laure's love. Following a sudden financial crisis, he must return to the stage to make some money and, in so doing, he resigns himself to forfeiting Laure. Adriani is about to sing Edgar in *Lucia di Lammermoor,* wherein he portrays circumstances similar to his own in regard to a misperception of unrequited love. He nearly forgets his music because of the anguish, disillusionment, and mistrust his love has occasioned. But his subconscious takes over and he portrays the poignant emotion of lost love to perfection. Laure, unbeknownst to Adriani, attends this performance and is transported by the beauty of his voice and the degree of suffering it indicates. Adriani and Laure are then reunited. Balzac uses a similar device in *Massimilla Doni,* where Genovese can only tell la Tinta of his love for her in an aria on the stage.

Like Célio, Adriani wrestles with the problem of an artist's responsibility to his public, but the purport of Adriani's hesitations does not imply mistrust of their taste but fear of their power. Self-exile does not alleviate Adriani's fear; he learns to overcome it only by working through it on stage. Laure, or more precisely, his love for Laure, brings Adriani back to music. But the important lesson he learns leads him to distinguish between the illusion and false emotions that produce "what is called in theater jargon 'effects,'"[24] and the real need to be in constant contact with the public, for "an artist dies when he separates completely from the public."[25]

Maître Favilla

Music contributed an important element to most of George Sand's stage productions, especially the rustic plays. The social restrictions of a young prima donna depicted in *Le Démon au foyer* (The demon at home) add another dimension to Sand's portrait of the musical world. *Maître Favilla* (1855; Master Favilla), however, incorporated music as a primordial facet of the plot and character portraits. The play opens on Herman and his father, Keller, going over the books of his recently deceased uncle, a great musician. They stand to inherit a large tract of land, a big house with an enormous library of musical scores, and a noble title. One odd matter they have not yet considered is the dead uncle's musical companion, Master Favilla, and his family. Favilla was, from all reports, at poverty level when Herman's uncle took him in. He and the uncle played duets and provided each other with musical companionship. The question of heredity becomes problematic: Favilla claims that the baron left everything to him, though he cannot substantiate his claim. Keller, a hard-nosed businessman, will not be cheated out of his inheritance and the coveted title. But, Herman awakens his father's sense of humanity, which prevents him from putting Favilla and his family out on the streets. The love interest that develops between Herman and Juliette Favilla causes great consternation for Keller and Marianne Favilla, Juliette's mother. Eventually, a solution to the inheritance question is found and the two young people are united.

Two additional musical links make the play interesting on this level. Herman and Juliette both take music lessons from Favilla, Herman studies violin and Juliette voice.[26] This common interest does not constitute the basis for their amorous attraction, but it does help create a common ground for their developing feelings. More intense and more interesting is the musical bond that defined the friendship between Master Favilla and the baron. Allusions to their closeness in musical taste establish an appreciation for the loss Favilla now feels.

Near the end of the play we understand the power of music. During the Saint Cecilia Day recital in honor of the patron saint of music, which is also a memorial for the deceased musician, Favilla appears to wake from his half-mad state at hearing Handel's music. The baron and Favilla had been playing duets when the baron fainted; the baron had sensed the end coming and had quickly scrawled a new will, leaving everything to Favilla. He presented it to Favilla, saying, "Favilla, this is my wish!" Favilla threw the will into the fire, for he did not want to be accused of accepting anything from the baron's estate. When he recovered from fainting and tried to face the shock of the baron's death, he could only remember the baron's wish for his inheritance. Now Handel's music unlocks a Proustian memory that brings everything together in an ordered manner. Juliette and Herman can now be united with no conflict of interest.

As with any dramatic production, the importance given to music relies on the ingenuity of the director. But Sand has written into *Maître Favilla* a number of details that cannot be overlooked: musical scores in the opening and subsequent scenes; a violin and a harp as functional props; music citations must accompany several scenes, including the vocal performance of Juliette. Jules Janin criticized the play for its antibourgeois theme, an aspect of the text that can hardly be denied. Sand retorted with a vehement attack in which she charged that overzealous realism usurps the public's imagination and ability to dream. *Maître Favilla* can certainly take its place among Sand's other successful musical works.

Art

The artist—musician and painter—enjoys a privileged place in Sand's world. She systematically worked an artist into most of her works, which often served as a pretext to advance her ideas on art. In part 3, chapter 8 of *Histoire de ma vie,* Sand exposes her ideas on the simplicity of art and the superior beauty of Nature over man-made art (*OA,* 1:806–807). She does away with the poet quite early: in *Lélia* she condemns him as a dreamer who wastes his time in hallucinatory reverie.[27] There are few writers in Sand's oeuvre, but musicians abound, as we have seen; there are also several painters. Sand herself had contemplated making her living painting snuffboxes when she first arrived in Paris. Her first visits through Le Louvre awakened her artistic eye. Later, Delacroix fostered in her, and in Maurice, the desire to acquire a discerning eye for the fine arts.

It is most interesting that the main work that has a painter as its principal character is *Elle et Lui* (1859), the novel Sand used as an account of her relationship with Musset. But this work has very little to do with painting, not even a few painting metaphors. Tévérino, in the novel of the same name, was once a model for painters and acquired some fundamental notions of art. His use of an artist's vocabulary helps his theorizing sound knowledgeable, even though the irony of his discourse usually serves to satirize the dull aristocrats.

The focus of *Les Maîtres mosaïstes* (1837) is a different sort of artist, for which Sand is indebted to Luigi Calamatta for information on engraving and the training involved in the trade. At Maurice's request, Sand wrote this novel with no love interest; consequently it remains a bit long and lacks interest for the adult reader.[28] The aspiring artist can also be the target of ridicule, as in *Marianne*. Philippe fatuously attributes all his waking attentions to his declared and not as yet inaugurated profession as painter. He is eventually advised by the country characters he looks down on that he should observe nature before going to the studio, for art is only a copy that diminishes the feelings inspired by God's artwork. Only Diane, in "Le Château de Pictordu" (1873), develops a gift for drawing that responds to a muse, as opposed to the mechanical technique of her father.

The true poet for Sand is not the writer of verse, but the creator of something unwritten. She states in *Aldo le rimeur* that the true scientist is a poet, where the word "poet" has the sense of "artist."[29] Music, as the divine language, takes us closer to God, which makes the musician a messenger of God. This messenger, unlike Mercury, is not sent by God, but attempts to reach God; but unlike Icarus, it is not a prideful gesture. Sand's artist, a sort of *vates,* does not belong on earth, but serves as an intermediary for the rest of us.

Chapter Seven
Plays

Le théâtre est l'art qui résume tous les autres.
(*OA*, 1:161)

Sand was never far from the theater. Her childhood dramatic experiences fill several pages of *Histoire de ma vie*, as she recalls acting out her "novels" in their Paris apartment. Even the ceremonies dedicated to Corambé have been seen as religious-dramatic inventions.[1] Subsequent dramatic experience can be traced as far back as the Convent of the English Augustinians in Paris. There Aurore wrote, directed, and acted in her own version of a Molière-like comedy.[2] And an important part of Sand's integration into Parisian life was an avid thirst for theater.

Sand wrote for the stage proper during a large portion of her writing career, yet her plays have rarely enjoyed much attention.[3] Several of them remain central to her social and literary principles; others demonstrate innovation in staging and dialogue.

Stage Plays

Cosima (1840) was Sand's first stage play, directed by Pierre Bocage at the Comédie-Française, with Marie Dorval in the title role. The story of Cosima examines the antithesis of a woman's boredom with home life and her husband's "macho" sense of honor. Sand proposes that honor of this sort constitutes a much more pervasive emotion than jealousy. The play is indicative of Sand's middle-of-the-road policy in regard to feminism: while the portrait of the woman made to stay at home presents a valid criticism of conventional gender roles, Sand's heroine succumbs to the stereotypical temptation of the bored housewife—infidelity.

After celebrating 1848 ideals in *Le Roi attend* (6 April; The king awaits), a story reminiscent of Moliere's *L'Impromptu de Versailles* where the "king" awaiting accession to power is actually "*le peuple*" (the common people), Sand next attempted a more dramatic production: adopting her rustic novel *François le champi* for the stage (1849). Bocage received high praise for his production of *François* at the Odéon. The detailed décor and carefully collected and orchestrated Berrichon music helped to make this production a success. It differs from the novel in several important respects, specifically the addition of a new character, Jean Bonnin, la Sévère's son. The spectator identifies him with the selfish deception of his mother near the end of the play. La Sévère's unrequited infatuation with François is also an innovation in the play.

Some structural changes create a perspective different from that of the novel, especially at the beginning and the end. The play opens after the death of Blanchet, with Madeleine weak in bed and François just coming back after an absence of six years to offer his help. The end and François's declaration of love to Madeleine cannot exploit the symbolically charged fountain scene in which Madeleine first sees François in the novel because the initial fountain scene precedes the opening of the play. Instead, Sand uses the device of a third party, Mariette, who overhears François and concludes that he loves Madeleine and tells her so. This ending is less dramatic than that of the novel, but it does fit with the other uses of asides and reminiscences that abound in the play.

Another rustic novel Sand rewrote for the stage was *Mauprat* (1853). The foreword offers a sort of apologia for transforming novels into stage plays. The author, quite aware of the tradition into which she transcribes this and other plays, explains the differences that separate the two forms: "It's not copying, it's creating a second time round."[4] The lively dialogue marks the passionate antipathy between Edmée and Bernard as well as the intimacy between Edmée and her father. The substantive omissions from the novel include Bernard's trip to America, which would have required superfluous staging difficulties, and the trial scene, a rather important segment of the novel. The biographical parallel to Sand's separation trial may well explain her desire to expurgate the trial scenes from the play.

Claudie (1851), another rustic play, increases the use of realism, or naturalism, as well as stage properties and décor. Claudie, the unwed mother of a deceased child, becomes the object of Sylvain's affections. Denis Ronciat, the father of Claudie's illegitimate child, discovers the birth and death of his son and attempts to regain Claudie's affections out of a sense of ill-placed guilt. When this fails, he vows to avenge himself. Spreading rumors of Claudie's loose morals, Ronciat manages to turn Sylvain's father, and for a short while Sylvain himself, against the woman they had come to love and respect. The play ends with Claudie's acceptance into the community and her probable marriage with Sylvain. Gustave Planche praised Sand for rehabilitating a fallen woman, which is the play's strong point.[5] Gautier referred to the play as the "country *Antigone*."[6]

The one-act play *Lucie* (1856) describes a similar situation, wherein the eponymous character is the illegitimate daughter of an unknown, who turns out to be Adrien, the main male character. Yet another similar situation, this time more realistically depicted, supplies the central action for *Marguerite de Sainte-Gemme* (1859). Anna, an orphan raised by de Luny's recently deceased aunt, loves Cyprien des Aubiers, whose mother is appalled at the idea of their marriage and whose father, a friend of de Luny's, is caught between the dreams of his youth and the reality of his present-day responsibilities. Anna's reputation is finally safeguarded and the two youths marry.

Les Vacances de Pandolphe (1852; Pandolphe's holiday) serves up another criticism of the materialism of the bourgeoisie. The shocked public expressed their disapproval that such an attack was presented in a jovial context (*Corres.*, 10:789–90; 11:329–31). A year later *Le Pressoir* (The wine press) also commented on bourgeois values, but this time in the context of a small town. Townspeople, Sand explains, represent the middle ground between country folk and Parisians. Most of the characters here are artisan-tradesmen. The wine press that serves as a metaphor for friendship and cooperation in the final act demonstrates the skill and diligence of these workers.

Le Mariage de Victorine (1851; Victorine's wedding) continues the story of Sedaine's *Philosophe sans le savoir* (1765). Sand's version presents a much more complicated interweaving of business, a sense of duty to employer, and dedication to the happiness of one's loved ones, ending with the moral that duty to job and employer ought not take precedence over familial responsibility.

Le Démon au foyer (1852) presents the vice of overprotection on the part of an impresario. The Maestro lauds Camille's voice while restricting her social life in order to preserve her voice. Her younger sister, Flora, who also sings, resents the attention her elder sister receives and revolts by fleeing with the Prince, who wishes to make her his mistress. After a duel and much jealous discourse, the sisters are rejoined and happiness reigns. The real culprit of *Démon* seems to be not the Prince, but the Maestro, who not only stifles his prima donna's social development but also endangers her reputation.

Flaminio (1854), adapted from Sand's 1845 novel *Tévérino*, places an odd figure center stage. Flaminio engages in smuggling, and to avoid the clutches of the authorities he takes on disguises. He dresses in fine clothes and calls himself Count Demetrius de Kologrigo (perhaps a deformation of the Italian for "the color gray," depicting his effort to remain unnoticed). He manages to establish himself as an industrial architect and thus praises capitalism. Flaminio's art is, in fact, a sort of imitation whose originality lies in the rearrangement of borrowed components. Sand thus comments on materialism and on the function of art in such a society.

After *Maître Favilla* (1855; see supra 103–4), Sand wrote *Françoise* (1856). This play deals with the theme of money and misalliance. Henri de Trégenec is falling in love with Dr. Laurent's daughter, Françoise, with whom he was raised. But when Henri discovers he has been disinherited because his father suspects Henri is not his child, he allows himself to be courted by Cléonice Dubuisson, the daughter of rich bourgeois parents. Thanks to the research of a friend and to the assiduity of Françoise, the truth of the bloodline is discovered and Henri's honor and inheritance are restored. Jacques, Henri's friend and confidant, ends up marrying Françoise, and Henri, Cléonice.

Apart from the obvious social commentary on arrivistes, this play shows some originality in its ending. All the work, on the part of three characters as well as the dishonored hero, goes toward reinstating Henri's good name. Yet, he does not end up with the girl, who recognizes the honesty of a friend. Sand's little socialist joke has Henri end up with Cléonice and become part of a family whose wealth overshadows their taste and good judgment.

Comme il vous plaira (1856) obviously draws its story from Shakespeare's *As You Like It*. Sand is careful to demonstrate her knowledge of Shakespeare's dramatic work in the foreword. While her efforts at genre definition are interesting, the resulting text lacks the imagination and lyricism of the English bard.

In *Le Marquis de Villemer* (1864) Sand recasts the story of her 1860 novel of the same name. For the most part the situation and characters are identical. An important omission and a minor change from the novel give the play a less complex turn. First, in the novel Urbain is writing a book on the history of the aristocracy's exploitation of the lower classes; this book does not appear at all in the stage play, though a few remarks identify the Marquis's political colors and, consequently, one of the reasons for Caroline's attraction to him. Second, Urbain's illegitimate son, as portrayed in the play, results from a secret marriage; in the novel, the son was born of the liaison between Urbain and a married woman, who subsequently died. The play is weakened by reducing the son's role, thereby removing an important factor in Urbain and Caroline's marriage.

L'Autre (1870; The other) casts the plot of *La Confession d'une jeune fille* for the stage. Sarah Bernhardt played the lead, and the play was a great success with the public. Unfortunately, it was forced to close in 1870 when the barricades went up. Karénine judges the play better written and more interesting than the novel.[7] All the chronological twists of the novel, which produce the suspense of not knowing all the identities or allegiances until the end, are straightened out in the play. The resulting frank presentation of events creates a flat exposition for the sake of greater coherence for the audience.

A few of Sand's plays never saw the footlights. *Gabriel* (1839), a novel in dialogue form, examines the capacity of women to reason and control their environment if they are given a "man's" education. Sand rewrote this play for the Nohant theater in 1851, under the title *Julia,* but that manuscript has been lost along with a later version entitled *Octave d'Apremont.*[8]

"Une Conspiration en 1537" (1831) and *Aldo le rimeur* (1833; Aldo the rhymester) never found their way to the stage. *Les Mississipiens* has also never been produced, nor has *Les Sept Cordes de la lyre,* both written in 1839. Most critics consider these works as armchair plays and classify them alongside other novels in dialogue form, such as *Cadio* (1867), which studies the plight of a family split by political principles in postrevolutionary Vendée, and *Lupo Liverani* (1869), Sand's reworking of a Tirso di Molina play.[9] The one-act play *Père Va-Tout-Seul* (1844) remains unstaged; *Le Pavé* (1862; The paving stone), *Le Lis du Japon* (1866; Japanese lily), and *Un Bienfait n'est jamais perdu* (1892; A good deed is never wasted) form a trio of one-act plays that Sand saw produced only at the end of her career in Paris. A number of Sand's works were adapted for the stage by others: *Les Beaux Messieurs de Bois-Doré* (1862), *Le Drac* (1864; The spirit), and *Cadio* (1868) by Paul Meurice, and *Les Don Juan de village* (1866) by Maurice Sand. Michel Carré put *La Petite Fadette* in verse, and T. Semet set it to music (1869, Opéra-Comique).

Theater at Nohant

Apart from a one-volume collection, *Théâtre de Nohant,* very few of the scenarios for the little theater at Nohant have been published.[10] Much can also be gleaned from Maurice Sand's *Masques et Bouffons,* which gives a history of commedia del l'arte theater.[11] From 1846 to 1863 the little theater at Nohant served not only as a source of entertainment during the long winter nights, but it also provided Sand with a testing ground for some of her dramatic concepts. Chopin encouraged this theater and even provided piano accompaniment for some of the performances. The performers came from the household staff and guests alike. In a long letter to her cousin René Vallet de Villeneuve, Sand explains the workings of the Nohant theater.[12] This all-consuming yet individual approach to lively dramatic productions forms the central plot of Sand's novel *Le Château des Désertes* (see chapter 6). Here improvisation meets its apotheosis. In this novel the importance of music and of the actors' preparation and attitude toward their roles offer a glimpse of the experimental nature of the little theater.

Le Druide peu délicat (The indelicate druid), the first play staged at the Nohant theater (1846), delivers the classic misalliance plot with a hint of superstitious folklore. At the rate of almost one performance per night over the next two months, the little theater at Nohant delighted its visitors, and the players themselves, with *La Belle au bois dormant* (Sleeping beauty), *Don Juan, Le Philtre* (The potion), *Le Mariage au tambour* (Drum wedding), and many others. Many of these scripts demonstrate Sand's penchant for fantasy, the fantastic, and the pastoral. Some of the stories recall Hoffmann, and a few are clearly inspired by him; others originate from Shakespeare.[13]

Although Sand initially intended to revive the lost art of the commedia del l'arte, she began to concentrate on more scripted plays after the success of her *François le champi* at the Odéon. Manceau urged Sand to write more for the Paris stage, but she kept the Nohant theater going as a testing ground. She asked Bocage and Hetzel to locate aspiring young actors who might enjoy some experience in her drama workshop. More than one future stage actor put in time on the boards of the Nohant theater; and most of Sand's Paris productions knew at least one preliminary version at Nohant.

The availability of the little theater at Nohant ceased in 1863 when Maurice requested that Manceau vacate the house. Sand and Manceau moved to small quarters just outside of Paris. There were no more productions at Nohant thereafter.

In 1847 Maurice Sand, with his friends Eugène Lambert and Victor Borie, began the serious development of a marionette theater. Sand described the history, development, and functioning of Maurice's endeavors in a text written only months before she died, "Théâtre des marionnettes." Lambert designed many of the backdrops, while Maurice fashioned the puppets and gradually increased the complexities of the theater's mechanics backstage and in the wings. Lighting added to the mood of the plays as did sound effects and music, provided by a guest, on violin or piano, or by a music box. Maurice planned a series on the French Revolution, which, ironically, the uprising of February 1848 interrupted.

Improvisation is, once again, the staple of this tradition. Maurice insisted that puppetry held the middle ground between a totally open setting of improvisation and the more rigidly scripted stage plays: "It's the attempt at a very well-regulated set of conventions which remains invisible (*OA,* 2:1270). Sand felt indebted to her son and the experience of the marionette theater for all it taught her in the realm of theatrics. "Nobody knows how much I owe to my son's marionettes."[14]

Dramatic Theory

On Acting   In many respects, Sand presented some of her most interesting notions on dramatic production in essays and letters. Before any actual association with the stage, she learned much about the craft of the actor from Marie Dorval. In a short essay written in 1833, Sand compares the art of Dorval to that of the more experienced actress Mademoiselle Mars.[15] Sand explains that Mars's technique stems from the eighteenth-century need for order and reason, which produces self-awareness and confident stage presence. Dorval, on the other hand, represents a more modern, freer approach to dramatic interpretation, which requires the actor to appear more natural. Sand finds Dorval's performance much more inspired. Sand would write a panegyric of Marie Dorval in a separate chapter of *Histoire de ma vie*.[16]

A few years after the essay Sand wrote another article on her favorite actress, "De Madame Dorval" (1837).[17] The article is a sort of reverie, with a narrator, Mario, who basks in the inspiration of Dorval's talent. His feeling of completion and oneness with the actress ends abruptly at the end of a performance. Sand examines here two important aspects of the actor's relationship with the public: first, the mutual transfer of emotion across space, and second, the ephemeral nature of performance arts, where the "magic" lasts only a instant.

How much should an actor's personal experience influence his acting? In *Le Château des Désertes*, Sand has her fledgling actors develop emotionally as well as professionally, insisting that the two necessarily go together. An actor according to this theory must draw on his life experience and relive it during a performance. A later piece, *Le Beau Laurence* (Handsome Laurence), the sequel to *Pierre qui roule* (1869; A rolling stone), agrees rather with Diderot's idea, in *Le Paradoxe sur le comédien*, that one's own personality must be set aside in order to portray the character of one's role. The hero, Pierre Laurence, gives another example of the farmer's son who has received an education and aspires to a poor Bohemian life. The much envied, proverbial Bohemian life of the actor is criticized by Sand in *Narcisse* (1858).

Improvisation remains an important element in Sand's vision of the actor. Consuelo discovers the art of free improvisation from Zdenko, who knows hundreds of Bohemian tunes and can embroider on the melodies with an innate ease that sets her to marvelling. She, above all other characters in Sand's world, appreciates the artistic and quasi-religious value of improvisation. Musical and dramatic improvisation in Sand's novels and plays provide similar examples that prove the concept that she places at the center of *Le*

Château des Désertes: the theater is a locus of trial, an authentic initiation, as in *The Magic Flute.*[18]

Philosophy and Realism Only in drama did Sand ponder, write, and apply theory. In matters of theater she felt the dangers of new territory. Already established as a novelist, perhaps she needed a more conscious approach to an exciting but uncertain career change. And as usual, she refused to pander to the public's lazy wishes and preferred to shake them up; indulging in her characteristic idealism. She felt strongly that the theater, most of all, very much needed to retain the freedom to manipulate fantasy.[19]

Sand's first published play, *Aldo le rimeur* (1833), is a metaphysical treatise on the relationship of art and science.[20] Sand calls *Aldo* a "*drame fantastique,*" a term she alternates with "*drame métaphysique*" and is spelled out most clearly in 1839 in her essay "Le Drame fantastique" in which she discusses the dream plays of Goethe (*Faust*), Byron (*Manfred*), and Mickiewicz (*Konrad*).[21] The theoretical essay, one of the best examples of Sand's seldom indulged literary criticism, concerns the use of supernatural beings for philosophical reasons rather than for dramatic effect. These characters articulate the polemic between thought and passion, reflection and despair, or what Sand calls the *moi* and the *non-moi*. In unusually modern terminology, Sand identifies all fantastic beings with the *moi,* the subject or main character, and his efforts to relate to the object, the other, the *non-moi,* or the other human characters.

Sand's own dream play, *Les Sept Cordes de la lyre,* written in the same year as her essay on the genre, does not rate a single mention here. She may have lacked confidence in it as a coherent work. She surely must have wanted to avoid comparison with Goethe. Much later, Sand would write a novel in dialogue form, *Le Diable aux champs,* in which many animals, not necessarily fantastic but certainly imaginary, combine the thoughts of the main characters in a similar function of subject versus object.

In the 1850s Sand effected a change in stage production with her Berrichon plays *François le champi, Claudie,* and *Le Pressoir.* She gave as much attention to detail in costuming and set design as to dialogue and music. She complained bitterly when festivals were made "prettier" or "more lively" to please the Parisian audience because this betrayed the somber attitude of the Berrichon countryman. Gautier quite liked the realism of *François le champi* and praised the ability of the production to take its audience inside a Berrichon thatched cottage.[22]

Sand published an essay on realism in 1857.[23] Although flattered to be considered an example of a realistic dramatist—and her work can be regarded as revolutionary—she outlined some problems inherent in the realist school. She extolled the virtues of fantasy and echoed the Romantic need to run the gamut from the obscene to the sublime. She would correspond with Flaubert on this subject, though they would never agree.

Sand's theater remains poorly known, even among Sand scholars. One reason for this is certainly the lack of availability of texts, although more critical interest might encourage the publication of a modern edition. It is hardly surprising that most of the scenarios of the Nohant theater never found their way into published form; for the most part, they represent an embryonic stage of a dramatic idea conceived among friends, where it was born and died with little development. Many of the Paris plays, on the contrary, catch the spirit of socialism and feminism, conveying current thoughts of Sand's era. These plays deserve further examination.

Delacroix, an old, dear friend of Sand's, denied her talents at dramatic writing. After attending a performance of *Mauprat,* he wrote in his journal that like most of her plays, it presented an interesting premise and carried some character development to the end of act 2. But there it stopped—and *Mauprat* comprises six acts! From that point on, there is no step forward. He feels her works—including her novels, which often lack taste and suitability—will never last.[24]

Such a harsh judgment, even from a friend, is rather understandable in reference to *Mauprat,* whose metamorphosis into a stage play lacks sufficient depth and stands in the shadow of its original form. In general, however, Sand's plays cannot be so readily dismissed. Zola would remind us later that Sand's dramatic talent was long denied, but after all her successful theatrical productions, she deserves to gain recognition, if not as a playwright, at least as someone with deep perception and a great gift for creation. If she suffered several failures in the theater, she also enjoyed many successes. *Le Marquis de Villemer* constitutes her greatest dramatic triumph; all Paris saw it. Still, Zola concludes, she was generally more complete in novel form, where she could give free rein to her dreamy, contemplative nature.[25] George Sand did construct a more coherent work in prose fiction, but certain dramatic innovations and some powerful ideological dialogue remain noteworthy.

Chapter Eight
Autobiographical Writings

George Sand accepted the autobiographical pact to tell her own story with herself as hero in several texts. The most famous instance is her memoirs, *Histoire de ma vie*. Georges Lubin has included in the two Pléiade volumes of this text a number of other autobiographical writings. The majority of these texts had not been reedited in nearly a century; a few had never been published. This valuable edition, enhanced by his esoteric notes, serves as the key reference tool for all Sand critics.[1]

Several additional texts qualify as autobiographical. Along with *Histoire de ma vie*, I shall examine *Journal intime, Entretiens du très-docte et très-habile docteur Piffoël, Sketches and Hints, Souvenirs de mars-avril 1848, Journal de novembre-décembre 1851, Promenades autour d'un village, Journal de Gargilesse*, and the novel *Elle et Lui*.

Histoire de ma vie

George Sand's memoirs, along with her correspondence, stand as the primary explicit revelation of her thoughts, aspirations, and weltanschauung. Yet, few biographers have studied this lengthy work, which numbered eleven volumes in its original edition. Karénine does comment on it quite often, but not in any ordered way. Subsequent biographies by André Maurois, Curtis Cate, and Joseph Barry barely mention *Histoire de ma vie*. Cate does not include it in his list of Sand's more important works, though he does cite Taine's appreciation of it as an autobiography far more honest than Chateaubriand's *Mémoires d'outre-tombe*.[2] Of the recent biographers, only Francine Mallet devotes several pages to a detailed description and analysis of Sand's memoirs.[3] Critics are beginning to uncover some important aspects of Sand's autobiography through recent serious studies of all sorts.[4] The value of *Histoire de ma vie* as a literary work as well as an historical document remains to be exploited.

For twenty years George Sand contemplated writing her memoirs. Although she first sketched them out in *Voyage en Auvergne* (1829) and further mentioned them in her early correspondence, only in late 1847 did she write the first volume of the story of her life. Friends encouraged her to continue, but the writing proceeded slowly. The events of 1848 halted any progress for some time. The postrevolution financial crisis hit the bookselling industry hard and the future of *Histoire de ma vie* remained uncertain. Yet, Sand continued to write faithfully. Another delay resulted from the 1851 coup d'état, and publishers were no longer sure what texts they dared print.

Finally, in late 1854 the long work appeared serially in *La Presse* with Girardin, while Delatouche published the book version almost simultaneously. Despite readers' general disappointment at not finding more secrets revealed, the piece was well received. Critics judged the pre-Sand section too long, and the latter years too laconic.

Histoire de ma vie comprises five parts, each divided into several chapters. One fifth of the book concerns Sand's ancestors, especially her father. Her mother's absence from this history jars the modern reader, even more so because Sand points to the necessity of including one's maternal family: "One is not the child of one's father only, but also somewhat, I believe, of one's mother. It seems to me one might be even more one's mother's child, and we hold dear to us, in the most immediate, the most powerful, the most sacred way, the belly which carried us" (*OA,* 1:15). Sand excuses this lacuna by citing Sophie's convenient memory loss on the subject of her years with Maurice Dupin. But Sand must have known more about her mother's life and ancestry than she tells us. Sophie appears from time to time throughout *Histoire de ma vie,* but the emphasis on Sand's father's life clearly points to a need for reconstituting the absent other.

Sand presents her father's life, in a section almost half the length of the part devoted to her own life, through his letters to his mother. Page after page of letters, rewritten by Sand, detail Maurice's military campaign experience and ambition. *Histoire de ma vie* thus includes a biography of Maurice Dupin followed by Sand's autobiography.[5] Sand defines the need for this long history: "Everything works toward history; *everything is history*" (*OA,* 1:78). The episode of her father's death reveals many details of primal interest to Sand critics: her mother's reaction and that of Sand's half-brother, everyone's mourning dress and attitude, the separation from her mother, and living with her grandmother (*OA,* 1:597–604).

The end of the autobiography also deserves brief comment. Sand's treatment of the adult years, including all of her writing career (part 5), is the shortest section of the book and a rather rapid overview of this period. Rather than a lapse in attention to detail, the sketchiness of this segment stems from Sand's promise not to embarrass any living person.[6] She also shares few details concerning her experiences with Musset or even her nine years with

Chopin. Sand exercises her right as author to select which details will become public. She will not reveal all her life; she dislikes the pride of confessions, especially when one cannot trust the reader to draw the best lesson from them.[7]

Sand's own historical intrusions reflect a metacriticism of multiple value. At the beginning of the eighth chapter of part 2 she states that the preceding section had been written entirely under the July Monarchy. When she takes up the work again in June 1848, the tenor of the writing is sure to be different. Illusions, maintained perhaps longer by her than by others around her, by this time have all dropped away (*OA*, 1:465). Such comments mark the beginning of Aurore's political awareness. Here intradiegetical references to Napoleon and the Empire, Moscow and Waterloo, followed by the Restoration, paint an historico-political backdrop for Sand's adolescent life. Not uninteresting is Sand's description of reading history as a novel; rather than historical theory, events and personalities attracted her. Further on she would describe her reactions to attending the funeral services of Louis XVIII and to the succession of Charles X to the throne.

The end of part 3 and the beginning of part 4 bring many details of convent life. When Aurore began to write in the convent, satire was her specialty. She would send her ironic texts home, knowing they would be appreciated there. But the Mother Superior, suspicious of the volume of correspondence, discovered the subject of Aurore's satires and put a stop to it (*OA*, 1:896–97). Her urge to write, however, was not totally thwarted in the convent. Aurore drew on her excellent memory of Molière, whom no one in the convent had read, to compose humorous scenarios for the girls to act out. At one point when she was on the point of disclosing her sources, a single sister, who knew a little Molière, advised her to keep quiet in order to avoid the theater's being closed down to the improper nature of her material (*OA*, 1:1001).

The next decade of Sand's life occupies only a hundred pages. She is forced to move in with her mother after her grandmother's death. The arrangement suited neither one very well, and Aurore went to spend some time with friends, the du Plessis family. Here she met Casimir Dudevant. After a short engagement, they were married, and barely ten months later her son, Maurice, was born.

The trip to the Pyrenees brought the occasion of meeting Aurélien de Sèze, generally thought to be Sand's first true love. His name never appears in the text. She refers to him once, after returning to Nohant, as "l'être absent" (the absent one).[8]

Meanwhile, her daughter, Solange, was born and Sand made the decision to take a stand in her life: departure for Paris. Once again, she makes no mention of Jules Sandeau in her writing, although he would appear in a later section where she explains the origin of her pseudonym (*OA*, 2:138–40). This section, part 4, chapter 13, and especially chapters 14 and 15, divulges Sand's suffering and idealism at the beginning of her writing career.

Part 5 of *Histoire de ma vie* recounts the part of Sand's life with which we have become familiar. She gives only ambiguous descriptions of her trip to Venice; once again, hardly any mention of Musset emerges in this travelogue. Just as in the fictional writings from the Venetian period, she has sprinkled Italian words throughout this section.

Sand allows herself the leisure to devote a few chapters to personalities around her. "Mme Dorval" earns a whole chapter, wherein ironically Sand explains her antiwoman feelings, thus heightening the importance she gives Marie Dorval. Delacroix, especially his dedication to the romantic ideals of beauty, goodness, and justice, also garners a large section. She also talks about Sainte-Beuve, Luigi Calamatta, and Charles Didier.

Sand dedicates a large number of pages to Michel de Bourges. From chapter 8 to chapter 12 he appears as the main figure in her life. Lamennais, Liszt, Leroux, and her mother also people these chapters, but Michel remains the principal actor. She discusses the importance of social issues and his role in her trial, as well as her role in the most important trial of his career. This section serves as complement to the "Lettre à Everard" in *Lettres d'un voyageur*.

Chopin is the focus of the last two chapters of *Histoire de ma vie*. Sand gives a sketchy account of the trip to Majorca, dwelling mostly on Chopin's sickness. The whole section on Chopin seems to speak mainly of his weakness and his coughing. She does talk some about his genius, but there are just as many passages about the problems of life in Paris with Chopin. Finally, the separation between Chopin and Sand marks the end of an important period and the end of her autobiography.

At the current stage of Sand criticism, one hardly reads *Histoire de ma vie* for its content. More important is the novelistic style in which she tells her own story. Reading the autobiography often recalls the experience of reading her novels, and it is sometimes difficult to remember Sand is at once the historical and the fictional heroine. She reveals just as much about Sand the writer as about Sand the person. We have yet to exploit this work sufficiently. *Histoire de ma vie* is becoming, and will remain, a staple for Sand criticism.

Other Autobiographical Works

Lettres d'un voyageur deserves brief comment here. Its value as autobiography remains boundless. Sand divulges intimate details about her thoughts and desires during rather difficult moments of her life. It is perhaps the form of presentation that provides the most interesting autobiographical element: she writes from the perspective of a male narrator, an older uncle figure who is sharing his life experience with a younger correspondent. She prefers to remain more or less anonymous while revealing personal and sometimes anxious emotions.

Between 1837 and 1841 Sand kept a journal of her thoughts, *Entretiens journaliers avec le très docte et très habile docteur Piffoël, professeur de botanique et de psychologie* (Daily exchanges with the very learned and very clever Doctor Piffoël, professor of botany and psychology; *OA*, 2:977–1018). As the long and humorous title suggests, the work provided a nonvulnerable context in which Sand could sound out her ideas without the threat of ridicule, even from herself. The text delivers the playful irony the title promises and at the same time offers Sand a forum for dialogue with herself, for the eponymous character is George Sand herself. "Pif" (slang for "nose") refers to the Dupin nose that George and Maurice sported. Sand also caricatures her own penchant for observing plants and people.

A self-deprecating parody of the Hail Mary provides an example of the characteristic irony of the piece. "Hail, Piffoël, full of grace, wisdom is with you. Blessed art thou among fools and blessed is the fruit of thy pain, boredom. Holy fatigue, Mother of rest, come to us poor dreamers, now and in the hour of our death. Amen" (*OA*, 2:986).

In the third clause, instead of sacrilegiously identifying herself with the Mother of God, she announces her degradation by deeming herself Queen of Fools. Having given birth to boredom instead of Jesus, she decries her work as unstimulating, soporific, and vacuous, which, in the extended metaphor, becomes a sin. Whether the sin be mortal or venial seems immaterial because death seems imminent.

Entretiens journaliers uses a device similar to dialogue, when an unnamed narrator addresses Dr. Piffoël on private matters. She states in the preface, "You only write a diary when passions have burnt out" (*OA*, 2:977). It is clear, however, that this text is not simply a private journal. Sand's attention to style and to the self-effacing technique of the dialogue, the distance she takes, and the third-person point of view indicate a fictional as well as an autobiographical endeavor. Yet, considering the irony of tone, the author, narrator, and hero are never very far removed from one another.

Another short autobiographical text, again fictionalized, describes Sand's turmoil at the death of her granddaughter. *Après la mort de Jeanne Clésinger* (1855; After Jeanne Clésinger's death) transforms George Sand's nightmare into a dreamy reworking of her guilt and her sense of loss. Sand imagines a voice calling her, whereupon she enters a parallel world. Here she encounters a young woman, strangely familiar, who remains unnamed for a good portion of the text. She calls the girl Jeanne; the name pleases her, though the girl says her name is Nata. (The real Jeanne's nickname was Nini.) Then Sand refers to the special corner of the garden at Nohant she had built with Jeanne, which they called the Trianon. The allusion awakens in Nata visions of a past life; Sand's dream then comes to an end. This lyrical text serves to distance grief and as such provides a perfect medium for coping with suffering. The oneirological and fantastic mode of this text announces the writings George Sand will dedicate to her other granddaughters at the end of her life, *Contes d'une grand-mère*.

Journal intime (Private Diary) was written in 1834, after the final break with Musset. Sand probably never intended it to be read by anyone except perhaps Musset himself. In all likelihood, she burned the manuscript. Paul de Musset had in his hands a copy from which he drew passages that he slightly altered to suit his purposes of rebuttal in *Lui et Elle*.[9]

The diary starts with a mood of melancholy caused by the music of a concert; Sand attempts to understand the reasons for her distress. She addresses the issue of Musset's jealousy over Liszt. Certainly she was not in love with Liszt. Perhaps Liszt had been attracted to her, but he never acted on it. She expresses raw emotions in regard to Musset, whereas the first two *Lettres d'un voyageur* present a more polished, more confident facade.

Sketches and Hints gathers a collection of notes and vague musings that Sand recorded between 1833 and 1868. The curious English title suggests an ironic manipulation of the popular "Keepsake," in vogue in France at this time. There are discussions of suicide, music, Hoffmann, Byron, Jean-Jacques Rousseau, Beethoven, and other personal memories. A few notes help to interpret the characterizations in *Lélia* as well as some of the symbolism in *Les Sept Cordes de la lyre*. Memories and notes are presented in a sort of stream of consciousness with no unifying thread. Near the end a page of verse, entitled "Trianon," describes the *locus amoenus* she constructed in the garden at Nohant with her granddaughter Jeanne.

Two short diaries communicate Sand's thoughts during periods of political crisis: *Souvenirs de mars-avril 1848* and *Journal de novembre-décembre 1851 (OA,* 2:1183–90; 1195–1222). Both texts mention the names of people who have become associated with the political movements of those eras, such as Mazzini and Ledru-Rollin, and names of newspapers, their roles and availability in Nohant. The general feeling of confusion after the elections of April 1848, and the general astonishment at the coup d'état of December 1851 come across readily in these journal texts. *Lettres d'un voyageur pendant la guerre* would give similar details about the reactions in the provinces to the events in Paris during the Franco-Prussian invasion and the subsequent Commune period. (See chapter 3.)

Journal de Gargilesse (January 1858 to April 1864) describes a series of trips to the house in Gargilesse with Manceau. Never intended to be published, this text is written in telegraphic style. Almost every entry begins with a description of the weather, followed by an evaluation of the previous night's sleep, then brief comments on work accomplished. The precise hour of the notation heads off each entry.[10]

Promenades autour d'un village (1857; Walks around the village) describes the "*vallée noire*" as if the narrator were showing it to visitors from Paris. Sand invents pastoral names that recall the characters of d'Urfé for the people in this small-scale travelogue. A few comments on realism versus idealism identify the state of Sand's thoughts at the time and correspond to discussions she was having with Flaubert at the time.

Elle et Lui

Shortly after the Sand-Musset "*affaire de Venise*" ended, Musset published a fictionalized apology, *La Confession d'un enfant du siècle* (1836). Octave and Brigitte bear a remarkable resemblance to Musset and Sand. Writing with slightly more perspective than when he produced *On ne badine pas avec l'amour* (1834), Musset is kind to Sand in *La Confession*. She accepted the apology; its poetic value and honesty moved her.

Sand observed strict discretion regarding Musset until his death in March 1857. When Musset died, his brother, Paul de Musset, contacted Sand to inquire about disposing of their letters. Sand promised to return Musset's to his brother, but not right away; she wanted to keep them at Nohant, where she might reread some of them before burning them.

In the early spring of 1858, Sand was searching for a subject for another novel. By early May, she had sketched out a short story called "Thérèse." We now know that some phrases in the final version of the story almost exactly match expressions that appear in the correspondence. Buloz, who earlier had dissuaded Sand from publishing her correspondence with Musset, renewed his misgivings at publishing this work. When Sand presented him with the completed *Elle et Lui*—a novel assuredly, but with many reminiscences—he only reluctantly agreed.[11]

Many elements in *Elle et Lui* differ from the historical lives of George Sand and Alfred de Musset. Instead of writers, in the novel the two protagonists are painters. Laurent's obscure background takes a back seat to the intrigue that surrounds the blond heroine, Thérèse Jacques, an illegitimate child brought up away from her mother, married a Portuguese count who was already married to a woman in Havana. The child Thérèse bore from that union was kidnapped by his father and brought to America, where he supposedly died. Dick Palmer, a cultured American, differs considerably from his real-life counterpart, Pagello. Palmer, a friend of Thérèse's father, knew her as a child and helped her reestablish herself after her marriage with the count was annulled. While he seems to be more intelligent and more magnanimous than Pagello, his excesses of jealousy eclipse what we know about the Venetian doctor's temperament. Palmer shows up again at the end of the novel to deliver, with no strings attached, the lost child whom he has searched out in America.

Despite the differences between Sand's fiction and Sand's reality, the number and the quality of similarities make *Elle et Lui* a transparent fictionalization of Sand's relationship with Musset. The heroine's name belies her history: Thérèse Jacques, the invented surname indicative of her obscure origins and simple status. The earthbound resonances of "Jacques" also recall the Virgilian "George." Laurent de Fauvel's name, on the other hand, calls attention to his aristocratic background. Thérèse's and Laurent's ages parallel those of Sand and Musset: twenty-eight to thirty, and twenty-four. Sand has also mimicked their personality traits: Thérèse keeps an air of mystery about her, presumably because of her unorthodox past, and Laurent cuts a young, selfish, and naïve figure.

The main area of duplication between reality and fiction comes from the professional activities of the two people involved: she is a portraitist and he is a landscape painter—vocations that parallel the separation of their actual careers of prose writer and poet or playwright.[12] Thérèse gives the work of doing Palmer's portrait to Laurent, much as Sand gave Musset her rough draft of "Une Conspiration en 1537," which he remolded into his celebrated *Lorenzaccio*. Sand often pictures the two characters at work, but Thérèse is by far the more diligent and the harder working of the two; Laurent only discovers the joys of regular work once the separation with Thérèse has been effected. Financial considerations have much to do with the discipline Thérèse maintains at work. Though she seems to lead a free life, she is frugal and must produce work regularly.

The triangle in *Elle et Lui* sets the woman up as the unattainable object of desire, a character similar to Indiana but less vulnerable. Thérèse gives in to Laurent only out of compassion, and to Palmer only out of a sense of duty. Instead of destroying the barriers that separate love and friendship, the triangle creates a high level of anxiety in each party and does not satisfy the need for union.[13]

Most readers will accept *La Confession d'un enfant du siècle* as an act of repentance. Musset presents Sand in a favorable light in this text and admits to weaknesses on his own part. Many critics insist that Sand shared none of Musset's generosity when she wrote *Elle et Lui;* that the book appeared after Musset's death only exacerbated critical and popular condemnation. At most, she showed some overall kindness: Laurent is good and compassionate. And Sand does end the novel in a simple display of understanding and forgiveness.[14]

One reader who immediately reacted to what he saw as libel was Paul de Musset. Hardly six weeks after *Elle et Lui* finished its serial publication, *Lui et Elle* appeared. In this version of the truth-become-fiction, the protagonists are musicians, Olympe, a songwriter of limited abilities, and Edouard de Flacony, a gifted composer—still the insistence on class differences. Paul's work lacks any stylistic interest, but it is a valuable stone in the edifice of this complicated story.

The publication of *Lui et Elle* caused an immediate demand for a book version of *Elle et Lui.* Sand's success clearly encouraged Louise Colet to take advantage of the publicity. She had briefly been Musset's mistress and decided to exploit the situation with her *Lui.* The book mostly compares Musset to Flaubert.[15] Yet another volume followed: *Eux et Elles: Histoire d'un scandale,* by Mathurin de Lescure.[16] His approach discredits the others. He states that *Elle et Lui* is a novel mixed with history, an untimely apology, a calumny against a dead man; that *Lui et Elle* is history with no novel, an honest but excessive pamphlet, a violent piece against women; that *Lui* is neither novel nor history, but instead a dithyramb inspired by passion, coquetry in book form. Autobiography to biography to fiction to historical fiction: these works represent a confusing but important addition to the Sand story.

Not all of Sand's texts discussed in this chapter qualify as autobiography, or at least not all satisfy the pact we have come to associate with the genre.[17] Yet they contain a wealth of information Sand decided to record. In many ways the correspondence as a document is just as important as several of those mentioned here. Now that M. Lubin's exhaustive edition has united all existing letters and references, we have a valuable and coherent text from which to work.[18] Moreover, Sand wrote many letters knowing they would be read by more than just the addressee by virtue of her stature in the literary community. George Sand added her own stamp to the concept of autobiography by giving it various forms and a varied importance. These texts will remain valuable as testimony to her historical, intellectual, and emotional life as well as to her sense of literary style.

Chapter Nine

Contes d'une grand-mère

After the Commune of 1870–71, George Sand withdrew from political discussions to an even greater extent than she had in 1848. But she did not abandon her idealistic aspirations for society. Her desire to know about the events in Paris conflicted with her vision of social reform, a conflict that characterizes *Journal d'un voyageur pendant la guerre* (1871). She finally disapproved of the Commune, as attested in her correspondence with Flaubert.[1] *Nanon* (1872), Sand's rewriting of the Revolution of 1789, also belies a nostalgic stirring of republican ideals.

From the end of the Franco-Prussian War to the end of her life, Sand wrote seven novels; after *Césarine Dietrich* and *Nanon*, *Ma Soeur Jeanne* (1874; My sister Jeanne) tells an enticing story of love and mistaken incest. *Flamarande* (1875) and its second volume *Les Deux Frères* (The two brothers) tell the story of Gaston, considered illegitimate by his father. Raised under the name Espérance, the child received a fine education despite his peasant surroundings. The novella *Marianne (Chevreuse)* (1876) introduces the problem of shyness in an amorous relationship between "older" people. Pierre, forty, and Marianne, twenty-five, both suffer from their timidity, though the woman proves to be much more resourceful than the man. An interesting *locus amoenus* sets the scene for the beginning of their intimacy. Finally, *La Tour de Percemont* (1876) is a Cinderella story. Marie de Nives's wicked stepmother devises many evil plans to torment her, but the lawyer makes certain they all backfire.

A large portion of Sand's literary production of this period revolved around her granddaughters. For the pleasure and edification of Aurore and Gabrielle Sand, the daughters of Maurice and Lina, she invented stories that combine fantasy with pastoral serenity: *Contes d'une grand-mère*. These stories, published between 1872 and 1873, mark her final literary endeavors and thereby serve as a sort of conclusion for her oeuvre.

The Stories

The stories that comprise *Contes d'une grand-mère* first appeared separately, then were published in two series in 1873 and 1876. This was not Sand's first attempt at story writing; already in 1837 she penned "Le roi des neiges" ("The Snow King") for Solange, which remains unedited, and in 1859 "La Fée qui court" (The Running Fairy). In a similar style and genre, *L'Histoire du véritable Gribouille* (1850; Story of the real fool) exploits a fantasy world. "La Coupe" (1865), written for Manceau, is a chilling story in which a fairy teaches us the promise of hope in death; it appeared in *La Revue des Deux Mondes* four months before Manceau died. "Ce que dit le ruisseau" (1863; What the stream says) presents the idea of pantheism; the protagonist tries to change the course of a stream to quiet its voice, but the voice of nature cannot be silenced.

"Laura" (1864) describes the fantastic world of geodes. Alexis, nineteen, and his cousin Laura, sixteen, take a trip "where everything is transparence and crystalization."[2] Laura leads her cousin, rather like Virgil leading Dante, into the "fairy-like regions of the crystal," speaking an unusual language, which Alexis soon begins to understand. Language and writing are important themes in this story. Alexis discovers we have two souls, one within us and one we do not know. Dream and reality combine and become confused in the fine balance that makes up the fantastic. "Laura" incorporates all the elements of the *Contes d'une grand-mère:* the orphan, travel, language, and metamorphosis.

Sand's stories have been ranked among those of La Fontaine, Perrault, E. T. A. Hoffmann, and Madame d'Aulnay.[3] While a taste for fantasy—the fantastic as well as the marvellous—pervades these texts, Sand's style offers less complexity than some, and less poetry than others. A certain sinister aspect, yet not so dark as in the Brothers Grimm, links Sand to Hoffmann; still, her tendency for didacticism and moralizing often overpowers the delight of the fantasy.

One pervading characteristic of these stories, a convention of the genre, is a bildungsroman development of the heroine. These stories nonetheless communicate optimism because the heroine—usually a little girl—discovers herself. Transmitting the Delphic code "Know thyself," Sand encourages her granddaughters and all readers, especially little girls, to explore their own talents and desires.

In "Le Château de Pictordu," Diane learns to draw well, better than her father, a professional portraitist; but she is troubled by her inability to draw the face of a veiled statue, which represents her mother. When she finally accomplishes this task, those around her stand in awe of the amazing likeness to her deceased mother, of whom she has never even seen a picture.

"La Reine Coax" (Queen Coax) tells the story of a woman who has become a frog; the title unflatteringly refers to her croaking. Margot meets the frog, who charms her and nearly coaxes her into a pond; but Névé, the swan, saves her. Ranaïde, the woman who became the frog, had erroneously suspected her husband, Prince Rolando, now Névé, the swan, of infidelity. To keep Rolando from discovering her lack of faith, Ranaïde transformed him into a swan and herself into a frog for two hundred years. Meanwhile, Margot's aristocratic but poor cousin realizes that Margot will inherit all the grandmother's wealth, and accordingly begins to court her. Margot is confused, especially because she does not consider herself pretty enough for marriage. The moral that one should not try to be what one is not is reinforced when Margot and her grandmother find a half-written letter from the cousin to his mother, stating that despite Margot's ugliness, he will try to talk her into marriage because one day she will be very rich.

Transformation is also the central theme of "Le Nuage rose" (The pink cloud). Catherine, a young shepherdess, hopes her great-aunt Colette, who has a reputation as a spinner of the finest thread, will pass her secret on to her. Impatient with not learning the secret right away, Catherine chases a pink cloud on the mountaintop, where she is sure the secret is hidden, for she believes her aunt spins thread from the clouds. Finally she learns that "cloud," in the local dialect, refers to anything fine and light, such as the high-quality thread Colette makes. And in Catherine's case, the pink cloud also symbolizes her whims, which must be kept in rein—only hard work and practice will make of her a talented spinner.

In "Les Ailes de courage" (Wings of courage) a boy called Clopinet because of his congenital limp learns to fly like a bird. Not able to pursue his dream of becoming a sailor like his uncle, Clopinet escapes and spends a few days listening to the voices he hears. The birds—he calls them "spirits"—tell him where to fly and how to fish and find food. He manages to get a job with the local pharmacist, who is also a taxidermist who specializes in birds. After a while, though, Clopinet feels claustrophobic and hears the call of the open air. He returns to his avian friends, taking one last flight, to his death.

The title "Le Géant Yéous" (Yéous the giant; probably Zeus, according to the narrator) refers to a rock formation that resembles a statue of a man. Miquel plots revenge on the rocky enemy that killed his father in an avalanche. He throws stones at Yéous until he knocks off the head. The statue's head reappears on its shoulders and it speaks, berating Miquel for his temper and willful destruction. Later Miquel succeeds in cleaning up all the rock and uncovers his father's tools and books; he learns to read, and cherishes these tomes. The land is now fertile and Miquel's family can return to live there in the new house he has built of stone. He has learned to admire the strength of nature, for "Whatever the circumstances, we're all stone breakers, more or less strong and patient" (*Contes,* 1:299).

In "Le Chêne parlant" (The talking oak tree) Emmi, who lives with his aunt and keeps her pigs, stays out in the forest one night. Afraid of the pigs, he climbs up an old oak tree. Despite a warning from a disembodied voice, he stays because the oak offers more security than his aunt's house. An old woman, La Catiche, happens along and urges Emmi to come with her. Though she appears suspicious, he is tempted by the promise of food and a roof. La Catiche, who learns to love and respect Emmi, bequeaths to him her large stockpile of money, begged penny by penny.

"Le Chien et la fleur sacrée" (The dog and the sacred flower) relates, in the first part, M. Lechien's former existence as a dog. This is not the only former life he can remember; he has also been a fish, an insect, a flower, and a rock. This progression, by the laws of metempsychosis, indicates progress, an advancement in species and talent. Lechien's main regret is having ignored other dogs. Perhaps his task as a human will involve improving that social failing. In the second part of the story, Sir William explains the Indian notion of the transmigration of souls. As an elephant, Sir William was called The Sacred Flower. He saved his trainer from torture at the hands of other humans, and the story ends with the promise that in the stage after human incarnation we will have wings.

The concepts of ontogeny and phylogeny are applied to rocks in "Le Marteau rouge" (The red hammer). Here Sand designs a way to induce rocks to tell their story. Through a series of transformations of form and function, the rock is shown to have "lived" an eventful existence. This never-ending story proves that matter never disappears, and thus gives the promise of progress.

"La Fée poussière" (The dirt fairy) tells a similar story, but with much more enthusiasm. The narrator recounts how the Dirt Fairy invites her to visit her subterranean world. In her laboratory, the Dirt Fairy fabricates all sorts of things from dust, with the help of her friend the fire, her servant the wind, and humidity and rain. Thus with the four elements at her disposal, she proudly modifies matter in a whirl of alchemical mystery that dazzles the girl.

"Le Gnome des huîtres" (The oyster gnome) tells of a man who loves oysters who roams the area from Paris to the Norman and Breton shores, searching for the best-tasting oysters. He meets another oyster connoisseur, a tiny man, who invites him to see his private collection of rare and ancient oysters. Sand comments on both the trivial pursuit of knowledge through classification as well as the meaningless search for the ideal.

The narrator of "L'Orgue du titan" (The titan's organ), an orphan of humble origins, finds refuge with a monk who teaches him the rudiments of music. During a long voyage through difficult terrain in Auvergne, the monk tries to scare the young boy with stories of giants who haunt the mountains. But the joke backfires when the monk's imagination, aided by a large quantity of wine, transforms a huge, flat rock into an organ. The rock formations—long, vertical indentations—look like the pipes of an organ, and in the region they carry the name "organ." The boy obeys his drunken master and "plays" the "organ." During the improvisations, a great crack of lightning and thunder jolts the couple, and they fall unconscious. Years later, whenever the narrator plays these variations, he feels his fingers growing longer with great pain.[4]

In another story, "Ce que disent les fleurs" (What flowers say), Sand gives the gift of divine language to all creatures on Earth: flowers, animals, the wind, and so on. The girl, who represents the memory of the narrator, responds to overpowering, seductive scents of flowers. The narrator assures us the olfactory sensation enjoys a close connection to divine language.

"La Fée aux gros yeux" (The fairy with the big eyes) presents a girl, Elsie, and her Irish governess, Miss Barbara, referred to as Miss Frog, or Miss Maybug, but most often as the Fairy with the Big Eyes. Though myopic, Miss Barbara can count the tiny threads of needle work with ease. She also has a deep repugnance for birds, especially bats. Elsie's brothers have a tutor called M. Bat. One night Elsie observes M. Bat appear and Miss Barbara disappear. The next day at dinner, she cannot help but notice that M. Bat relishes the bloody beef he is served, while Miss Barbara eats hardly anything.

Recurring Themes

Orphans   In over half the stories in *Contes d'une grand-mère* the hero is an orphan, or has been orphaned in some way. Diane, in "Le Château de Pictordu," has lost her mother, and her father has remarried. Diane's relationship with her stepmother resembles that of many fairy-tale characters and provides an added incentive for her to seek solace outside of the family unit. Angelin, the narrator in "L'Orgue du titan," is an orphan. The local priest and musical director of the church has taken charge of his education. Emmi ("Le Chêne parlant") has lost his parents and is being raised by his uncaring aunt. He tends the pigs and is not unaware that should he make some silly mistake, he will be relegated to sleeping with his wards. In a moment of self-pity and solitude, Emmi decides not to return to the "orphanage" that his aunt's farm represents and takes up residence in an old oak tree.

Miquel loses his father in "Le Géant Yéous." The mother is a weak character in this story. Miquel is left to deal with his grief, his sense of loss, and the completion of his adulthood: assuming responsibility and rehabilitating his respect for Nature. Catherine, in "Le Nuage rose," has no father. At Catherine's request, her mother leaves her with her great-aunt in the Alps because Catherine wants to learn the secret of spinning clouds into fine thread. The case of Margot in "La Reine Coax" and of the girl narrators in both "La Fée Poussière" and "La Fée aux gros yeux" is less defined. Their family situations are never made clear, but they have no mothers or fathers within the textual confines.

Clopinet ("Les Ailes de courage") presents a case of self-exile. He chooses not to follow his father's plans for him, a decision that symbolizes his refusal to accept his physical handicap as a reason to give up hope for independence. Replacing the sea as a symbol of freedom, the heavens fulfill the same need for openness and independence.

The danger of the lesson Clopinet learns resides in the invitation to run away from your parents when their plans do not coincide with your own. But here, as in all the situations of orphaned children, Sand emphasizes that children need to learn how to make decisions and to find the best path for decision making. Sand's goal remains that of teaching children responsibility and self-discovery, which includes the realization that they have the capacity and capability to make up their own minds. The love and charity usually associated with parenthood cannot be assumed as part of the bargain in the case of replacement parents. An orphan must learn to discern between disinterested kindness and self-serving sympathy.

Travel   We have already seen in a previous chapter the importance of travel for Sand. *Contes d'une grand-mère* exploits a similar need to explore and discover the exotic. The narrator in "Le Gnome des huîtres" travels in search of something better. Ostensibly looking for the best oysters in France, he merely wants to renew countless times the sensual experience of tasting different mollusks. He learns little from his travel and returns home having "proven" exactly the premise he had set out to prove. Sand, in an obvious inversion of the travel motif, makes light of those who travel because it is chic, not because they seek self-edification, which is the ultimate purpose of travel.

The best conditions for travel in the *Contes* stem from a child's need to distance herself from a familiar situation in order to discover herself more fully. Although travel as self-examination removed from the biased influence of parents provides an excellent opportunity for self-discovery, Sand tells us, moderation must always be exercised. While traveling to the snow-covered summits of the Alps automatically lends a more fantastic aura to Catherine's dreams, the trip to the peak where the pink cloud beckoned her could have been dangerous because Catherine might have been caught in an avalanche.

Clopinet's travels represent the most liberating getaway of the *Contes*. As fantastic as his flying abilities may seem, the reader leaves Earth with him and appreciates a rarely tasted independence and remembers the freedom of a child's innocence. The final image of the story, Clopinet flying off into the heavens, represents death. Death as travel unites ancient myths and contemporary concepts of metempsychosis.

Language   Children's discovery of language remains one of the most fascinating aspects of childhood. Sand's keen awareness of language finds an important place in her stories. Language as vocabulary enters into play in almost every story: botanical terms in "La Reine coax"; natural science vocabulary in "Le Gnome des huîtres" and in "Le Fée aux gros yeux"; geological terminology in "Le Marteau rouge"; regional expressions for geological formations in "Le Nuage rose"; ornithological nomenclature in "Les Ailes de courage"; even philosophical words and concepts in "Le Chien et la fleur sacrée." The young characters of the stories also experience the use of language with nonhuman, sometimes inanimate, and often unidentified entities. Diane talks with the veiled statue; Margot converses with a frog and a swan; Emmi speaks with the oak, and the narrator of "La Fée Poussière" talks with the dust ball. All the flowers talk in "Ce que disent les fleurs," and only a child has the innocence to comprehend.

Catherine hears a voice beckoning her to approach the mountaintop. And while the "voice" Angelin and Maître Jean hear in the mountains of Auvergne can be attributed to the quantity of regional wine they have drunk, that both of them hear the same music at the same time substantiates the existence of the sounds. A similar phenomenon occurs in "Carl" (1843), where nature seems to repeat the melody the narrator sings. Finally, Miquel hears the voice of the Giant Yéous.

Perhaps the most interesting phenomenon of language learning occurs in "Les Ailes de courage." Clopinet hears voices early on in the story, but he cannot discern their origin or meaning. He does, however, pay attention to the voices; eventually he learns to intuit significance from them and little by little he begins to comprehend. Sand has transposed the process of language learning from a human to an avian situation. Unlike second language or foreign language learning, Clopinet has had to realize that these "voices" are actually communicating ideas to him and that he must infer meaning. In contrast to learning a first language, however, Clopinet will not learn to imitate the sounds. Clopinet's learning to understand the new language parallels his newfound appreciation of his own capacities and his sense of resourcefulness. Language, in this sense, implies freedom.

For Sand, the power of language supplies an inexhaustible source of inspiration, which also leads to freedom. The girl in "Ce que disent les fleurs" learns not only to adapt to a different kind of language in order to understand the flowers, but she also learns not to assume that difference must indicate madness. Angelin, too, accepts the pain of memories and the power of music to spark memories and emotions.

Metamorphosis   Changing from a dependent child to a responsible adult is perhaps the single most difficult transition for humans. Transformation takes on complex and far-reaching symbolism in the *Contes*. Often the metamorphosis involves an inanimate object becoming a live one—for instance, the statues in "Pictordu" and "Yéous." The Pygmalion element is not lost on the reader. Rock also comes to life in "L'Orgue du titan" with music and remonstratory pain. Rock in "Le Marteau rouge" also represents life by retelling its history of changing forms. The fairy's ability to transform dust into different forms in "La Fée Poussière" also appeals to our notion of forming and transforming clay. Nor can we ignore the obvious biblical reference of "dust to dust."

The perceived changes of the cloud in "Le Nuage rose" lead Catherine to distinguish fantasy from reality. The changes in "Le Gnome des huîtres" and "Le Chien et la fleur sacrée" tell the story of natural history. Metempsychosis and the transmigration of souls in a romantic text lead naturally to socialist notions of progress. These texts demonstrate Sand's characteristic synthesis of the individual and society.

"La Reine Coax," "La Fée aux gros yeux," and "Les Ailes de courage" show the metamorphosis of beings, from one animal to another. In the first instance, a woman's jealousy results in a magical spell that turns her into a frog and her unsuspecting husband into a swan. In the second story, M. Bat's change into a bat teaches us no more than Miss Barbara's metamorphosis into a moth, except perhaps that too close an adherence to one's subject of study can prove dangerous. Clopinet's change, however, plays on the ever human desire to fly and thus to gain the freedom of the skies. Clopinet's transformation is real insomuch as he loses his limp. Clopinet's ultimate metamorphosis is, of course, death.

Conclusion

As with the *Contes d'une grand-mère,* many of George Sand's works teach a lesson by example. Critics, contemporary and modern, have called her didactic and moralizing, which is often the case. We have seen, in the case of the stories written expressly to teach her granddaughters lessons, that the message usually involves self-discovery, self-awareness, and self-esteem. Therein lies the fundamental spirit of Sand's feminism: thinking for herself and getting an education equal to that of a man. Though perhaps lacking the militant stance of a Flora Tristan, Sand's tenets represent nonetheless an important step forward for nineteenth-century French women.

Beyond the general feminist context of the majority of Sand's texts, other elements of the *Contes* recap typical aspects of the Berrichon author's writings. Orphans, of course, bring to mind *François le champi,* but examples of orphaned children or abandoned people abound in her work. Consuelo represents the orphan, trained by a caring and sympathetic adult, who goes on to fulfill her potential and to change the lives of those she touches. Emilien, in *Nanon,* is orphaned in a sense and at the same time he abandons his family to adopt the republican ideals he has learned to respect. The solitary figure, one who is either forced to face life alone or who has chosen to grapple with some intimate problem by himself, represents for Sand someone who becomes strong as a result of finding a source of power and perseverance within himself. This is the nature of the Sandian hero.

Finding the force to continue in life often takes the form of travel in Sand's novels. Consuelo's travels take her through exciting and dangerous adventures, all of which contribute to her character, but not without testing her limits and her principles. The travels described in *Le Compagnon du tour de France* give a highly idealized version of instructive travel. The guild system, though barely operative in the 1840s as Sand described it, provided just the symbol to combine autodidacticism, socialism, and the link between individual and social growth. Adriani's travels also managed to remove him from the routine of the professional world at the Opéra and to refresh his outlook on life. Even a trip intended solely for scholarly instruction, such as that in *Valvèdre,* ends up providing much more important personal development for Francis and Alida.

Language, poetry, literature, or art in general often holds center stage in Sand's novels. She offers aphorisms as well as involved discussions on the function and purpose of art in society. The Saint-Simonian influence is evident, though well tempered by Sand's more individualistic approach. Sand's masterpiece, *Consuelo,* once again stands out as a perfect example. The comments on the responsibility a musician owes his public apply to all artists and indicate the development of the conscientiousness that will characterize modern artists, what Sartre later called "engagé." From Geneviève's dedication to the perfectly realistic representation of flowers in *André* to the Maestro's devotion to beauty in opera in *Le Démon au foyer,* from Célio's attention to technical detail in *Le Château des Désertes* to Adriani's faithful portrayal of real emotions, the artist in Sand's world suffers first from the attempt to create beauty and second from the desire to share that beauty with the public.

More than almost any other author of her time, with the notable exception of Nerval, Sand uses dreams to divulge information about her characters. Dreams or a dream state add mystery to such varied works as *Lélia, Spiridion, Le Meunier d'Angibault, La Filleule, La Daniella,* not to mention several of the *Contes d'une grand-mère.* Some of the dreams are mere devices to advance the plot, but many reveal untapped desires the characters have hidden from themselves and thus provide an opportunity for personal growth.

Sand was aware of her penchant for idealization. She happily admitted to Balzac that while he portrayed men as they were, she painted them as they ought to be. There can be no denial that George Sand's style added fresh pages to the history of French literature. In almost every work, she wrote passages of startling poetic value. If her character portraits tend toward the flat or perfect type, her portrayal of emotions always ring true. The wealth of Sand's oeuvre remains to be exploited. More than a "trade" or a "job to put bread on the table," writing represents George Sand's freedom.[5] This is perhaps her most valuable legacy.

Notes and References

Chapter One

1. *Correspondance,* ed. Georges Lubin (Paris: Garnier), 1:262–92; hereafter referred to in the text as *Corres.*

2. This document has not been recovered. George Sand does not mention it in any correspondence or in her memoirs. Most biographers of Sand, including M. Georges Lubin, believe such a letter existed judging from Sand's allusions to Casimir's maliciousness. It also best explains the sudden financial arrangement and Aurore's subsequent departure for Paris.

3. *Oeuvres auobiographiques,* 2 vols., ed. Georges Lubin (Paris: Gallimard, 1971), 2:135; hereafter referred to in the text as *OA.*

4. *Le Dernier des Beaumanoir,* a tale incorporating the idea of necrophilia. It includes the story of a priest who raped a woman, thinking she was already dead. Sand read the book and found it vile, although she admitted it was what seemed to be selling. See Sand's letter to Boucoiran in *Corres.,* 1:826.

5. *OA,* 2:150. As M. Georges Lubin points out in his note, this was not Sand's first visit to Kératry, and she no doubt collapsed her reactions to the older man into one, bilious confrontation.

6. Maurois avoids classifying the relationship. His quotations from the letters show his desire to believe that theirs was a lesbian affair. The tenor of his biography, however, communicates a value judgment that casts a so-called perversion on all of Sand's personal life. Cate simply cites Arsène Houssaye's description of the relationship between Sappho and Phaon-Erinna. Although he says this was only embroidered gossip, he offers no other explanation without denying the possibility of this one. Joseph Barry declares, in his characteristic style, that there is no doubt that Sand and Dorval were involved in a lesbian affair.

7. It is interesting to note that George Sand does not write of the Mérimée incident in her memoirs. The few letters to Marie Dorval and Sainte-Beuve constitute her only written witness to this bungled affair. Mérimée's correspondence gives a few more indications. The standard version of this story comes from a brief pamphlet, published in 1934 by Maurice Parturier, *Une expérience de Lélia, ou le fiasco du comte Gazul.* See also Mérimée's short story, "La Double méprise," for a fictionalized version of the incident.

8. *Europe littéraire,* 9–22 August 1833. This vicious reaction would result in a duel fought between de Feuillade and Gustave Planche. No one was hurt, and Musset wrote a satirical poem about the whole affair.

9. In Florence, Musset drank in local color to set his play *Lorenzaccio,* for which Sand had given him her notes. Once again, her frustration at his lack of disci-

pline and his exasperation at her seemingly endless source of energy to write evinced a fundamental obstacle to their relationship.

10. "Une mauvaise maladie." See M. Lubin's notes in *Corres.*, 2:730–31 and 3:812–13.

11. *"Il n'y a que la dissertation de madame de Staël qui soit vraiment ce qu'elle veut être, un écrit correct, logique, commun quant aux pensées, beau quant au style, et savant quant à l'arrangement. —Je n'ai trouvé d'autre soulagement dans cet écrit que le plaisir d'apprendre que madame de Staël aimait la vie, qu'elle avait mille raisons d'y tenir, qu'elle avait un sort infiniment plus heureux que le mien, une tête infiniment plus forte et plus intelligente que la mienne. Je crois, du reste, que son livre a redoublé pour moi l'attrait du suicide"* (Mme de Staël's essay alone is what it purports to be: a piece of writing that is proper and logical, with commonly held ideas, beautiful style, and intelligent presentation. I found no other palliative in this text than the pleasure of learning that Mme de Staël loved life, that she had a thousand reasons to hold on to it, that she was infinitely more fortunate and more intelligent than I. Moreover, I believe that her book has increased my attraction to suicide) (*Lettres d'un voyageur,* "Lettre IV," *OA,* 2:752).

12. Curtis Cate, in his excellent biography *George Sand,* points out that from a literary point of view the Musset-Italy episode brought little to George Sand's career. On the other hand, Musset managed to reap a large benefit: *Lorenzaccio, On ne badine pas avec l'amour, La Confession d'un enfant du siècle,* and, of course, some of the material and images found in *La Nuit de mai* and *La Nuit d'octobre.* (New York: Avon, 1975), 348–49.

13. Although there were most likely other factors that contributed to Sand's abandoning her novel "Engelwald," the most pertinent reason was the Corsican Fieschi's attempt on Louis-Philippe's life in July 1835. The story of "Engelwald" also deals explicitly with an assassination plot on the life of Napoleon. Already George Sand's activities with her Berrichon friends had been watched; now her relationship with Michel de Bourges put her under further suspicion. She set the novel aside to protect herself and Buloz. Although she continued to work on the novel intermittently, she kept delaying delivering it to Buloz because it would certainly cause her problems with the tribunal during the trial with Casimir. She eventually destroyed the manuscript in 1864.

14. Charles Didier (1805–64), born in Geneva, went to Paris in 1830. He was the author of *Rome souterraine* (1833) and several other novels and articles that never won him literary fame. He was poor as a result of an unfortunate financial deal, went blind, and ended his own life at the age of fifty-eight.

15. It is interesting to note how this public trial would be fictionalized by Sand in her novel *Mauprat* (1837).

16. Liszt took his inspiration from the Spanish folk tune, "El Contrabandista," written by Manuel Garcia, la Malibran's father. "Le Contrebandier" was first published in the January 1837 issue of *La Revue et gazette musicale de Paris.* See chapter

1 of my doctoral thesis, "The Modes of Music in the Works of George Sand," Ph.D., University of Pennsylvania, 1985. *DAI* 85:15439.

17. When George Sand went to visit Liszt and Marie d'Agoult in Geneva, she discovered they had gone to Chamonix and had left word for Sand to join them there. When she arrived at the hotel in Chamonix, she discovered Liszt and Marie had registered under the name 'Fellows,' no doubt to poke fun at the police registry. In like manner, George Sand registered herself and her children as the family "Piffoël," from the slang "pif" (nose), to make fun of her large nose. These nicknames stuck, and the two friends often used them in correspondence. For passages pertinent to Michel de Bourges, see *Entretiens journaliers*, 3 June 1837, *OA*, 2:982.

18. Joseph Barry, *Infamous Women: The Life of George Sand*, (Garden City, N.Y.: Doubleday, 1977), 233; see also Marie d'Agoult, *Mémoires* (Paris: Daniel Ollivier, 1927), 97.

19. For appearances of George Sand in other Balzac novels, consult also *Les Illusions perdues* for a version of her relationship with Sandeau, and *La Muse du département* for her role as a provincial litterateur. Balzac also wrote much of his impressions of George Sand to his mistress and future wife, Mme Hanska. Also consult Janis Glasgow, *Une Esthétique de comparaison: Balzac et George Sand: "La Femme abandonnée" et "Metella"* (Paris: Nizet, 1978), and her forthcoming article, "George Sand's Multiple Appearances in Balzac's *La Muse du département*," in *Acts of the Seventh International George Sand Conference*, Hofstra University, October 1986 (Westport, Conn.: Greenwood Press, forthcoming).

20. See William G. Atwood's *The Lioness and the Little One: The Liaison of George Sand and Frederic Chopin* (New York: Columbia University Press, 1980).

21. Sand had set aside *Spiridion* to write the musical, philosophical, dramatic dialogue *Les Sept Cordes de la lyre*.

22. See Thérèse Marix-Spire, *Les Romantiques et la musique. Le Cas George Sand 1804–1838* (Paris: Nouvelles Editions Latines, 1954), 620–21.

23. Cf. *Une Correspondance romantique: Madame d'Agoult, Liszt, Henri Lehmann* (Paris, 1947), 140–42, 165–68. On Marie d'Agoult and the Vicomtesse de Chailly, see Wladimir Karénine, *George Sand* (Paris: Ollendorff, 1899–1926), 2:278–85.

24. Sand's love and devotion to Pauline Garcia seems to eclipse her feelings for Marie Dorval. To her *Entretiens journaliers*, 18 February 1841, she confides: *"C'est la seule femme depuis dix ans que j'aie aimée aussi tendrement. C'est la seule femme depuis Alicia la religieuse que j'aie aimée avec un enthousiasme sans mélange, et je crois bien que dans toute ma vie, elle sera la seule que je puisse et doive chérir et admirer avec raison, avec certitude"* (She's the only woman that I've loved so tenderly for ten years. She's the only woman that I've loved with unmitigated enthusiasm since Sister Alicia, and I do believe that, in my whole life, she will be the only one whom I can and ought to hold dear and admire surely and certainly) (*OA*, 2:1014).

25. The baby, Jeanne-Gabrielle, would die a week later.

26. This sequel to *Lucrezia Floriani* would eventually appear under the title *Le Château des Désertes* (The Castle of Les Désertes) in 1851.

27. See *Corres.*, 8:470ff.

28. See the chapter of Joseph Barry's biography of George Sand called "Muse of the Revolution," 281–97.

29. An actual theater had been built within the château at Nohant, and during the years Chopin lived there Sand and her guests amused themselves improvising in the style of the commedia del l'arte. See chapter 7.

30. *Corres.*, 10:659–64: "I am not Mme de Staël." She was, of course, referring to the enmity felt by Napoléon I toward Mme de Staël, whom he exiled from Imperial France.

31. Cited by Barry in *Infamous Woman*, 326.

32. Taine and Henry James are just two favorable critics. Maurois, on the other hand, says that the novels of this period were not very good because they remained novels "with a purpose." He says that Valvèdre is nothing but a creature of reason, the hero of a "socially conscious" novel from which the irrationality of life is wholly absent (André Maurois, *Lélia, the Life of George Sand*, trans. Gerard Hopkins (New York: Harper & Bros., 1953), 418.

33. Karénine, *George Sand*, 4:413.

34. Curtis Cate points out that among the destroyed manuscripts was a document written in Geneva during the visit with Liszt and Marie d'Agoult in 1836, called *Les Petits Piffoël* (*George Sand*, 678). This document certainly would have given us more information on Sand's attitudes and activities at that time.

35. *Nanon, Ma Soeur Jeanne* (My Sister Jeanne), *Flamarande, Les Deux frères* (The two brothers), *Marianne Chevreuse, La Tour de Percemont* (The tower at Percemont) as well as several articles published in *Le Temps*. She left an unfinished manuscript, *Albine Fiori*.

Chapter Two

1. *"Je composais à haute voix d'interminables contes que ma mère appelait mes romans.... Elle les déclarait ennuyeuses à cause de leur longueur et du développement que je donnais aux digressions. C'est un défaut que j'ai bien conservé, à ce qu'on dit"* (*OA*, 1:541–42).

2. Cf. Philippe Berthier, "Corambé: interprétaion d'un mythe," *George Sand*, ed. Simone Vierne (Paris: CDU-SEDES, 1983), 7–20.

3. *Voyage en Espagne*, in *OA*, 2:467–74. See also *Histoire de ma vie, OA*, 1:555ff.

4. For the story of the cricket and some sketchy commentary on *La Marraine*, see *OA*, 2:100–101.

5. M. Lubin makes reference to this other version in *Corres.*, 1:562n. "Histoire du rêveur" was published as part of the volume with "Jehan Cauvin" (Paris: Montaigne, 1931) and reprinted with an introduction by Thierry Bodin in *Présence de George Sand*, no. 17 (June 1983):4–39.

6. She asked Félix Pyat, a friend of Jules Sandeau, to help her with the ending

(*Corres.*, 1:761–63). In a letter to Jules Boucoiran (*Corres.*, 1:817–20), Aurore says she was told the novel was too morally upright for the public to believe. She says that Henri Delatouche, whose advice and help she requested, had found it detestable but that she ought to be able to do better with some experience in life (*OA*, 2:151).

7. *La Mode,* May 1831.

8. Karénine, *George Sand,* 1:337.

9. For further discussion of this topic, see Karénine, *George Sand,* 1:335–37; Tatiana Greene, "De J. Sand à George Sand: *Rose et Blanche* de Sand et Sandeau et leur descendance," *Nineteenth-Century French Studies* 4, no. 3 (Spring 1976):171. Thérèse Marix-Spire (*Les Romantiques*) also points out the many resonances of Rose's character in later novels; see in particular pp. 144, 166–67, 235–36, 242–43.

10. Karénine, *George Sand,* 1:338–39.

11. Aurore had already written a short piece by herself, between "La Prima donna" and "La Fille d'Albano," after discovering the cathedral at Bourges. The tale, "Jehan Cauvin," takes place on the feast of the Sacred Innocents in 1529 and describes the unlikely visit of Calvin to Bourges. There is an indecent spectacle in the cathedral with much music, which did not lack beauty, especially due to the ingenious coupling of beautiful children's voices with the organ. Calvin, says Aurore, was scandalized by the cacophony. Thérèse Marix-Spire cites this story as an indication of Aurore's increasing powers of observation, especially in the realm of sound imagery (*Les Romantiques,* 239–44). Sand mentioned "Jehan Cauvin" to Emile Régnault in several letters, telling him she was sending the "article" off to Jules Sandeau (*Corres.*, 1:849–52) and telling him that her "*oeuvres légères sur les cathédrales*" could put him to sleep on nights when he suffered from insomnia (*Corres.*, 1:901–902). Jean Gaulmier also points out that a short passage in one letter to Régnault (*Corres.*, 1:834–38, esp. 837) appears almost exactly in the story. See the published volume edited by Gaulmier, *Histoire d'un rêveur suivie de Jehan Cauvin* (Paris: Montaigne, 1931), 135–36; also cited in Lubin, *Corres.*, 1:837 n. 1.

12. The author's full pseudonym appeared with the publication of her second novel. Whereas the Christian name was first printed with the traditional French spelling, Sand dropped the "s" perhaps for the feminine resonance afforded by the mute-"e" ending, or perhaps to give an Anglicized spelling to accompany the English-sounding surname.

13. Cf. the insightful article by Lucy McCallum Schwartz, "Tradition and Innovation in Women's Literature," in *George Sand: Collected Essays,* ed. J. Glasgow (Troy, N.Y.: Whitston Publishing, 1985), 220–26.

14. For a discussion of the father figure as object of the heroine's love in George Sand, see Kathryn J. Crecelius, *Family Romances: George Sand's Early Novels* (Bloomington: Indiana University Press, 1987); chapter 3, in particular, deals with *Indiana.*

15. Karénine, *George Sand,* 1:370. Pierre Salomon, in his edition of *Indiana* (Paris: Garnier, 1962), suggests that the second volume was too short and that G.

Sand was encouraged to add an ending that would be more commercially viable (v–vi). Arlette Béteille ("Où finit *Indiana?* Problématique d'un dénouement," in *George Sand: Nouvelles recherches,* ed. Françoise van Rossum-Guyon [Amsterdam: CRIN, 1983], 62–73) gives a convincing analysis in favor of the closure argument.

16. See discussion in Barry, *Infamous Woman,* 141–43 and Cate, *George Sand,* 199–201. Cf. also the exhaustive study Françoise van Rossum-Guyon has done on the reception of *Indiana,* "Les Enjeux d'*Indiana* I, métadiscours et réception critique," published in a collection of essays of which she is the editor, *George Sand: Recherches nouvelles* (Amsterdam: CRIN, 1983), 1–35, esp. 19ff.

17. "Pauline" appeared in the *Revue des Deux Mondes* on 15 December 1839 and 1 January 1840. It is included, with an introduction by Alex Szogyi, in the collection of short stories edited by Eve Sourian, *George Sand: Nouvelles* (Paris: Des femmes, 1986).

18. "La Marquise," introduced by Isabelle Naginski, *George Sand: Nouvelles,* 74. It is interesting to note that Sand sent a copy of this story to Marie Dorval. The links between the Marquise's adoration for Lélio the actor and Sand's for Dorval have served as proof of the actual nature of the author's relationship with the actress, and the similarity is indeed striking. For more discussion on this topic, see Barry, *Infamous Woman,* 151–59; also Pierre Reboul, *Lélia* (1960; reprint, Paris: Garnier, 1985), xli–xlii.

19. This aspect of illusion and the theater was already a potential element of "Pauline"; Sand would bring this problem out when she took up this manuscript again later.

20. Karénine, *George Sand,* 1:447–48.

21. For more insight into the erotic nature of these texts, consult the thoughtful article by Nancy Rogers, "Psychosexual Identity and Erotic Imagination in the Early Novels of George Sand," *Studies in the Literary Imagination* 12, no. 2 (1979):19–35.

22. See Cate, *George Sand,* 217.

23. Sand ended up selling the book to Dupuy to spite Buloz's initial reaction to it, although she earned about a third as much as Buloz would have paid her.

24. K. Crecelius states that Lélia is the first woman to suffer from this romantic ailment in France, *Family Romances,* 98.

25. These notes are to be found in an appendix to Planche's *Correspondance,* 2 vols., ed. Maurice Regard (Paris: 1955); they can also be found in Reboul's introduction to *Lélia,* xxvii. Also see Sand's notebook, *Sketches and Hints,* in *OA,* 2:614–16.

26. See Corrie Kruikemeier, "Fêtes et cérémonies: la structure mythique de *Lélia,*" in *George Sand: Recherches nouvelles,* ed. Françoise van Rossum-Guyon (Amsterdam: CRIN, 1983), 74–92.

27. Reboul, *Lélia,* lviii, and Cate, *George Sand,* 229.

28. Crecelius, *Family Romances,* 102.

29. See Mireille Bossis's intelligent argument, "La Femme Prêtresse dans les romans de George Sand," in *George Sand: Collected Essays,* 250–70.

30. Reboul, *Lélia*, 1x; Crecelius, *Family Romances*, 98; Maurois, *Lélia*, 147.

31. See I. Naginski's criticism of Reboul's commentary in her introduction to "La Marquise" in *George Sand: Nouvelles*, 43. Also, consult the insightful article by Béatrice Didier, "Le Corps féminin dans *Lélia*," *Revue d'histoire littéraire de France* 76, no. 4 (1976): 634–43.

32. The essay "Obermann," which appeared in the May 1833 issue of the *Revue des Deux Mondes*, broached several such topics. This essay was reprinted in the collection *Questions d'art et de littérature* (Paris: Calmann-Levy, 1878). See also Isabelle Naginski's fine article, "The Literary Relationship of Sand and Dostoevsky," in *George Sand: Collected Essays*, 110–25.

33. Crecelius, *Family Romances*, 113. She was also hurt by the treatment her son, Maurice, received from classmates, doubtless transferred from their parents' judgments; see *OA*, 2:177.

34. Letter to Christine Buloz in May 1836, *Corres.*, 3:362; also letter to Buloz in June 1837, *Corres.*, 4:120–22.

35. See P. Reboul, "D'une Lélia à l'autre," in *Lélia*, esp. 337–41.

36. This formula is found several times in the novel, in the mouths of various characters. It also appears in the converse, or affirmative form, although slightly less often.

37. See Karénine, *George Sand*, 2:83.

38. Sand contracted with Buloz for *Jacques* only seven weeks after "Metella" appeared in the *Revue des Deux Mondes*, that is, three days before leaving with Musset for Italy.

39. Karénine discusses at length the superiority of these women, *George Sand*, 2:413–27.

40. While I recognize that comparing the conditions of inheritance and property in *Mauprat* to those of the Napoleonic Code is anachronistic because the novel takes place wholly before the Revolution, Sand's own civil circumstances at the time of the novel's creation cannot be ignored, especially in the important matter of property rights.

41. Sand rewrote *Mauprat* for the stage; it was performed at the Odéon Theater in November 1853. While the general reception at the revival of a romantic piece was good, critical review was less favorable. See Gay Manifold, *George Sand's Theatre Career* (Ann Arbor, Mich.: UMI Research Press, 1985), and chapter 7 of this book.

Chapter Three

1. "*En un mot, je voulais faire le propre roman de ma vie et n'en être pas le personnage réel, mais le personnage pensant et analysant*" (In a word, I wanted to write the real story of my life and not be the actual character, but the thinking and analyzing character) (*OA*, 2:298–302, esp. 299).

2. See Cate, *George Sand*, 310–15.

3. *Nouveaux lundis*, 12:122–23, cited in Lubin, *OA*, 2:640.

4. Sand confessed to Sainte-Beuve that she preferred the fantastic to the real-

istic (*Corres.*, 2:444). Also see p. 434, where Sand tells Sainte-Beuve that she is afraid her story is but a pastiche of E. T. A. Hoffmann, which she also mentions in the preface to the story in an ulterior edition.

5. Sand started, or at the very least conceived, the story while still in Venice (*OA*, 2:208).

6. Annarosa Poli asserts that Sand does give an excellent portrait of the cosmopolitan population of Venice in the eighteenth century, *L'Italie dans la vie et dans l'oeuvre de George Sand* (Paris: Colin, 1960), 157.

7. Sand did not like *L'Uscoque* and resented its being preferred to *Spiridion*; letter to Buloz, *Corres.*, 4:613.

8. Poli finds that *Leoni* is closely inspired by Casanova's *Memoirs* (*L'Italie*, 64, 155).

9. Crecelius compares the Sand and Prévost novels from a Freudian and a feminist point of view (*Family Romances,* chapter 6). She comments on the use of the talking cure and the ironic twist at the end of *Leoni,* which breaks the narrative expectations set up by the original *Manon.*

10. Annarosa Poli points out in her extensive annotated bibliography, *George Sand vue par les Italiens (essai de bibliocritique)* (Paris: Didier, 1965), that, while the Italians generally received many of Sand's works well, especially *André, Les Maîtres sonneurs, Mauprat,* and even the metaphysical works *Spiridion* and *Les Sept Cordes de la lyre,* they were shocked that Sand would use the tradition of the dishonest Italian so familiar in the texts of Balzac and Eugène Sue (47). She also cites Gaetano Barbieri, who regrets that Sand made Leone in the tradition of the dishonest Italian cheater (20).

11. Karénine, *George Sand,* 2:158.

12. Poli, *L'Italie,* 124, 189.

13. *La Daniella,* ed. Simone Balayé (Paris: Ressources/Slatkine, 1979) part 1, 1; hereafter referred to in the text.

14. *La Daniella,* 1:117. Poli points out that the very detailed travelogue was mostly Manceau's idea and execution (*L'Italie,* 280).

15. Poli insists that the novel only holds together because of the anticlerical agenda, yet she also says that the love story would be simply boring if not for the well-drawn minor characters (*L'Italie,* 309–316). The anticlerical theme surely shocked contemporary readers, but I believe their reaction has exaggerated the importance of this theme in the novel.

16. Poli, *L'Italie,* 113. Travel is an important element of *Consuelo*. For an important discussion of this topic, see René Bourgeois, "Le Voyage heureux: Feinte et Naturel," in *La Porpora: Entretiens sur Consuelo,* ed. Léon Cellier (Grenoble: Presses Universitaires de Grenoble, 1976), 69–75.

17. See Poli, *L'Italie,* 153.

18. Poli states that the idea for *Jacques* surely came to Sand after Musset's departure, as the situation in the novel recalls that of the Venetian trio. She quotes from Pagello's *Da Parigi a Genova*: "*Ella scrivera il suo romanzo intitulato Jacques, dove mi*

finse protagonista esagerando il mio carattere morale" (She'll write her novel entitled *Jacques*, where she made me the main character, exaggerating my moral makeup) (Poli, *L'Italie*, 150, n. 6).

19. See Poli, *George Sand*, 47, 49.

20. Karénine, *George Sand*, 3:510 and 637.

21. See the focused article by Marie-Paule Rambeau, "*Cadio* ou les leçons de l'histoire," in a special issue of *La Bulletin des Amis de George Sand*, "George Sand et la Révolution Française," new series, no. 9 (1988):32–37.

Chapter Four

1. I discount, in this discussion of Balzac's rustic elements, *Les Chouans* (1829), which is more clearly a historical novel whose rural resonances have a complex military and social import. The social aspects of this novel stem more from the characters' historically politico-religious allegiance than from their condition as "provincials."

2. Zellweger gives a convincing argument to deny Balzac's influence on Sand in the development of the rustic genre: the manuscripts of *Jeanne* and *La Mare au diable* were completed when *Les Paysans* appeared. See Rudolf Zellweger, *Les Débuts du roman rustique: Suisse-Allemagne-France, 1836–1856* (Paris: Droz, 1941), 119.

3. Because Sand's use of the term "rustic novels" is somewhat vague, I have adopted a more precise one that also permits me to include a few other novels under this heading. I base my definition of the rustic novel largely on Zellweger's, to wit: "*nous englobons dans ce travail, sous le nom de romans rustiques, la totalité des romans, nouvelles, idylles, histoires, récits et contes en prose qui ont comme théâtre la campagne et comme principaux acteurs les paysans. Seront ainsi écartés les récits de petite ville, les histoires de pêcheurs et le conte alpestre, de même que ceux qui font la navette entre la chaumière et le château ou le village et la ville. Par contre, nous n'excluons pas les livres dans lesquels la peinture fidèle des habitants de la campagne n'est point la préoccupation principale, mais où elle sert surtout de prétexte à des démonstrations morales ou autres. L'écrit pédagogique est en effet une des formes les plus caractéristiques du roman rustique à sa première époque*" (We include in this study under the name of rustic novels all novels, novellas, idylls, stories, accounts, and short stories in prose that have the countryside as their theater and country folk as the main actors. We shall therefore leave aside small town accounts, fisherman stories, and the mountain short story, as well as those that shift back and forth between castle and cottage or town and country. On the other hand, we shall not exclude books in which the faithful portrait of country residents is not at all the main issue, but wherein it functions especially as a pretext for displaying morals or other matters. Pedagogical writing is, in fact, one of the most typical forms of the rustic novel at its beginnings) (*Roman rustique*, 2). Paul Vernois, in his follow-up work *Le Roman rustique de George Sand à Ramuz: ses tendances et son évolution (1860–1925)* (Paris: Nizet, 1962), adds that those who had traditionally denigrated the rustic novel confuse it with the regional or

regionalist novel, which has the tendency to paint the quaintness of provincial life without devoting any space to the value of country manners and traditions: "*Le roman rustique confronte l'homme à la Terre et non à la Province. Vouloir l'enfermer dans la géographie et le réduire au folklore c'est, proprement, le déshumaniser et le trahir*" (The rustic novel pits man against Earth and not against the provinces. Relegating it to geography and reducing it to folklore is nothing more than dehumanizing and betraying it) (14–17).

4. *Jeanne*, ed. Simone Vierne (Meylan, France: les Editions de l'Aurore, 1986), 28.

5. *La Mare au diable*, ed. Pierre Reboul (Paris: Garnier/Flammarion, 1964), 23.

6. Zellweger points out that Sand seems to be the only creator of this genre not to realize the originality of her approach (*Roman rustique*, 127).

7. One will notice the similarity with the situation of Brulette, in *Les Maîtres sonneurs*, where she must decide among three suitors. The song "Les Trois Fendeux," which Sand rewrites to fit her context, demonstrates a genial use of folklore—specifically folk music, which is of primordial importance to the plot and structure of this novel—to enhance the plot and characterizations.

8. *La Mare au diable*, ed. Pierre Reboul, 16–17. Zellweger states that Sand "sins against verisimilitude less in the rustic novels than in any others"; yet he goes on to specify that it is the heart and soul of her "paysans" that she paints carefully and not so much their exterior traits. Her depictions, he says, are correct in the detail but idealistic on the whole (*Roman rustique*, 132–33).

9. André Fermigier questions whether this is really Berry or Berrichon, but, in the end, does it matter? See his introduction to *François le Champi* (Paris: Gallimard/Folio, 1976), 32.

10. The "pierres jaumâtres," or "jomâtres," are strange rock formations, reputed to date from prehistoric times. The regional legends attribute mystical powers of druidic origin to them and the promise of a hidden treasure amidst them.

11. The criticism for *Fadette* comes from Durand, quoted in Marie-Louise Vincent, *Le Berry dans l'oeuvre de George Sand*, vol. 2 of *George Sand et le Berry* (Paris: Champion, 1919; reprint, Geneva: Slatkine Reprints, 1978), 86. Vincent reassures us of the authenticity of the other novels, 88–90.

12. Sand, maintains Zellweger, is able to separate dramatic effect from the purely folkloric (*Roman rustique*, 132).

13. Jean Gaulmier, in his insightful article "Un exemple d'utilisation immédiate du folklore: genèse et structure des *Maîtres sonneurs*" (*Actes du VIᵉ Congrès national de littérature comparée*, 1964), 143–50, states that in *La Mare au diable* "*le folklore n'intervient que de manière adventice, pour ainsi dire documentaire, dans une sorte d'appendice extérieur au récit*" (folklore intervenes only in an incidental way, like a documentary so to speak, in a sort of appendix outside of the story) (149), whereas *Les Maîtres sonneurs* represents "le folklore vivant" (living folklore) (150).

14. Vincent, *George Sand et le Berry*, 2:218. Sand also discusses regional superstitions in *OA*, 1:835–38.

15. *Moeurs et coutumes du Berry* appeared as two articles, both in *Illustration*: 28 August 1851 and 14 August 1852. *Les Visions de la nuit dans les campagnes* was published in the same journal in the four installments between December 1851 and February 1855. The collection *Promenades autour d'un village* (1866) also contains the story of discovering *Les Tapisseries du Château de Boussac* (otherwise known as the Unicorn Tapistries), *les Bords de la Creuse*, and *Gargilesse*. The second half of the thick volume carries reprints of *Les Sept Cordes de la lyre*, *Lettres à Marcie*, *Carl*, *Le Dieu inconnu*, *La Fille d'Albano*, *Cléopâtre*, *Fragment d'une lettre de Fontainebleau*, and *Coup d'oeil général sur Paris*. A recent edition of *Promenades autour d'un village*, *suivies du Journal de Gargilesse* (Saint-Cyr-sur-Loire, France: Christian Pirot, 1984), contains drawings by George Sand, Maurice Sand, Jules Veron, Eugène Grandsire, and Christiane Sand.

16. *Promenades autour d'un village* (1866), 160–62.

17. *La Petite Fadette* (Paris: Gründ, n.d.), 80–81.

18. *Fadette*, 231.

19. Sand is known to have used Jaubert's lexicon of Berrichon dialect and vocabulary. See Monique Parent's work in *Hommage à George Sand* (Strasburg: Publication de la Faculté des Lettres, 1954). Zellweger points out that Sand seems to have approached the problem of language with a better thought out system than any of the major rustic authors (*Roman rustique*, 316–17). Vernois upholds Sand's progress in her honest attempts to relay Berrichon language to Parisian readers, always looking for the ideal style (*Roman rustique*, 35).

20. Sand does succumb to a banal representation of dialects ten years later in *L'Homme de neige*, a long, bizarre tale of an Italian who travels through Europe and learns many languages, including a provincial dialect of Swedish. The narrator intersperses terms that supposedly have no translation and that must then be explained in French. The result is far from satisfactory, which fits, all in all, with most other aspects of the bizarre text.

21. For this and other points of comparison between Sand and Emily Brontë, see Patricia Thomson's chapter "*Wuthering Heights* and *Mauprat*" in her *George Sand and the Victorians* (New York: Columbia University Press, 1977), 80–89.

22. Zellweger, *Roman rustique*, 316.

23. *Les Maîtres sonneurs*, ed. Marie-Claire Bancquart (Paris: Gallimard/Folio, 1979), 57. Sand tells us about her evenings listening to stories told by Berrichon farmers (*OA*, 1:836–37).

24. See further discussion in Nicole Mozet's introduction to *Nanon* (Meylan, France: Editions de l'Aurore, 1987), 22–24.

25. See Gay Manifold's *George Sand's Theatre Career* (Ann Arbor, Mich.: UMI Research Press, 1985), 63–64.

26. See ibid., 45.

27. Such is, according to Brigitte Lane, "*la fonction initiatique (sinon*

révolutionnaire) du roman champêtre sandien" (the initiatory [if not revolutionary] function of the Sandian country novel), from her thoughtful article "Voyage et initiation dans *La Mare au Diable*," *Etudes françaises* 24, no. 1 (Spring 1988): 71–83.

Chapter Five

1. Sand transformed the novel into a stage play in 1854 under the title *Flaminio*.

2. In his introduction to *Le Compagnon du tour de France* M. Lubin says that no matter what critics say, this is not a utopian novel (Tour-de-la-Var, France: Editions d'Aujourd'hui, 1976), i.

3. See Jean-Pierre Lacassagne, *Histoire d'une amitié: Pierre Leroux et George Sand, d'après une correspondance inédite 1836–1866* (Paris: Klincksieck, 1973), 8, 13. See also the excellent notes established by Thierry Bodin in the Aurore edition of *Horace* (Meylan, France: Editions de l'Aurore, 1982).

4. See Léon Cellier's introduction to *Consuelo* (Paris: Garnier, 1959) for a detailed discussion of socialist theories in the text.

5. *Le Meunier d'Angibault* (Verviers, Belgium: Nouvelles Editions Marabout, 1977), 191.

6. Ibid., 230, 232.

7. *Le Péché de Monsieur Antoine*, 2 vols., ed. Georges Lubin (Plan de la Tour, France: Editions d'Aujourd'hui, 1976), 2:167.

8. In *Oeuvres de George Sand* (Paris: Hetzel, Lévy, 1852–55 and 1856–57).

9. *Questions politiques et sociales*, 228. Jean Larnac thinks it was a tactical error on Sand's part to use the word "communist"; it was even naïve, according to him, to write to the aristocracy at all (*George Sand Révolutionnaire*, 102–112). The prologue presented at the Théâtre Français on 9 April 1848, "Le Roi attend" (reprinted in *La Cause du peuple*, no. 2), also uses the term "communism."

10. "Socialisme," also in *Questions politiques et sociales*, first published in *La Cause du peuple*. Other political writings of this period that might interest readers are the twenty-five issues of *La Bulletin de la République* Sand penned between March and May 1848; "La Question sociale," *La Vraie République*, 4 May 1848; a letter to Karl Marx, printed in German in issue 64 (3 August 1848) of the *Neue Rheinische Zeitung*; and the article "A propos de l'élection de Louis-Bonaparte à la Présidence de la République," in *La Réforme*, 22 December 1848. See also Georges Lubin's enlightening article, "L'Evolution des idées politiques de George Sand jusqu'en 1848," *Revue des travaux de l'Académie des sciences morales et politiques*, 123 (1970), 61–76.

11. Larnac points out the ambiguity in Sand's term "*peuple*," as it sometimes refers to the proletariat, but it often seems to designate the entire electoral body (*George Sand*, 133).

12. Cf. Philippe Berthier, "Corambé: Interprétation d'un mythe," *George Sand*, Cerisy-la-Salle Conference, 1981, ed. Simone Vierne (Paris: CDU/SEDES, 1983), 7–20.

13. *OA*, 1:954. The whole story of the conversion extends from p. 946 to p. 956.

14. *OA*, 2:721–24; see also Sand's "Lettre à M. Lerminier sur son examen critique du Livre du Peuple" and "Sur la dernière publication de M. F. Lammenais," both reprinted in *Mélanges* (Paris: Perrotin, 1842–44).

15. See the excellent chapter on *Lélia* in Marc Moret's book, *Le Sentiment religieux chez George Sand* (Paris: Marcel Vigné, 1936), chapter 3.

16. Sand draws the analogy elsewhere between a person's tolerance for alcohol and religious devotion; it is not the quality of the wine but the individual's organism that makes the difference. Similarly, the fault of religion does not lie within the organization, but within the receptacle (*OA*, 1:707–708).

17. See Eve Sourian's article, "Les Opinions religieuses de George Sand: Pourquoi Consuelo a-t-elle perdu sa voix?" in *George Sand: Collected Essays*, ed. Janis Glasgow (Troy, N.Y.: Whitston, 1985), esp. 131–33. Sourian finds that the second version of *Lélia* is still pessimistic. I disagree with this interpretation and posit that the 1839 version marks a clear progress toward an optimism that will form a system in *Spiridion*. For Leroux's credo as expressed by George Sand, see also Moret, *Le Sentiment religieux*, 157–58. See also Henry Dartigue's good but rather outdated article, "La religion de George Sand," *La Revue chrétienne*, 1904, 137ff.

18. See Frank Bowman's insightful article, "George Sand, le Christ et le royaume," *Cahiers de l'Association international des études françaises* 28 (1976): 243–62; he continues his investigation in *Le Christ aux barricades, 1789–1848* (Paris: Editions du Cerf, 1987), 264–69.

19. Many critics have said that Leroux actually wrote much of *Spiridion*. Moret studied the manuscript and feels quite sure that Leroux's involvement with the writing of the novel was minimal. See Moret, *Le Sentiment religieux*, 160. See also Jean Larnac, *George Sand révolutionnaire* (Paris: Editions Hier et Aujourd'hui/ Collection Grandes Figures, 1947), 15–25, 37 n.1.

20. Jean Pommier, *George Sand et le rêve monastique: Spiridion* (Paris: Nizet, 1966), 68–70.

21. See Moret, *Le Sentiment religieux*, 175.

22. Pommier, *Le Rêve*, 85–86.

23. Ibid., 88–91.

24. Tatiana Green, "George Sand, hérétique," in *Bulletin de l'Association des Professeurs français d'Amérique* (1985), 143.

25. See Frank Bowman, "George Sand, le Christ et le royaume," 250.

26. Foreword to *Jean Zyska* (Paris: Lévy Frères, 1867), 3.

27. According to censorship laws of the beginning of the Second Empire, this novel violates the morality of the times. *La Presse*, where the novel was first serialized, was given two warnings, then a third warning and a temporary suspension.

28. Sand was just as uneasy, however, about taking on the yoke of a church often more intolerant than the Vatican. See Moret, *Le Sentiment religieux*, 215.

29. Another atheist character, rare for George Sand, appears in *Confession*

d'une jeune fille. Frumence, the nephew of an abbot, knows the teachings of the Church very well and has proven to his intellectual and emotional satisfaction that God does not exist. During his beloved's nearly fatal sickness, he swears before God to make her his wife. Challenged in this religious invocation, he defends himself by insisting that he was thus naming "*une des plus douces hypothèses que l'esprit humain puisse concevoir, c'est pour désigner le bien absolu dont nous portons en nous-mêmes l'aspiration*" (one of the sweetest hypotheses the human mind can conceive, for designating absolute goodness to which we all aspire) (2:260). While the narrator goes on to say that Frumence had not budged an iota from his well-conceived set of principles, I feel this is a weakness in his character that the narrator fails to recognize and that Sand fails to develop.

30. While Sand advances the notion that the devil is no longer fashionable, she affords him a place of some importance, first in the title of this novel and, second, by the pains to which she goes to prove his uselessness. She states in the preface that she plans this novel as the first of a series, the others to be called *Le Diable à la ville* and *Le Diable au voyage.* These she would never write, but the intention, no matter how serious, to dedicate so much time and space to the devil demonstrates to what extent the theological problem occupied her mind at this time. Other instances of the devil are to be found in *La Mare au diable,* although this more readily represents the issue of superstition and religion, and in the comic play *Le Démon au foyer* (The Demon at home) (1852). Baudelaire, in his *Mon Coeur mis à nu,* states that the devil had doubtless duped Sand, despite her declaration in the preface to *Quintinie* that Hell did not exist or, at least, that good Christians did not believe so (*Oeuvres complètes,* ed. Marcel Ruff [Paris: Seuil, 1968], 633); also in André Maurois, *George Sand,* trans. Gerard Hopkins (New York: Harper & Bros., 1953), 402–3.

31. Sandra M. Gilbert and Susan Gubar, *Madwoman in the Attic: The Woman Writer and the Nineteenth-Century Literary Imagination* (1979; reprint, New Haven, Conn.: Yale University Press, 1984), 67 and passim.

32. While it is true that two generations earlier the Marquis de Sade had shocked the reading public with his sexually frank writings, Sand's goal was not to shock but to examine the psychological circumstances of frigidity within the larger context of women's slavery in a patriarchal society.

33. Janis Glasgow has published a new edition of *Gabriel* (Paris: Des femmes, 1988); Gay Manifold is currently preparing an English translation of the play.

34. Simone Vierne discusses further implications of the contradictions between the supposed feminist theme and stereotypically female attributes in her provocative article "Le Mythe de la femme dans *Consuelo,*" in *La Porpora: Entretiens sur Consuelo,* ed. Léon Cellier (Grenoble, France: Presses Universitaires de Grenoble, 1976), 41–50. For another interpretation, see also Eve Sourian's "Les Opinions religieuses de George Sand: Pourquoi Consuelo a-t-elle perdu sa voix?" cited in note 17.

35. *Jacques* (Paris: Hetzel, 1853), 10.

36. Cf. Kathryn Crecelius, *Family Romance,* where this query is one of the main elements of the thesis and is especially well presented in the introduction.

37. Cf. Arlette Michel, "Problèmes du mariage chez George Sand d'*Indiana à La Comtesse de Rudolstadt,*" *Romantisme* 16 (1977):34–45.

38. Karénine, *George Sand,* 4:501.

39. See Eve Sourian's critical article on these two novels, "Amitiés féminines dans *Isidora* et *Constance Verrier*: polarités et classes sociales," *George Sand Studies* 8, nos. 1 and 2 (1986–87):28–37.

40. Also printed in *Corres.,* 8:391–92.

41. *Corres.,* 8:400–408; also reprinted in *Souvenirs et idées* (1904). For further discussion of this matter, see Barry, *George Sand,* 289ff. For a more complete discussion of the context of the women's movement in France at this time, see also Edouard Dolléans, *Féminisme et mouvement ouvrier: George Sand* (Paris: Editions ouvrières/Collection "Masses et militants," 1951), chapter 1.

42. The text of this letter can be found in the volume *Impressions et Réminiscences.*

Chapter Six

1. Yvette Bozon-Scalzitti studies Sand's equation of noise and music as it relates to childhood scenes of passion and violence and how it is developed in her fiction: "George Sand, le bruit et la musique," *Orbis litterarum* 41 (1986):139–56.

2. Thérèse Marix-Spire suggests this was indicative of the lack of common interests that led to the breakup of their marriage in *Les Romantiques et la musique, le cas George Sand, 1804–1838* (Paris: Nouvelles Editions latines, 1954), 231.

3. Madeleine L'Hopital, *La Notion d'artiste chez George Sand* (Paris: Bovin, 1946), 111.

4. For more on this topic, consult the informative article by Thérèse Marix-Spire, "Du piano à l'action sociale. Franz Liszt et George Sand, militante socialiste," *Renaissance* 2–3 (1945):187–216.

5. In *Entretiens journaliers avec le très docte et très habile docteur Piffoël, professeur de botanique et de psychologie, OA,* 2:981.

6. The most recent book on the subject is Marie-Paule Rambeau's *Chopin dans la vie et l'oeuvre de George Sand* (Paris: Les Belles lettres, 1985), an excellent treatment of both people, with extensive research into Sand's novels and especially into Chopin's compositions.

7. She says of Chopin, "*Il a fait parler à un seul instrument la langue de l'infini*" (with just one instrument he spoke the language of the infinite) (*OA,* 2:421). L'Hopital notes that, prior to this, she had said of Liszt, "He alone could make a piano come alive" (*La Notion d'artiste,* 110).

8. Thérèse Marix-Spire willing attributes the hackneyed style of this story to Sandeau, but she insists that the subject is pure Sand (*Les Romantiques et la musique,* 232).

9. L'Hopital says Sand wanted to "rival" Liszt with this work (*La Notion d'artiste,* 116); Sand does mention in the foreword that it was on a dare from Liszt and others that she undertook the project.

10. An excellent article by Béatrice Didier, "Problèmes de sémiologie musicale dans *Consuelo*," *La Porpora: Entretiens sur Consuelo,* ed. Léon Cellier (Grenoble, France: Presses Universitaires de Grenoble, 1976), 131–45, discusses the relation between the musical signifier and the musical signified, giving a textual approach to the study of music in fiction.

11. See Frank Paul Bowman, "Notes toward the Definition of the Romantic Theater," *L'Esprit Créateur* 5, no. 3 (1965):121–30. This *drame philosophique* adapts itself to the genre Sand herself defined as the *drame fantastique* in an article in *La Revue des Deux Mondes* entitled "Essai sur le drame fantastique: Goethe, Byron, Mickiewicz" (December 1839), 593–645. Supernatural beings articulate the polemic between thought and passion, reflection and despair, what Sand calls the *moi* and the *non-moi* (596–97). As with "Le Contrebandier," in *Les Sept Cordes* we are dealing with a mixed genre, which offers both advantages and problems.

12. Brian Juden says that this piece "represents, in one single symbol, the unison of the arts under the aegis of love" in his exhaustive study *Traditions orphiques et tendances mystiques dans le romantisme français (1800–1855)* (Paris: Klincksieck, 1971), 508.

13. That the sole woman of the work has a natural talent for music while the man represents cold reason hardly sets up this drama as a feminist text. Hélène will demonstrate some powers of scientific observation and reason later in the work. Consuelo will help somewhat to rectify this gender-bound dichotomy.

14. *Les Sept Cordes de la lyre,* ed. René Bourgeois (Paris: Flammarion, 1973), 132.

15. Here we are reminded of the lesson Sand gave in "La Prima donna."

16. Sand uses actual musical notation in the text of *Carl* (1843). This story demonstrates the force of music on the memory and the emotions and describes the reincarnation of someone's soul as it identifies itself through music. A strong element of madness links this text to *Adriani*.

17. *Consuelo,* 3 vols., ed. Simone Vierne and René Bourgeois (Meylan, France: Editions de l'Aurore, 1983), 1:56.

18. Pierre Salomon, Marie-Thérèse Rouget, Marie Jenny Howe, Francis Gribble, William Atwood, Joseph Barry, Curtis Cate, and several others identify Chopin as the inspiration for Prince Karol. See *Histoire de ma vie, OA,* 2:443–44, and Lubin's note 3, p. 443. Sand is not entirely wrong to point out that Karol's character and Chopin's are quite dissimilar; and Karol has no artistic talents, which makes him totally incomparable to Chopin. Still, a sickly man with aristocratic pretentions and Catholic guilt as a result of cohorting with a marked woman could easily describe both Karol and Chopin. Marie-Paule Rambeau brings new and convincing evidence to confirm the identity of Karol and Chopin in her well-documented and well-presented *Chopin dans la vie et l'oeuvre de George Sand* (Paris: Les Belles Lettres, 1985), part 2, chapter 1, esp. 229–33.

19. L'Hopital, *La Notion d'artiste,* 212.

20. *Le Château des Désertes,* ed. Jean-Marc Bailbé (Meylan, France: Les Edi-

tions de l'Aurore, 1985). Sand first wrote this novel in 1847, but it remained unpublished until 1851.

21. For more discussion on the problem of the artist's relations with the public, see L'Hopital, *La Notion d'artiste,* 226–30.

22. *Les Maîtres sonneurs,* ed. Marie-Claire Bancquart (Paris: Gallimard/Folio, 1979), 414–15. See also the interesting article by Dauphiné James, "Ecriture et musique dans *Les Maîtres sonneurs* de George Sand," *Nineteenth-Century French Studies* 9, nos. 3–4 (1981):185–91.

23. *Otello,* 3.1; lyrics taken from Dante, *Inferno,* canto 5; also serves as the epigraph to Byron's *The Corsair.*

24. *Adriani,* ed. Maurice Toesca (Paris: Editions France-Empire, 1980), 212.

25. Ibid., 224.

26. As in *Consuelo,* the man plays an instrument and the woman sings; again Sand upholds socially determined gender roles.

27. L'Hopital, *La Notion d'artiste,* 97.

28. Karénine, *George Sand,* 2:152–53.

29. *Aldo le rimeur,* in *La Revue des Deux Mondes,* September 1833.

Chapter Seven

1. See Dorrya Fahmy, *George Sand: auteur dramatique* (Paris: Droz, 1935), 9.

2. Sand recounts this experience with humor in *Histoire de ma vie, OA,* 1:998–1001.

3. Dorrya Fahmy, *George Sand: auteur dramatique* (Paris: Droz, 1935), gave the first book-length study of Sand's theater. Since then there have been a few doctoral dissertations: Valentine Petoukhoff, "George Sand et le drame philosophique," Ph.D. diss., University of Pennsylvania, 1975; and Lenore Kreitman, "George Sand's Symbolique Vision: A Fading Yet Future Fantastic," Ph.D. diss., University of Pennsylvania, 1976. Gay Manifold's *George Sand's Theatre Career* provides us, finally, with an exhaustive survey of Sand's theatrical experience. This is an excellent tool for further research in Sand's theater.

4. *Théâtre de George Sand* (Paris: Hetzel, 1860), 3:i.

5. Planche, *Revue des Deux Mondes,* 1 February 1851, cited in Manifold, *George Sand's Theatre Career,* 67.

6. *Claudie* suffered from the censorship of the new Republic. See Censor's Report, cited in Gisela Schlientz, *George Sand: Leben und Werk in Texten und Bildern* (Frankfort: Insel Verlag, 1987), 235; Gautier's comment is also cited by Schlientz, *Leben und Werk,* 237.

7. Karénine, *George Sand,* 4:589.

8. Paul Meurice was given both versions; see G. Manifold, *George Sand's Theatre Career,* 79, 138. A new edition of *Gabriel* has recently been published by "des femmes," with an introduction by Janis Glasgow; Gay Manifold is also currently preparing an English translation for publication.

9. *Condenado por desconfido.* She insists hers is not a simple transcription or translation of the Spanish play, as was so often the case with classical playwrights.

10. *Théâtre de Nohant* (Paris: Lévy, 1864, 1866). I am indebted to Gay Manifold's research for much of the textual information on the little theater. See chapter 4, "A Theatre of One's Own," of her *George Sand's Theatre Career,* 107–46. See also Debra Linowitz Wentz's book, *Les Profils du "Théâtre de Nohant" de George Sand* (Paris: Nizet, 1978).

11. Maurice Sand and Paul Manceau, 2 vols., *Masques et Bouffons* (Paris: Lévy, 1860 and 1862).

12. *Corres.,* 9:787–90; see also *Le Théâtre et l'acteur* and *Théâtre des marionnettes, OA,* 2:1247–76.

13. See the chapter on "L'Univers fantastique de George Sand" in Wentz's *Les Profils,* 13–40.

14. Cited by Maurice Toesca, *Une Autre George Sand* (Paris: Plon, 1945), 164.

15. *L'Artiste,* 17 February 1833.

16. Part 5, chapter 4, *OA,* 2:222–49. See the story "La Marquise" for additional discussion of the outmoded, classical method of acting.

17. "De Madame Dorval," 27 January 1837, *Journal de Toulouse,* reprinted in *Questions d'art et de littérature* (Paris: Calmann-Lévy, 1878).

18. J.-M. Bailbé, "Le Théâtre et le vie dans *Le Château des Désertes,*" *Revue d'Histoire Littéraire de la France* 79 (1979):609; also in his prefatory notes to the novel (Meylan, France: Editions de l'Aurore, 1985), 20–21.

19. See Fahmy, *George Sand: auteur dramatique,* 160–66.

20. Published in *La Revue des Deux Mondes,* 1 September 1833, *Aldo le rimeur* is Sand's second play, the first being "Une Conspiration en 1537," which she handed over to Musset, who used it as fodder for his *Lorenzzacio.*

21. "Le Drame fantastique," *La Revue des Deux Mondes,* 1 December 1839, 593–645.

22. Théophile Gautier, *Histoire de l'art dramatique en France depuis vingt-cing ans,* cited by Gay Manifold, *George Sand's Theatre Career,* 45.

23. "Le Réalisme," *Le Courrier de Paris,* September 1857; this is a response to Champfleury's manifesto of realism, "Du Réalisme: Lettre à Madame Sand" (1855), in *Le Réalisme,* ed. Geneviève Lacambre and Jean Lacambre (Paris: Hermann, 1973), 171–76. Champfleury holds up Wagner as the paragon of musical realism, Courbet as that of realism in painting, and George Sand of dramatic realism.

24. Eugène Delacroix, *Journal,* 28 November 1853, cited in Schlientz, *George Sand,* 240.

25. Émile Zola, *Documents littéraires: George Sand,* in Schlientz, *George Sand,* 276.

Chapter Eight

1. *Oeuvres autobiographiques,* 2 vols., ed. Georges Lubin (Paris: Gallimard, 1970–71). A few fragmentary translations of *Histoire de ma vie* exist in English, the most recent being that of Dan Hofstadter, *My Life* (New York: Harper & Row, 1979). At the time this volume is going to print, a full-length version of Sand's memoirs in English translation, edited by Thelma Jurgrau, is being published by the State University of New York at Binghamton. A three hundred-page abridged Dutch translation is also being prepared by Ank Maas.

2. Cate, *George Sand,* 637.

3. Mallet, *George Sand* (Paris: Grasset, 1976), 333–43.

4. Among others are the writings of Béatrice Didier, notably "Femme/ Identité/Ecriture: A propos de l'*Histoire de ma vie* de George Sand," *Revue des Sciences Humaines,* October–December 1977, 561–76. See also Lucienne Frappier-Mazur, "Nostalgie, dédoublement et écriture dans *Histoire de ma vie,*" *Nineteenth-Century French Studies,* 17, nos. 3 & 4 (Spring-Summer 1989):265–275; Yvette Bozon-Scalzitti, "Vérité de la fiction et fiction de la vérité dans *Histoire de ma vie*: Le Projet autobiographique de George Sand," *Nineteenth-Century French Studies* 12, no. 4 (Summer 1984) and 13, no. 1 (Fall 1984):95–118.

5. Maas, "*Histoire de ma vie,*" 176, 189.

6. Lubin also suggests her waning interest in the project (*OA,* 1:xxii).

7. Letter to Charles Poncy, *Corres.,* 8:188–89. See also *OA,* 2:110. For further discussion concerning the relation between reality and fiction, see the probing article by Yvette Bozon-Scalzitti, "Vérité de la fiction."

8. *OA,* 2:99. One will recall similar oblique references to Chopin in *Un Hiver à Majorque.*

9. *OA,* 2:953–71; see Lubin's introductory notes, 947–51.

10. *Journal de Gargilesse* was published for the first time in a recent edition (Saint-Cyr-sur-Loire, France: Christian Pirot, 1984), along with *Promenades autour d'un village,* with drawings by Maurice Sand, Christiane Sand, et al.

11. Consult Thiery Bodin's informative presentation of the history of the text in the most recent edition of *Elle et Lui* (Meylan, France: Editions de l'Aurore, 1986).

12. See Anne Callahan's insightful article, "Elle e(s)t Lui: L'endroit et l'envers de l'autre romantique," *George Sand: Collected Essays,* ed. Janis Glasgow (Troy, N.Y.: Whitston, 1985), 242. See also Jeanne Fuchs's study, "George Sand and Alfred de Musset: Absolution through Art in *La Confession d'un enfant du siècle,*" in *Proceedings of Seventh International George Sand Conference* (Westport, Conn.: Greenwood Press, forthcoming).

13. Callahan, "Elle e(s)t Lui," 243.

14. Curtis Cate calls Sand's novel vindictive; Henri Guillemin allows that she was generally fair toward Musset, despite the otherwise bilious treatment he gives her and the novel in his introduction to the Swiss edition (Neuchatel: Ides et Calendes, 1963); Thiery Bodin admits that at least the ending of the novel is kind.

15. An English translation of Colet's book, by Marilyn G. Rose, has recently been published (Athens: University of Georgia Press, 1986).

16. Lescure, *Eux et Elles* (Paris: Poulet-Malassis et de Bavise, 1860).

17. Pierre Lejeune indicates related genres that do not satisfy all the conditions of the definition of autobiography: memoirs, biography, personal novel, autobiographical poem, diary, autoportrait, *Le Pacte autobiographique* (Paris: Seuil, 1975), 14.

18. Lubin has arrived at volume 22, corresponding to 1872, in the volumes of Sand's *Correspondance*.

Chapter Nine

1. Conference paper by Murray Sachs, "Reason of the Heart: George Sand, Flaubert and the Commune," *Proceedings of the Seventh International George Sand Conference* (Westport, Conn.: Greenwood Press, forthcoming).

2. *Laura,* in *Voyage dans le cristal,* ed. Francis Lacassin (Paris: Union Générale d'Edition, 1980), 33.

3. Philippe Berthier, ed., *Contes d'une grand-mère,* 2 vols., (Meylan, France: Editions de l'Aurore, 1982), 5–8.

4. I discuss the musical and psychological ramifications of this story in my conference paper, "Musical Fantastic in *L'Orgue du titan,*" MLA Conference, Chicago, December 1985.

5. *"la littérature . . . m'offrait le plus de chances de succès comme métier, et, tranchons le mot, comme gagne-pain"* (Literature gave me the best chance of success as a trade and, let's be frank, as a way to put food on the table) (*OA,* 2:101).

Selected Bibliography

PRIMARY WORKS

For novels, bibliographic information refers to the first appearance in volume form; where a serial publication precedes, the date is given in parentheses. For plays, parenthetical dates refer to the stage premiere. A number of the following titles are now available in modern, critical editions; bibliographic information for these follows the first citing.

Complete Works

Oeuvres de George Sand. Paris: Bonnaire, 1838–42.
Oeuvres de George Sand, nouvelle édition revue par l'auteur. Paris: Perrotin, 1842–43.
Oeuvres complètes de George Sand illustrées, with drawings by Tony Johannot and Maurice Sand. Paris: Hetzel, 1852–56.
Théâtre de George Sand. 3 vols. Paris: Michel-Lévy, 1860.
Théâtre complet de George Sand. 4 vols. Paris: Michel-Lévy, 1866–67.
Oeuvres complètes. 32 vols. Geneva: Slatkine, 1978.

Novels and Short Stories

Adriani (1854). Paris; Cadot, 1854; France-Empire, 1980.
André (1835). Paris: Bonnaire, 1835; 1987.
Les Beaux Messieurs de Bois-Doré (1857). Paris: Serrière, 1857; Albin Michel, 1976.
Césarine Dietrich (1870). Paris: Michel-Lévy, 1871.
Le Château des Désertes (1851). Paris: Michel-Lévy, 1851; Aurore, 1985.
Le Compagnon du tour de France (1840). Paris: Perrotin, 1841; Aujourd'hui/Les Introuvables, 1979; Compagnonnage, 1979; Presses universitaires de Grenoble, 1988.
La Comtesse de Rudolstadt (1843). Paris: L. de Potter, 1844; Garnier, 1959; Aurore, 1983.
La Confession d'une jeune fille (1864). Paris: Michel-Lévy, 1865.
Consuelo (1842). Paris: L. de Potter, 1843; Garnier, 1959; Aurore, 1983.
Contes d'une grand-mère (most of the stories first appeared in magazines separately). Vol. 1, Paris: Michel-Lévy, 1873; vol. 2, Paris: C. Lévy, 1876; Aujourd'hui/Les Introuvables, 1979; Aurore, 1982–83.
La Daniella (1857). Paris: Librairie nouvelle, 1857; Geneva: Slatkine, 1979.

Le Dernier amour (1866). Paris: Michel-Lévy, 1867; Geneva: Slatkine, 1981.

La Dernière Aldini (1837). Paris: Hetzel, 1855.

Elle et Lui (1858). Paris: Hachette, 1859; Aurore, 1986.

François le champi (1847). Brussels: Méline, Cans et Compagnie, 1848; Paris: Cadot, 1850; Gallimard/Folio, 1976; LGF/Livre de poche, 1977.

Horace (1841). Paris: L. de Potter, 1842; Aurore, 1982.

Indiana. Paris: Roret et Dupuy, 1832; Aujourd'hui/Les Introuvables, 1979; Gallimard/Folio, 1984; Garnier, 1985.

Isidora (1845). Paris: Souverain, 1846.

Jacques. Paris: Bonnaire, 1834.

Jeanne (1844). Brussels, Hauman, 1844; Paris: L. de Potter, 1845; Aurore, 1986.

Lélia. Paris: Dupuy, 1833; 2d version, Bonnaire, 1839; Aujourd'hui/Les Introuvables, 1976; Garnier, 1986; Aurore, 1988.

Leone Leoni (1834). Paris: Bonnaire, 1835.

Lettres à Marcie (1837). Paris: Perrotin, 1844.

Lucrezia Floriani (1846). Paris: E. Proux, 1846.

Mademoiselle la Quintinie (1863). Paris: Michel-Lévy, 1863; Geneva: Slatkine, 1979.

Mademoiselle Merquem (1868). Paris: Michel-Lévy, 1868; Ottawa: Presses universitaires d'Ottowa, 1981.

Les Maîtres sonneurs (1853). Paris: Cadot, 1853; Gallimard/Folio, 1979; Garnier, 1981.

La Mare au diable (1846). Paris: E. Proux, n.d.; Gallimard/Folio, 1973; Flammarion, 1975; with *Mauprat,* Hachette, 1979; with *François le champi,* Garnier, 1981.

Le Marquis de Villemer (1860). Paris: Naumbourg et Paetz, 1860–61; Casterman, 1976.

"La Marquise" (1832), "Mattéa" (1835), "Métella" (1833), "Lavinia" (1833). Paris: Bonnaire, 1837; *Nouvelles,* also with "Pauline," ed. Eve Sourian, Des femmes, 1986.

Mauprat (1837). Paris: Bonnaire, 1937; Flammarion, 1985; Gallimard/Folio, 1981.

Le Meunier d'Angibault (1845). Paris: Desessart, 1845; LGF/Livre de poche, 1985.

Monsieur Sylvestre (1865). Paris: Michel-Lévy, 1866; Geneva: Slatkine, 1980.

Mont-Revêche (1852). Paris: Cadot, 1853.

Nanon (1872). Paris: Michel-Lévy, 1872; Aurore, 1987.

Le Péché de Monsieur Antoine (1845). Brussels: Lebèque et Sacré fils, 1846; Paris: Souverain, 1846–47; Aujourd'hui/Les Introuvables, 1979; Aurore, 1982.

La Petite Fadette (1848). Paris: Michel-Lévy, 1849; Flammarion, 1967; LGF/Livre depoche, 1973; Garnier, 1981; with *François le champi,* Hachette, 1979.

Rose et Blanche (signed J. Sand). Paris: Renault, 1831

Simon (1836). Paris: Bonnaire, 1836.
Spiridion (1838). Paris: Bonnaire, 1839; Aujourd'hui/Les Introuvables, 1976.
Téverino (1845). Paris: Desessart, 1846.
L'Uscoque (1838). Paris: Bonnaire, 1838.
Valentine. Paris: Dupuy, 1832.
Valvèdre (1861). Paris: Michel-Lévy, 1861.

Autobiographical Works

Histoire de ma vie (1854). Paris: Lecou, 1854–55. In *Oeuvres autobiographiques*. Paris: Gallimard/Pléiade, 1970–71; Stock, 1985.
Un Hiver à Majorque (1841). Paris: Souverain, 1841; Aurore, 1985; LGF/Livre de poche, 1984.
Lettres d'un voyageur (1834–36). Brussels: Scribe, Tecmen et Compagnie, 1837; Paris: Bonnaire, 1837; Flammarion, 1971.

Plays

The year and theater of a play's premiere are given in parentheses; bibliographic information for published edition follows.

Cadio, in collaboration with Paul Meurice (1868, Porte Saint-Martin). Paris: Michel-Lévy, 1868.
Claudie (1851, Porte Saint-Martin). Paris: Blanchard, 1851; Librairie Théâtrale, 1851.
Cosima (1840, Théâtre Français). Paris: Bonnaire, 1840.
Le Démon au foyer (1852, Gymnase). Paris: Giraud et Dagneau, 1852.
François le champi (1849, Odéon). Paris: Blanchard, 1849.
Gabriel (never produced). Paris: Bonnaire, 1840; Des femmes, 1988.
Maître Favilla (1855, Odéon). Paris: Librairie nouvelle, 1855.
Le Marquis de Villemer (1864, Odéon). Paris: Michel-Lévy, 1864.
Le Mariage de Victorine (1851, Gymnase). Paris: Blanchard, 1851.
Mauprat (1853, Odéon). Paris: Librairie Théâtrale, 1853.
La Petite Fadette, verse parts by Michel Carré, music by Théodore Semet (1869, Opéra-Comique). Paris: Michel-Lévy, 1869.
Les Sept Cordes de la Lyre (never produced). Paris: Bonnaire, 1840; Flammarion, 1973.

English Editions

The Bagpipers. Chicago: Academy Chicago Publishers, 1977.
Consuelo. Jersey City, N.J.: DaCapo, 1979.
The Country Waif. Translated by Eirene Collis. Lincoln: University of Nebraska Press, 1977.

The Haunted Pool. Translated by Frank Potter. Berkeley, Calif.: Shameless Hussy Press, 1976.

Indiana. Translated by George B. Ives. Chicago: Academy Chicago Publishers, 1978.

Intimate Journal. Translated by Marie J. Howe. Chicago: Academy Chicago Publishers, 1978.

Leone Leoni. Translated by George B. Ives. Chicago: Academy Academy Chicago Publishers, 1978.

Letters to Marcie. Translated by Betsy Wing. Chicago: Academy Chicago Publishers, 1988.

Lucrezia Floriani. Translated by Julius Eker. Chicago: Academy Chicago Publishers, 1985.

Marianne. Translated by Siân Miles. New York: Carroll & Graf, 1988.

Mauprat. Translated by Stanley Young. Chicago: Academy Chicago Publishers, 1977.

My Convent Life. Translated by Maria E. McKaye. Chicago: Academy Chicago Publishers, 1977.

Valentine. Translated by George B. Ives. Chicago: Academy Chicago Publishers, 1978.

Winter in Majorca. Translated by Robert Graves. Chicago: Academy Chicago Publishers, 1978.

SECONDARY WORKS

The specific bibliography for various works being too extensive, I have included here only recent, general titles that treat George Sand and her works.

Bibliographies

Brynolfson, Gaylord. "Works on George Sand, 1964–1980: A Bibliography." In *George Sand Papers: Conference Proceedings, 1978,* edited by Natalie Datlof, 189–233. New York: AMS Press, 1982. Excellent review of secondary source material for dates mentioned.

Poli, Annarosa. *George Sand vue par les italiens (essai de bibliocritique).* Paris: Didier, 1965. Exhaustive overview of reception and treatment of Sand in Italy, especially by contemporary audience.

Spoelberch de Lovenjoul, Vicomte Charles. *George Sand: Etude bibliographique sur ses oeuvres.* 1914; reprint, New York: Burt Franklin, 1971. The standard compendium of Sand's oeuvre, very reliable.

Books and Parts of Books

Barry, Joseph. *Infamous Woman: The Life of George Sand.* Garden City, N.Y.: Doubleday, 1977. In conjunction with Cate's book, the best modern biography on Sand.

Cate, Curtis. *George Sand.* New York: Avon, 1975. With Barry's book, the best modern biography available, despite the method of documentation, which is difficult to consult.

Cellier, Léon, ed. *La Porpora: Entretiens sur Consuelo.* Grenoble, France: Presses Universitaires de Grenoble, 1976. Some good articles on Sand's masterpiece.

Crecelius, Kathryn J. *Family Romances: George Sand's Early Novels.* Bloomington: Indiana University Press, 1987. Interesting study of triangular relationships; unfortunately the thesis is not borne out throughout the book.

Dickenson, Donna. *George Sand: A Brave Man—the Most Womanly Woman.* Oxford: Berg, 1988. An uneven treatment that fails to dispell the legends that surround George Sand.

Goldin, Jeanne, ed. *George Sand: Voyage et écriture. Études françaises* 24, 1 (Spring 1988). Montreal: Presses de l'Université de Montréal, 1988. Collection of very interesting essays on the important relationship in Sand's works between traveling and writing.

Glasgow, Janis, ed. *Sand: Collected Essays.* Troy, N.Y.: Whitston, 1985. Some very good articles from the 1981 Sand conference in San Diego.

Karénine, Wladimir. *George Sand: Sa vie et ses oeuvres.* 4 vols. Paris: Ollendorff, 1899–1926. The best biography, even if not the most modern; an exhaustive study with more literary commentary than any other biography.

Lacassagne, Jean-Pierre. *Histoire d'une amitié: Pierre Leroux et George Sand, d'après une correspondance inédite 1836–1866.* Paris: Klincksieck, 1973. A good, modern treatment of the socialism question.

Mallet, Francine. *George Sand.* Paris: Grasset, 1976. A solid biography, though in many ways disappointing.

Manifold, Gay. *George Sand's Theatre Career.* Ann Arbor, Mich.: UMI, 1985. Excellent and long overdue treatment of Sand's theater in Paris as well as in Nohant, with pertinent comments on Sand's place in the development of theater practices.

Maurois, André. *George Sand,* translated by Gerard Hopkins. New York: Harper & Bros., 1953. Formerly the standard, modern biography, now out of favor with most Sandists because of the thinly veiled misogynist tone.

Poli, Annarosa. *L'Italie dans la vie et dans l'oeuvre de George Sand.* Paris: Colin, 1960. Important and well-documented study of a major influence on Sand's writing.

Pommier, Jean. *George Sand et le rêve monastique: Spiridion.* Paris: Nizet, 1966. The best book-length study of Sand's religious thought, even though it focuses largely on a single work.

Rambeau, Marie-Paule. *Chopin dans la vie et l'oeuvre de George Sand.* Paris: Les

Belles lettres, 1985. Admirable study from both literary and musicological perspectives, discussing mutual influences and the problems of influence studies.

van **Rossum-Guyon, Françoise,** ed. *George Sand: Nouvelles recherches.* Amsterdam: C.R.I.N., 1983. A fine assemblage of recent scholarship with modern critical approaches.

Schlientz, Giesela. *George Sand: Leben und Werk in Texten und Bildern.* Frankfort: Insel Verlag, 1987. Very good documentation, presented with iconography as dictated by the publication series; she brings new and interesting visual support to underscore biographical and literary commentary.

Thomson, Patricia. *George Sand and the Victorians.* New York: Columbia University Press, 1977. The best comparative study to date.

Vernois, Paul. *Le Roman rustique de George Sand à Ramuz: ses tendances et son évolution (1860–1925).* Paris: Nizet, 1962. Valuable work linking Sand to a tradition.

Vierne, Simone, ed. *George Sand.* Cerisy-la-Salle conference, 1981. Paris: CDU/ SEDES, 1983. Superb collection of essays by prominent scholars discussing Sand in modern critical terms.

Wentz, Debra Linowitz. *Les Profils du "Théâtre de Nohant" de George Sand.* Paris: Nizet, 1978. An interesting commentary on Sand's sense of the fantastic, but somewhat limited in scope because of the narrow corpus.

Articles

Balayé, Simone. "Consuelo: Déesse de la Pauvreté." *Revue d'Histoire Littéraire,* July 1976, 630–31. An important article that adds to the interpretation of the conclusion of Sand's masterpiece.

Bowman, Frank Paul. "George Sand, le Christ et le royaume." *Cahiers de l'Association internationale des études françaises* 28 (1976): 243–62. Solid article on Sand's religious thought, including thorough bibliography and excellent treatment of Sand's key religious novels.

Bozon-Scalzitti, Yvette. "George Sand, le bruit et la musique." *Orbis litterarum* 41 (1986): 139–56. A superb article on the psychological inferences of music in Sand's work.

_____. "Vérité de la fiction et fiction de la vérité dans *Histoire de ma vie:* Le Projet autobiographique de George Sand." *Nineteenth-Century French Studies* 12, no. 4 (Summer 1984), 13, no. 1 (Fall 1984):95–118. Excellent discussion of the psychological need to write autobiography.

Didier, Béatrice. "Le Corps féminin dans *Lélia.*" *Revue d'Histoire littéraire de France* 76, 4 (1976), 634–43. A daring treatment of the problem of female sexuality in narrative.

_____. "Femme/Identité/Ecriture: A propos de l'*Histoire de ma vie* de George Sand." *Revue des Sciences Humaines,* October–December 1977, 561–76. One of the best studies of Sand's autobiography, linking it to feminism and the advent of a writing career.

Frappier-Mazur, Lucienne. "Code romantique et résurgences du féminin dans *La Comtesse de Rudolstadt.*" In *Le Récit amoureux,* edited by Didier Coste, 53–70. Paris: Editions du Champ Vallon, 1986. Admirable discussion of romance and sexuality in Sand's masterpiece.

————. "Nostalgie, dédoublement et écriture dans *Histoire de ma vie.*" *Nineteenth-Century French Studies,* 17, 3 & 4 (Spring-Summer 1989): 265–275. Excellent psychological study of *Histoire de ma vie* and the problems of gender changes.

Greene, Tatiana. "De J. Sand à George Sand: *Rose et Blanche* de Sand et Sandeau et leur descendance." *Nineteenth-Century French Studies* 4, 3 (Spring 1976): 167–76. Good study of Sand's literary coming of age.

————. "George Sand, hérétique." *Bulletin de l'Association des Professeurs français d'Amérique* (1985), 139–58. Important addition to study of Sand's religious thought.

Michel, Arlette. "Problèmes du mariage chez George Sand d'*Indiana* à *La Comtesse de Rudolstadt.*" *Romantisme* 16 (1977): 34–45. Original treatment of an important but poorly understood issue for Sand.

Miller, Nancy K. "Writing (from) the Feminine: George Sand and the Novel of Female Pastoral." In *The Representation of Women in Fiction,* edited by Carolyn G. Heilbrun, 124–51. Baltimore: Johns Hopkins University, 1983. A fair assessment of Sand's place in feminist fiction and of the problem of feminism in the pastoral.

Mozet, Nicole. "Signé 'le voyageur': George Sand et l'invention de l'artiste." *Romantisme* 17, no. 55 (1987): 23–32. Travel and writing linked in a provocative article.

Naginski, Isabelle. "*Lélia*: Novel of the Invisible." *George Sand Studies* 7, no. 1–2 (1984–85): 46–53. Very good treatment of the dark side of a complex novel.

————. "The Serenity of Influence: The Literary Relationship of George Sand and Dostoevsky." *George Sand. Collected Essays,* ed. Janis Glasgow. Troy, N.Y.: Whitston, 1986, 110–25. A landmark essay for Sand's influence on the Russian novelist as well as for the problem of influence studies.

Powell, David A. "Discord, Dissension, and Dissonance: The Initiation in Sand's *Les Maitres sonneurs.*" *The Friends of George Sand Newsletter* 6, nos. 3 and 4 (1987): 54–61. Good study of music and the artist's plight among fellow artists.

Schor, Naomi. "Reading Double: Sand's Difference." In *The Politics of Gender,* edited by Nancy K. Miller, 248–69. New York: Columbia University Press, 1986. An excellent study of Sand's feminist politics and some interesting remarks concerning political inconsistencies in *La Petite Fadette.*

Sourian, Eve. "Amitiés féminines dans *Isidora* et *Constance Verrier:* polarités et classes sociales." *George Sand Studies* 8, nos. 1 and 2 (1986–87): 28–37. Perspicacious look at an important and as yet untreated topic in Sand's work.

Index